Organized Crime and Politics in Jamaica

Organized Crime and Politics in Jamaica

BREAKING THE NEXUS

Anthony Harriott

Canoe Press

Jamaica • Barbados • Trinidad and Tobago

Canoe Press
7A Gibraltar Hall Road   Mona
Kingston 7   Jamaica
www.uwipress.com

12 11 10 09 08   5 4 3 2 1

Harriott, Anthony.
Organized crime and politics in Jamaica: Breaking the nexus /
Anthony Harriott.

p. cm.

Partial contents: Political corruption and organized crime /
Lloyd Waller and Anthony Harriott.

Includes bibliographical references.

ISBN: 978-976-8125-89-7

1. Crime – Political aspects – Jamaica. 2. Political corruption –
Jamaica – History. 3. Political violence – Jamaica. 4. Patronage,
Political – Jamaica. I. Waller, Lloyd. II. Title.

HV6868.5.H378 2008   364.97292

Book and cover design by Robert Harris.
Set in Bembo 11/15 x 24
Printed in the United States of America.

Contents

List of Illustrations / *vi*

Acknowledgments / *vii*

Introduction: The Challenges Presented by
Organized Crime / *1*

1 Politics and the Rise of Organized Crime in Jamaica / *12*

2 Controlling Organized Crime: Elements of a Strategy / *77*

3 Political Corruption and Organized Crime / *115*
Lloyd Waller and Anthony Harriott

4 Who Pays the Piper Calls the Tune? Party Financing,
Political Debts and Organized Crime Networks / *142*

5 In Lieu of a Conclusion: Prospects for Controlling
Organized Crime / *160*

Notes / *178*

References / *190*

Index / *199*

Illustrations

Tables

Table 1.1   Drug Seizures, 1986–2006   /   *38*
Table 1.2.   Control of Criminals by Organized Crime: Homicide
                Data from Selected Communities, 2000–2006   /   *46*
Table 2.1   Level of Maturity of Organized Crime Groups   /   *102*
Table 3.1   How Jamaicans Define Corruption   /   *122*

Figures

Figure 1.1   Kilograms of ganja seized in the Caribbean, 2004   /   *37*
Figure 3.1   Corruption in the political administration   /   *123*
Figure 3.2   Corruption in the state bureaucracy   /   *124*
Figure 3.3   Perceived causes of corruption   /   *125*
Figure 3.4   Procurement contracts and criminality   /   *126*
Figure 3.5   Involvement of politicians in serious crimes   /   *127*
Figure 3.6   Contribution of construction to gross domestic
                product   /   *131*
Figure 3.7   Structure of the construction sector   /   *132*
Figure 4.1   Cost of elections per capita   /   *147*

Acknowledgements

MY WORK HAS BEEN MOTIVATED as much by a felt need to satisfy my intellectual curiosities as by the impetus to respond to social pressures. Like so many others, I hardly ever have the luxury of simply pursuing my curiosities. I was pushed into writing this book. I was pushed by the destructiveness and velocity of violent crimes in Jamaica and my responsibility to conduct research that supports solutions to this and other difficult social problems.

A number of persons as institutional actors, and others, as individuals free of any such obligations, have helped with the process. I am especially indebted to my colleagues at the University of the West Indies. The dean of the Faculty of Social Sciences was generous enough to provide me with the required financial support so that I could present a draft of what subsequently became chapter 1 at the annual meeting of the Academy of Criminal Justice Sciences that was held in Seattle in March 2007. Just prior to this, I was invited to a seminar on "The Impact of Organized Crime on State Structures and Democratic Governance in Central America and the Caribbean" that was jointly organized by the United Nations and FRIDE (Fundacion para las Relaciones Internationales y el Dialogo Exterior) and held in New York City in January 2007. These conferences afforded me the opportunity to have some useful direct exchanges with other scholars and development professionals who were working on this issue in Latin

America, Central America and a few other developing countries. Since then, a number of conferences and seminars have been held on this issue in Jamaica. The newly formed Institute of Criminal Justice and Security at the University of the West Indies and the United Nations Development Programme held one such conference in May 2007. The idea of the book germinated during the planning phase of this conference. I thank all of my colleagues and associates who participated in this activity as the push forced me to clarify issues that I had been mulling over at my own pace. It also helped me to focus on issues related to prevention and control strategies and to become more involved in these issues with a degree of specificity, and at a level of concreteness, at which I had not felt competent to engage. It is not that I have become more competent, but rather that the pace of events and the social pressures have dissipated these reservations.

Professors Bernard Headley and Richard Bennett, and Dr Peter Phillips, a former minister of national security in the Government of Jamaica, were kind enough to read sections of the manuscript. I have benefited from their helpful and supportive comments.

A number of persons helped with the most difficult aspects of writing this book. Danielle Brown and Nicola Satchell (in alphabetical order) helped with much of the data collection and fact checking. Renay Folkes patiently searched the stacks of the main library of the University of the West Indies (Mona campus) and the electronic archives for several useful newspaper articles and many of my footnoted sources. Cecile Maye-Hemmings and Danielle Brown did the copy editing.

The principal of the Mona campus of the University of the West Indies, Professor Gordon Shirley, provided some of the financial support that was needed to send the manuscript to press. Linda Speth and the staff of the University of the West Indies Press were, as they always are, very professional, very patient and very wise. I am most grateful to them all.

Despite the best efforts of those listed above, this book suffers from many imperfections. I take full responsibility for them, and tolerate them in the hope that, despite these imperfections, the book will serve a worthwhile purpose in informing and stimulating further public debate on the subject.

Introduction

The Challenges Presented by Organized Crime

THE "HIGH POLITICS" OF powerful state actors often define and rank the problems of the country, shapes policy, mobilizes support for these policies and allocates resources to ensure that the state has the operational capacity to deliver the programmes that give effect to these policies. Despite the democratic constraints imposed by public opinion and non-state interests, high politics makes things happen, sometimes without regard for the legal status of these objectives and the methods used to achieve them. High politics may be contrasted with the "low politics" of community activism that involves the average citizen and which is largely concerned with local outcomes.

There is also "high crime". This is crime that nets huge sums from enterprise and predatory activity. It is, however, not simply high-yield crime. It involves powerful actors who form intricate networks that largely operate above and beyond the reach of the law. They are placed above the law by their location in protective networks that are politically powerful enough to restrain law enforcement even without overt instructions for their restraint, and placed beyond the law by the incapacities of law enforcement. High crime may be contrasted with the "low crime" of street-level actors who operate at the low end of the illegal opportunity structure and who do not enjoy, to a similar measure, the protective networks of the powerful criminal elite.

Then there are networks that bring the two sets of high actors into active collaboration in order to attain their respective sets of goals (power, wealth, high income, high social status and other valued social goods). High politics is joined with high crime, and directly and indirectly influences in various ways both low politics and low crime. These sets of high actors, when operating together, seem to add a special quality to the crime problem. For want of a better term, we call this range of criminality organized crime. Jamaican organized crime largely operates at this intersection of high politics and high crime – although there are other varieties of organized crime that are not as intimately associated with high politics.

The Crime-Politics Nexus

The crime-politics nexus is most pronounced in the case of organized crime. If Jamaican politics is in some ways responsible for the extraordinarily high rate of violent criminality that the country is now experiencing, then successive political administrations since the 1970s are even more responsible for the emergence and rise of organized crime. The political methodology of the political parties is profoundly and directly implicated in the rise of organized crime. As will be discussed later in this text, politics has stimulated the demand for violence, a demand that has been met by organized crime. Public policy has supported the "garrisoning" process in which organized crime is embedded within the community as a part of the system of community governance. Successive political administrations have also fostered the enterprise character of organized crime by giving these groups and networks procurement and other service provision contracts.

The relationship between politics and crime has stimulated the curiosity of criminologists who wish to understand crime, and political scientists who wish to understand the backstage workings and true nature of the political system. In the early post-independence period, the relationship between politics and crime was largely manifested as political violence and

research on this subject was mainly restricted to studies of political violence (see, for example, Lacy 1977). However, the role of politics as an
explanatory variable in ordinary crime has not been completely neglected
(see Headley 1994). The relationship between crime and politics has
evolved beyond the use of thugs to intimidate opponents. It now involves
more complicated partnerships in racketeering and enterprise crimes; it has
developed and now sets organized crime at the heart of this problem.

In this volume, an attempt is made to link both lines of inquiry. The
nexus between politics and crime is explored by analysing the rise of
organized crime in Jamaica. This book represents a dedicated attempt to
treat with a particular and current expression of this nexus between politics
and crime, that is, organized crime. It describes the rise of organized crime
in Jamaica, its efforts to consolidate a hold on the cities and towns of
Jamaica and (to a limited degree) its transnationalization. This development
is accounted for in terms of its distinct structural roots and facilitators. The
analysis is further extended by the exploration of two critical aspects of the
problem – political corruption and party financing. By focusing on the
crime-politics nexus, we locate the crime problem in the mainstream of
polity and society. Institutionalized patterns of behaviour, including the
methods of political mobilization and organization, core aspects of political
culture are interrogated, not as a purely moral discourse, but rather in an
attempt to better understand the political and social processes.

Discussions of crime in Jamaica are generally considered to be almost
useless if they are not seen as "solution seeking". This work attempts
to move the discussion beyond an analysis of the problems to possible
approaches to solving and resolving them. It makes two shifts in the
discussion about crime in Jamaica. The first is to dedicate the discussion
to the special category of organized crime, and the second is to interrogate
the existing approaches to solving this problem and to sketch some
alternatives.

Much has been written about possible solutions to the Jamaican crime
problem (Ministry of National Security 2007; WKC 2002; PERF 2001;
Wolfe et al. 1993; NACCV 1984, 1990, 2002). These reports, most of them
official reports that were commissioned by the government of Jamaica,
while in some cases identifying organized crime as an important problem,

are, however, unclear on how specifically this problem ought to be tackled (beyond the promulgation of new legislation). And yet organized crime may be regarded as the centre of gravity of the Jamaican crime problem.

Discussions of organized crime, and of solutions to the more general crime problem, have largely been avoided in the academic literature. There are good reasons for this. Difficulties attend both projects. Probing the activities of powerful and powerfully connected high-end criminals presents problems of information access that makes the systematization of data collection difficult. This study had to rely primarily on what is already in the public domain. Even though privileged access to information was limited, readers may expect that an independent treatment of organized crime is likely to be somewhat different from the official discourses about crime, which tend to be understandably silent about its links to the centres of power. Regarding solutions to the problems presented by organized crime, this also presents the special challenges discussed in chapter 2.

As a dedicated analysis of organized crime and the crime-politics nexus, this book focuses on the crimes of the politically powerful. It does not emphasize the relationships between organized crime and corporate sector. Less violent forms of organized crimes and their relationships to the business classes are not given microscopic treatment. This work clearly focuses on the politically attached and more territorial and violent forms of organized crime. Why organized crime and not some other category of crime? Why not direct attention to, for example, white-collar crime? These questions are answered in the text, and it is hoped that these answers are not taken to mean that other aspects of the problem of high-end crimes and the crimes of the powerful that are not discussed here are unimportant. The questions that are posed above are valid questions. They retain their validity even in a context of high levels of street violence, but they nevertheless signal the difficulty of arriving at a shared understanding of the nature of Jamaica's crime problem.

The crime problem is too often viewed in ideological or group-interested terms. From these perspectives, the most threatening crime types are always those that are concentrated in the groups with which we have the least affinity. People who are stopped by the police for traffic violations are given to asking the officer, "Why don't you concern yourself with violent criminals instead of us?" Elements of the urban poor (who are often tired of indiscriminate policing methods) will urge a redirection of policing to the investigation of white-collar criminals. Corrupt state officials and loyal party affiliates argue that public sector corruption is not as consequential as private sector corruption. This approach is not peculiar to Jamaicans. Leon Radzinowicz, the late British criminologist, related the experience of being telephoned by a New York City mafia leader who inquired of him why "criminologists [were] so busy writing about the mafia while doing so little about muggings" (Radzinowicz 1979, 9). One is always open to the charge of not properly directing one's intellectual energies. And the older one gets, the more damning these charges are. They are perhaps more a problem of different perspectives than a problem of different interests. People, however, tend to demand that the authorities ignore their preferred offences. And if these offences are not ignored, then it is claimed that the authorities are biased and oppressive (a not altogether groundless claim). This diversionary technique is not peculiar to Jamaica, but in Jamaica it takes on the character of a legitimacy discourse that is directed against the state authorities, and an authenticity discourse (and ideological litmus test) when directed against researchers.

Vulnerabilities to Organized Crime

Organized crime is recognized as a threat to Jamaica's national security (Ministry of National Security 2007). Threats are best understood in context. For example, a cold is normally not a major threat to a healthy adult, but for someone with a major immune system disorder, a cold may be life-threatening. Any threat to the country is thus best understood in the context of an evaluation of its relevant vulnerabilities. This is the minimum requirement for proper contextualization.

These vulnerabilities include a weak criminal justice system; profound socio-economic problems, such as high rates of real youth unemployment and underemployment; the structure of the economy, especially its tourism dependence; the high impact of externalities, such as international drug markets; and a somewhat criminogenic political system that is underpinned by a factious class-colour-gender divide but, taking a long historical view, an increasingly integrated society. To describe a criminal justice system as weak suggests several features (Buscaglia and van Dijk 2003). As is generally understood, first, it is unable to convict the powerful, including members of the economic, political and criminal elites including the leaders of organized crime or "dons" as they are called. This weakness may be due to its incapacity or the impact of undue political and social influences on it. A second feature of such systems is that it tends to elicit a low level of confidence that it will deliver justice (protect the vulnerable, convict the guilty, exonerate the innocent, and treat people fairly). A third feature of a weak system is that it is generally unable to protect the populations that it serves, or at least large sections of these populations, from criminal victimization. A measure of a weak system is the low rate of usage of it by the population and especially by the more vulnerable subpopulations.

According to these criteria, Jamaica has a weak criminal justice system. In contemporary Jamaica, powerful law-breakers enjoy near immunity with respect to lawful police action. The leaders of organized crime, as a group, enjoy near freedom from prosecution unless they lose political influence, violate the rules of the game, or are investigated by external law enforcement (exclusively or in partnership with local law enforcement) and are extradited to another jurisdiction. An unambiguous expression of the weakness of the system is seen in the killing of crime leaders by the police. The exceptions to this, that is, the cases of convictions before the courts, prove the general rule (these exceptions are discussed in chapter 2).

As noted above, a second indicator of the strength of the system is the level of confidence and trust that the population has in it. The level of public confidence in the various components of the criminal justice system is fairly low and has been low for some two decades. A survey that was conducted by the Centre for Leadership and Governance at the University of the West Indies (Mona campus) in 2006 recorded that 69.4 per cent of a representative sample of the populations were of the opinion that "the administration of justice favours the rich" (see Powell 2007, 56). This is similar to findings by Carl Stone some fifteen years earlier when he reported that 68 per cent of the population felt that judges did not "deal fairly with poor people" (see Stone 1991b, 10). In early 1998, only 18 per cent of a sample of the Jamaican population reported that they felt comfortable in giving the police information of criminal activity (see Harriott 1998, 4). Such is the low level of trust in the police. Regrettably, in the period between these surveys, no one had seriously and systematically acted on the data that had been provided. The expressions of low levels of confidence and trust are not limited to attitudes, but extend to patterns of behaviour that are consistent with these negative attitudes. The rate of usage of the system varies with the types of criminal victimization, but reporting rates are notoriously low. Only 20 per cent of all crimes are reported.[1] Serious crimes involving organized crime groups are even less likely to be reported. For example, recent surveys indicated that extortion is fairly prevalent, yet very few cases have been reported to the police and convictions for this crime are exceedingly rare. Many forms of racketeering that defraud the state of hundreds of millions of dollars are not even popularly regarded as crimes. Moreover, attempts to simply name these activities as corruption are contested.

These are not problems that can be solved by simply making quantitative adjustments to the system, such as increasing the number of police officers and police stations, judges and court houses, and prison warders and prisons. More profound changes in methods of work, in mentalities and conduct norms, and in the nature of the relationships with the people are required.

The conditions that incubate and sustain high-end street crimes are spatially concentrated. There are approximately 595 squatter settlements in the country. Most of them are located in the urban areas.[2] In most of these settlements, the material conditions that cause high rates of crime are acute. These include high rates of youth unemployment, and low levels of "employability", that is, low levels of educational achievement and absence of the required skills sets. High rates of poverty,[3] social exclusion and the unresponsiveness of the state agencies help to reduce community and individual resilience to crime.

These are not problems that can be solved in the short term. A consistent pattern of development that brings opportunities, access to quality education and skills training, work and income opportunities, and which cultivates relationships based on respect and strengthens the critical institutions of the state and society is required.

The difficulties presented by these social problems are compounded by the apparent incapacity and, perhaps at times, even an official unwillingness to effectively respond to the problems presented by organized crime. Law enforcement has successfully resisted reform. The justice system is in need of modernization. There are problems of access, slow and unreliable processing of cases, and disrespectful treatment of various categories of users of the system (offenders, victims, witnesses). The upshot of this is greater self-help by victims and the entrenchment of the accompanying code of silence that facilitates all types of criminality, but particularly violent criminality. The economic cost of fixing the system is high and the country faces considerable constraints in attempting this. The economy has been stagnant for almost two decades and the debt burden is weighty. These are the objective realities and limitations, as well as symptoms of poor governance.

Jamaica's vulnerabilities also include tourism dependence and external pressures. The issue of tourism dependence and the real and potential effects of crime on tourism have been extensively discussed elsewhere and includes the vulnerability of this economic sector to reputational damage by patterns of violent crime that occur within Jamaica's borders as well as the activities of Jamaican transnational crime networks in the major tourism markets abroad (Harriott 2007b; Alleyne and Boxill 2003).

The international drug markets seem to magnetize local organized crime groups. They are viewed as huge and lucrative markets that present opportunities that can radically alter one's material circumstances in ways and at a speed that is not otherwise possible. These markets stand at the apex of the illegal opportunity structure.[4] Their attraction is quite similar to the lure of licit, high-reward, but highly competitive career opportunities for individuals. The young man with nothing but his skills as a footballer hopes to play in the English League, and, in so doing, become enormously wealthy and important. Young males with limited talent invest considerable time and resources in the pursuit of careers in entertainment in the hope of becoming big stars. Materially acquisitive aspirations are very high among sufficiently large numbers of unskilled and undereducated young males. These aspirations tend to shift the gaze of the risk-taking aspirant away from the conventional careers to the unconventional.

Drug trafficking and its associated crimes are particularly damaging in their consequences. It generates high murder rates. It fuels corruption in law enforcement and the administration of justice. It corrupts the political process and sections of the general population including some of the communities of the urban poor. Drug income may also distort the economy and create a dependency on these criminally acquired funds. On this basis, a permissive attitude toward and tolerance of organized crime and non-violent enterprise forms of criminality, such as fraudulent schemes, which target the resources of both the state and private citizens develops. This problem is discussed in chapters 1, 2 and 3.

Jamaican politics has been developmental, but also criminogenic. Its criminogenic sources include its methods, that is, the systematic use of violence to achieve electoral objectives and clientelistic mobilization which exerts a pressure for corrupt raiding of the resources of the state. The successful use of both violence and corruption for political purposes is made possible by corrupt networks that extend into the state bureaucracy. These methods encourage party permeation of the state and undermine good governance. The process is made easy by weak state institutions that are not very resistant to party permeation. Thus, the parties may engage in criminal partnerships with organized crime groups. Members of the political administration may act as facilitators of systematic patterns of criminality. In both of these cases, the career criminals are outside of the parties and the state and may be junior partners. However, beyond this, these partnerships eventually lead to the migration of high-end criminals into government and the state and to criminality among state and party leaders and functionaries. The institutions themselves run the risk of becoming criminal actors. The collusion between the political parties and organized crime is not just the outcome of materially self-interested motivations; it is an adaptation to state incapacity that permits co-rulership of the communities of the urban poor. This underpins the seeming failure of the state to effectively respond to organized crime. There is, therefore, a need to improve the capacities of the state and to indeed transform it.

These vulnerabilities explain the rapid rise of organized crime in Jamaica, intimate and underline its actual and potential impact on the economy, polity and society, and emphasize the need for informed and effective leadership at the level of the political administration as well as the state institutions. Yet, despite a number of efforts, there is an apparent inability to develop a national consensus and a sense of purpose with respect to the control and prevention of violent crime. National consensus means that agreement and disagreement on a programme of crime prevention and control is not patterned along the social and political fault lines. For example, the poor and the rich do not necessarily favour opposing policies. Males may not hold to a different programme from females. Supporters of the two major political parties may be similarly divided. The extent of majority support for a particular policy is less important than the pattern of support for the policy. A consensus pattern is more promising than a large but polarizing majority. A major challenge of leadership is to achieve consensus.

Consensus-building begins with having a common understanding of the crime problem. A common understanding is facilitated by objective inquiry, by a large enough number of researchers producing similar findings and arriving at similar conclusions. Developing a common understanding, as a politically significant reality, is, however, easily torpedoed by political competitiveness. The threat of losing the support of interested constituencies and paying a political price for subordinating party-power interests to the national interests presents a disincentive for consensus. And yet the parties which are so mired in the problem are central to its solution.

Thus far, the efforts to develop a common purpose and consensus at the level of policy and programmes have foundered.[5] A precondition for a national consensus is a measure of trust among the political actors in the high politics of the country, and some confidence in the responsible state institutions. Building trust and confidence among the policymakers means redeeming national politics by breaking the nexus between crime and politics. The vicious cycle that makes the response to organized crime ineffective begins with corrupt politics. A shift to a virtuous cycle may thus develop with political change.

International experience suggests that success hinges not just on the activity of the political leadership (although this is vital) but that the actions of the public are critical to the outcomes. Public opinion and civic activism against high-end and violent crimes are vital. The low politics of civic activism may help to resolve some of the problems of crime-control policy and political competition in the high politics of the country.

Outline of the Book

These chapters represent a dedicated attempt to understand organized crime in Jamaica. They provide an overview of the phenomenon and account for its rise in terms of its distinct roots (rather than relying on a general explanation of crime) and how it is facilitated (through politics in particular). Much of this is done in chapter 1. The analysis is then extended by exploring two aspects and expressions of the nexus between organized crime and politics. These are corruption and party financing. These aspects are presented in chapters 3 and 5 respectively. As an attempt is made to explore solutions to the problem, the book is structured such that follow-ing on the discussion of each problem is a chapter that broadly sketches some unpaved pathways to the solutions. This is done in chapters 2 and 4. Each chapter builds on the previous chapter, but has its own integrity and was written as a stand-alone essay.

This book focuses on the relationship between organized crime and politics. There are some obvious gaps in its treatment of organized crime, such as the international dimension of the problem and its relationships with private businesses. The first, has been attempted elsewhere (Harriott 2005), and the second is a matter for future research. There are many other aspects of this work that urge further research. Our understanding is still somewhat limited. This book is simply an effort to open up the discussion and to stimulate further work.

1

Politics and the Rise of Organized Crime in Jamaica

JAMAICAN ORGANIZED CRIME HAS become a powerful force in the country and a significant player in the underworld of the metropolitan centres of the United States and the United Kingdom. It is thus both internal and external. Major groups have accumulated vast fortunes from the international drug trade, extortion and other rackets. Using this criminally acquired wealth, organized crime has penetrated various sectors of the formal economy as participants in symbiotic relationships with previously legitimate businesses and as independent operators. It operates in the illegal and legal spheres, bridging and combining both. It dominates a significant number of the communities of the urban poor in the main cities, both protecting and preying on them. It systematically engages in criminality outside of its territory while "policing" it inside. Organized crime is grounded in these communities but reaches the upper rungs of the social hierarchy. In its complicated relationships with communities and with the political parties, it is respectively both patron, and client and patron. On these bases, it is able to influence political outcomes by funding the electoral campaigns of political party candidates and delivering the votes in intra and inter-party contests. It is an important factor in street politics and in violent confrontations between the parties or "uncivil politics". In the political sphere it thus spans high and low (local) politics. Organized crime wields considerable coercive power in selected communities *and* enjoys a robust referent power among young males in these localities. It bridges the above mentioned contrasting categories: internal and external, local and national, illegal and legal, predatory and protective, criminal and "police", patron and client, coercive and seductive. In this way it demonstrates its flexibility and complexity and signifies the enormity of the challenge that it presents for the society.

Organized crime is a new phenomenon in the Caribbean region. The arguable exception is Cuba's pre-1959 experience with American mafia groups, but these were largely offshore operations in which Cuba was simply the host.[1] Much of the extant work on this phenomenon, which, as will be discussed later, takes various forms and extends to a wide range of activity, has largely been restricted to analyses of drug trafficking and has been pitched at the regional level (Maingot 1999, 1994; Griffith 1997). Khan-Melnyk (1994) has explored the drug trade in Jamaica, but problematized the trade as an international relations issue, and Headley (2002) discussed the response of the government to a constructed "narco-terrorism", or rather, the violence of organized crime and other criminal groups. As has been the case with the regional studies, the principal concern of the Jamaica studies has been with drug trafficking (which is not exclusively an activity of organized crime) and drug policy. There has, however, been some work on the so-called yardies and posses or organized crime groups and networks in the United States (Josephs 1999; Headley 1997) and the United Kingdom (Small 1995), but very little has been written on the activities of organized crime within the borders of Jamaica.[2]

In this chapter, the nature of organized crime and its development in Jamaica are described, and the conditions and structural features that have facilitated this development identified. Organized crime is distinguished by the nature of its relationships to institutions and actors in conventional or mainstream society. Its penetration of the political system and its relationship to official corruption, that is, its implications for good governance are therefore described. On the basis of this analysis, the broad approaches or strategies that have been adopted to deal with Jamaican organized crime are discussed.

The upper-world relationships of organized crime extend beyond the political institutions and parts of the state bureaucracy.[3] A similar effort therefore ought to be made to explore the linkages to critical economic institutions and particularly the financial system, but this requires a more comprehensive treatment than is attempted here. The historical processes that have incubated organized crime are of considerable importance for understanding its development. This chapter mainly concerns itself with a preliminary exploration of the dimensions of this history. The picture that is presented here is thus partial.

Here it is argued that the emergence, prominence and power of organized crime represent a transformation of criminality in Jamaica that has taken place over the last two decades. To the extent that organized crime may be regarded as a transforming force, it is a force for a more robust criminality (self-transforming), and to the extent that its ties to local and national governments permit, it is a force for poor governance and maladministration (and possible regime modification in a predatory direction). It has deep causal and explanatory processes that are internal to Jamaican society, such as the persistently high rates of youth unemployment and historically high levels of inequality that find expression in the marginalization of the urban ghetto poor, and the patterns of political mobilization and integration of the urban poor into the political system (as is, for example, expressed in the garrison phenomenon). External conditions have also contributed to its rise, particularly the opportunities presented by the growth of the illicit drug markets in North America and Europe. Some of these factors and the processes attending them generally explain the high levels of violent crimes and the processes that eventually gave rise to organized crime. Jamaican organized crime emerged and flourished in a context of high levels of violent crime, weak law enforcement, high levels of state corruption, access to the international drug markets and subcultural tolerance of some categories of crime, particularly entrepreneurial forms such as ganja (cannabis) trafficking.

The Threat of Organized Crime

This rise of organized crime is illustrated by the career of the Clansman group. Originating in one of the garrison communities of the city of Spanish Town, Jamaica's first capital, the Clan is one of the better known and more powerful groups.[4] Like so many other groups, it has spawned affiliate and imitator groups in other towns.

On 30 October 2005, Donovan Bennett, known as "Bulbie", the leader of the Clan, was killed by the police at one of his homes. He had successfully evaded the police for some ten years while his group operated openly. His death triggered mass protests that succeeded in shutting down the old capital, which in 2001 had a population of approximately 131,500 (PIOJ 2005). The protest forced the closure of places of business and schools, blocked the main roadways, and brought public transportation within the city to a halt. The killing of Oliver "Bubba" Smith, the leader of the rival One Order network, in the summer of 2004 produced a very similar upheaval.[5] This violent upheaval was, however, less engaged with the high politics of the country. For example, they did not demand a change in the minister of national security. This reflected the power differential between the two networks, one of which was affiliated to the ruling party and the other the Opposition. Their protests reflected their differential accesses to the power centres in the country.

The power of the Clan to shut down the town was derived from the group's demonstrated capacity and will to engage in large-scale violence, the popular support that the group commands in the communities of the poor and its penetration of critical sectors of the local economy. For example, the group's particularly powerful hold on public transportation via control of the major transportation centres, ownership of some of the transportation stocks and an extortionist relationship with the independent taxi and bus operators allows it to quite easily shut down this vital sector on which other economic and social activity turns. Moreover, the reputation of these groups for engaging in open violence between themselves and with the security forces is such that the shooting death of one of their leaders is sufficient reason for citizens to stay home in anticipation of retaliatory violence.

These protests were an interesting show of political influence and social power. A target of the protestors was the minister of national security, Peter Phillips, who was denounced for ending Bennett's immunity. He was labelled a traitor to the ruling party for failing to deflect the gaze of law enforcement away from the activities of highly valued party affiliated criminals. The protestors called for his removal from his ministerial position (*Gleaner*, 6 November 2005). This theme was to be repeated when another leader of organized crime, Donald Phipps, who was also affiliated to the ruling party, was arrested and later convicted for murder.[6] These developments occurred in the context of a competitive election for a new party president and prime minister of the country. Phillips was a candidate in this electoral contest and organized crime sought to exploit the moment to leverage its political influence.

Bennett's funeral was attended by thousands of persons of all ages. The support of the people from the home community of the Clansmen was evident. According to a middle-aged man who was in attendance and who was (from a safe distance) animatedly contending with the police officers who were present, "dis a fi wi thing".[7] This expression indicated a complete identification with Bennett and his Clansmen and open unapologetic ownership of this type of criminal enterprise. Bennett was a "don", a new breed of what Volkov (2002), in a different context, calls violent criminal entrepreneurs. They symbolize a newfound power and influence. Some members of the communities that are dominated by the group, but which also benefit from its patronage and protection, interpret this as *their* power and influence (and in some sense it is). In Jamaica, organized crime is anchored in a larger subculture and tradition of subverting legal authority.[8]

The dons symbolize the transformation of crime that has occurred – a transformation that was facilitated by exploiting the major international markets in drugs and the opportunities presented by state corruption and political sponsorship. At the time of his death, the police estimated the value of Bennett's personal wealth to be approximately J$100 million (*Sunday Observer*, 20 November 2005, 1). This seems to be quite modest when compared with the net worth of some of the other known criminal entrepreneurs. However, this sum appeared to be simply an estimate of the value of his known personal property and would represent an underestimation of his wealth as it did not take into account the value of his legal and illegal businesses or "corporate" assets.

The above highlights five critical aspects of organized crime. These are:

1. Its treatment of crime as enterprise or business activity.
2. The extension of these activities from the underground to the formal economy via various linkages and partnerships.
3. Its social support among the people.
4. Its political engagement and influence.
5. Its use of managed violence to achieve its objectives.

The protests were exhibitions of organized crime's economic, social and political power.

Presumably there are other types of major threats of a political nature, such as international terrorism.[9] Organized crime does not present an overt strategic challenge to the state. If it did, there would be less uncertainty among the authors of the National Security Strategy in identifying organized crime as *the* major (not *a* major) threat to the country. Organized crime groups may establish their own quasi-governmental administration in some localities and may have the capability to violently disrupt social activity, inflict considerable harm on the economy, and even to make political demands on the government, but they do not contest for control of the political administration as an independent force that is external to the political system.[10] Organized crime rather tends to influence the political process *from within* as a part of the existing circuits of power. Even street protests such as the Bulbie demonstrations described earlier are intended to amplify its internal influence. Such actions may hasten meetings with the relevant member of parliament and ensure that the concerns of the protestors are thereby filtered into the internal decision-making process of the parties and government.

In Jamaica, organized crime thus corrodes the political system from within. Although in other national contexts organized crime may have evolved from (or at least was influenced by) prison alliances between ordinary criminals and repressed anti-system oppositionist political groupings, as was the case with the Thieves World in the former USSR (Volkov 2002,

54–59) and the Comando Vermelho in Brazil during the period of military dictatorships (see Dowdney 2003, 29–32), or may have been mobilized by these political movements, as was the case in China during the anti-communist campaign of the nationalist Kuo Min Tang (see Liu 2001, 27–31), it has not presented any oppositionist political challenge to demo-cratic *regimes*. It may seek to influence policies that adversely affect its inter-ests by the resort to terrorism, as occurred in Colombia, but this must be distinguished from attempts to effect regime change or to supplant an administration.

In some cases, such as in southern Italy, some strains of organized crime may have had their antecedents in social banditry. Some of the iconic fig-ures in the history of violent crime in Jamaica are remembered as "social bandits" who adopted anti-system rhetorical postures and who shared the proceeds of their crimes with their communities. Cinematic productions have cast Ivanhoe Martin, known as "Rhygin", a figure from the late 1940s, in this mould.[11] And not without some evidential support, Dennis "Copper" Barth, who was killed by the police on 29 April 1978, is similarly regarded.[12] So too was Derrick "Shabba" Adair, one of his associates. Of Adair, almost thirty years after his death in 1978, his brother reportedly said the following:

> Is a whole heap of poor people benefit from those robberies [Adair was a member of a group of robbers]. My brother was too generous. The bad men of those days [the 1970s] did not operate like how dem youth ya deal with people now; *they used to treat people right* [my emphasis] and, because of their kindness to the poor and unfortunate, they were well protected. Poor people were their strength. (Karyl Walker, "Robin Hood Lucks Out at 23", *Sunday Observer*, 16 December 2007, 9)

Here, facts are embellished and harnessed to a myth-making project that tries to project a benevolent and justly redistributive criminality.

In contemporary Jamaica, organized crime is not to be mistaken for social banditry or its approximation. The party allegiances of some groups and networks may force or even induce some ideological and political pos-turing, but these groups have not acted independently as ideologically driven agents that challenge the state and the social order and seek to redis-tribute wealth to the urban poor.[13] It provides some benefits to the poor, such as providing welfare support and making loans to street vendors, but this is typically done in ways that incorporate the beneficiaries into the criminal enterprise, or at least promote social facilitation. For example, organized crime may provide to these vendors funds that are received abroad and used to purchase goods for importation into Jamaica. On the sale of the goods locally, the soft loans are then repaid in Jamaican currency. By these means criminally acquired funds are repatriated. Although organized crime groups and networks may appear to be helpful to the poor, they are certainly not anti-system subaltern movements. However, the goodwill gained from the benefits that are provided to the communities in which these groups operate fortifies the support for organized crime and gives this support active protective expression within these communities, particularly in encounters with the police. The leaders of these groups typically wish to acquire large personal fortunes, status, power and political influence. In the process they seek to govern the lives of the people who live in the communities controlled by them. Their administration of the communities is thus based on a combination of support for the members of the organized crime groups as valued members of the community and a predictable application of violence to enforce their will.

Organized crime has different faces. It is capable of being violently disruptive and confrontational in its conflicts with the state and yet it partners with it in the co-rulership of the urban communities in which it operates, and plays an active role in the maintenance of the existing social and political relationships. With regard to its role in system maintenance, for example, impressionistic evidence suggests that the place of women in the Jamaican underground economy is more unequal and limiting than it is in the formal economy and mainstream society. This is certainly true of the drug trade where women are largely confined to high-risk/low-reward roles, such as that of transnational couriers, or "mules". Similarly, with regard to its politics, organized crime remains closely linked to the political system and is an institutional actor that helps to integrate the urban poor into the system and to bolster party control by erecting and maintaining one-party monopolies in the communities.

Permeation of the Political System

This relationship with the political mainstream indicates that the system itself has a latent capacity for political degeneration. Degeneration has been occurring and could continue to occur, for example, via a slow process of increasing the number of garrison constituencies, thereby making the system more politically monopolistic on a constituency by constituency basis.[14] Some 20 per cent of all constituencies and approximately 60 per cent of all urban constituencies have already been fully or partially garrisoned.[15] By this process, the danger to democracy that is presented by the politics–organized crime nexus is always seen as local. However, beyond its local jurisdiction, organized crime has already played a role in violently crushing street protests,[16] and in a few cases, intimidating journalists and public figures who may be critical of "their" government[17] or, as will be discussed below, their party leader.

Changes in the dominant coalition within a political party that favours the personalities, groupings and social forces that tend to rely mostly on street politics and corrupt methods of rule could further reinforce and indeed extend these kinds of developments to the point of silencing dissenting voices within their own parties and among the general public. As will be shown later, in recent times, organized crime groups have been mobilized for this purpose. This element has however been present in the internal political life of the parties, especially in the garrison constituencies, for at least two decades. For example, Pearnel Charles, a member of parliament, former minister of government and former deputy leader of the Jamaica Labour Party (JLP), may credibly claim to have been a victim of physical attacks and intimidation by members of party-affiliated organized crime groups. These attacks occurred in July 1992 when he was a prominent critic of the leader of his party. Even after releasing several white doves, he and his supporters were forced to hastily retreat from a party conference at which it was expected that he would have contested for the post of party leader or in other ways "embarrassed", or in the language of the gangsters, "disrespected" the party leader.[18] A decade later, when Seaga was eventually removed as leader of the party, he too claimed that he and his allies in the party were the victims of the activities of these elements.[19]

Despite their territorial moorings, the leaders and operatives of the criminal groups are not simply pawns in the political game, they are active agents sensitive to the shifts in power and help to make and to consolidate those shifts thought to be in their interests. The Jamaican experience however suggests that leadership of any democratically suspect and politically degenerative process within either political party and in government must come from sections of the political elite; organized crime is simply a willing, able, experienced and self-interested assistant.

Changes in the dominant coalition within a party may be effected in various ways but could involve organized crime playing an increasingly important role in the internal politics of the party and in national elections, that is, by progressively increasing its influence within and degree of control over the political process. This process typically begins with local influence and is most evident in the garrison communities. There, they are able to determine key outcomes, and, in some cases, may even have veto power over major party decisions, such as those to do with candidate selection in local government elections. Such political influence is derived from social support within the communities. From their community base, the more powerful entrepreneurial groups are then able to extend their influence to the constituency level, where they may exercise a degree of control over the party machinery so that they are able to determine, or at least influence, candidate selection at the constituency level. Candidates may be co-opted via funding arrangements and may even be out-manoeuvred by dons who are part of contending party coalitions at the national level. On this basis, some leaders of organized crime groups and networks may become a force in national party affairs and exercise influence over other public processes, such as the awarding of contracts and resource allocation. In turn, a feedback effect may occur, where party dependence on corrupt funding serves to reinforce the influence of organized crime within the party structures. Deep inter-dependencies are therefore developed. Organized crime may further enhance its influence by the process of funding a party or selected party candidates in conditions where the prospects for alternate funding streams are limited, such as when the economic elites, who normally provide the lion's share of campaign funds, withdraw from the coalition that is led by a particular party. This forces the party or some candidates to rely more on illegal funding sources. Such a development may signify a shift in the social base of the coalition. Elements of organized crime may thus become part of the dominant coalition within the funding-dependent party. This outcome would not be irreversible. Changes in the political fortunes of the party and of organized crime may be expected to lead to internal realignments.

This process of empowerment, political entrenchment and interdependence between the political elites and criminal elites is associated with the maturity of organized crime. It is a process whereby politics is "criminalized", that is, there is an increasing resort to criminal methods in politics, and criminality is easily politicized as a protective strategy.[20] The more extensive use of criminal methods in politics is, for example, evident in the use of fraudulent and racketeering schemes to extract large sums from various state agencies to support electoral contests, soliciting kickbacks from private contractors who work for the state, vote buying and voter intimidation. The politicization of criminality is of colonial filiation, but was most pronounced during the 1970s. In the contemporary period, it is most evident in a number of gang wars. Contending criminal groups, especially the organized crime groups that are closely affiliated to the major political parties, are usually quick to name ordinary criminal conflicts as political conflicts. This allows them to mobilize the support of the politically homogenous communities in which they operate and the public support of their members of parliament and other political leaders. Once this is successfully accomplished, the efforts of the police as enforcers of the law are easily nullified. For example, they may be asked to perform peace-keeping duties and to erect buffer zones between the warring groups rather than to arrest the participants.

Organized Crime: The Motor of Violent Crimes

Although it does not directly challenge the state, organized crime nevertheless presents one of the greatest challenges facing the country since independence. It has become the motor of Jamaica's crime problem for several reasons. First, it serves to advertise the success of crime, including violent crime. Its leaders have become highly visible models of material success and social success more generally. Jamaica now has "Super Dons" whose personal assets are valued at hundreds of millions of dollars. Their success is evident in the open displays of opulence, such as the ownership of mansions that are fitted with all sorts of expensive and eye-catching but aesthetically tasteless features such as gilded stairways, external granite walls, fleets of sports utility vehicles, and exhibitionist displays of consumerism. Importantly, it is also manifested in the dons' access to seemingly unlimited numbers of attractive women, and perhaps, just perhaps, more importantly, in their social and political influence. Wealth, money, pleasure, status and power are the desired valuables.

That these social goods may be acquired by criminal means is profoundly subversive of the social order in profoundly social ways. This is particularly true of status acquisition which was formerly the only primary social good (among those listed above) that could not be purchased with criminally acquired wealth. Status acquisition was wedded to the means used to acquire the other goods on which it is based and to valued service to the society, that is, to adherence or, at least, visible adherence to conventional norms.[21] Thus white-collar criminals could acquire status and respectability if their illicit activity was undetected, but violent and highly visible street criminals could not do so. The extent of tolerance of innovative means (grey and illegal) and the diffusion of subcultural norms have, however, eroded the significance placed on means-related conduct norms. Criminally acquired wealth has thus become more fungible. The primacy of money as a value (and the unhinging of law) and the success of organized crime via its bridging relationships to the upper-world of powerful, high-status actors (including very public association with members of the political elite) have undermined this social restraint or limit on criminality.

Second, it has made a successful business of violence. The lucrative extortion racket is an example of this as it allows the groups to monetize their reputations for violence. It motivates and encourages copy-cat extortionists who must now establish the credibility of their claims by engaging in reputation-building violence. Violence thereby becomes more prevalent as a strategy for success in building a criminal career.

Third, it commands considerable means of violence. The major groups are thus able to destabilize the society when engaged in wars among themselves and confrontations with the security forces.

Fourth, organized crime groups have been able to use their criminally acquired wealth to corrupt some of the key institutions of the country including the police force,[22] elements in the state bureaucracy and the political parties. The extent of the problem is illustrated by the following anecdote. Shortly after his arrest and during his extradition proceedings, a major drug trafficker reportedly offered to pay the equivalent of the entire budget allocation of the police force if his extradition was successfully blocked (personal communication).[23] Corrupt institutions tend to be unresponsive to the needs of the people and to become increasing by self-serving. Official involvement in partnerships with organized crime accelerates this process and gives elements in the political administration and the state bureaucracy an interest in blocking cardinal principles of good governance such as accountability and transparency.

Fifth, it has set up and maintains defensible territory, that is, safe havens that give it near immunity from police action. Entry into these areas by the police may precipitate armed battles that are costly in lives lost and may also be politically costly for the police and the political administration. By increasing these costs to law enforcement and the political administration, the garrisons ensure their near complete immunity and security as criminal safe-havens.

Finally, its embeddedness in larger networks of national influence, especially its influence in the political parties, is particularly threatening. This presents the country with the prospect of legislators who are indebted to the crime networks being sent to parliament, and who may frustrate efforts to pass legislation to effectively deal with organized crime and use their influence to weaken the police services and anti-corruption agencies (via resources allocations, undermining of the merit principle, imposition of a compliant leadership and other methods). In 2001, the then minister of national security and justice, K.D. Knight, warned that this prospect was real (*Gleaner*, 25 October 2001).

This idea of organized crime as the main security threat to the society was not always accepted. In the late 1990s, new programmes in the Ministry of National Security and Justice were still largely based on the erroneous idea that domestic violence was the most prevalent and problematic form of homicidal violence and the centre of gravity of the country's crime problem. This construction of the problem served the interests of the police well (they argued that such killings were not preventable by police action and therefore they should not be held accountable for the high homicide rate), and was informed by police data which categorized all forms of inter-personal violence as domestic violence. A mediation unit was consequently set up in the Jamaica Constabulary Force and was given the charge to control domestic violence. This was greatly needed, but was unlikely to have, and indeed did not have, an impact on the homicide problem. Later, there was a better appreciation of the problem, but this was then specified as gang violence, with little distinction being made between youth gangs and organized crime. This assessment, in part, led to the formation of the Peace Management Initiative, which has had some success in pacifying youth gangs and has done much useful work to bring peace to some of the embattled communities, but has made little impression on the country's homicide rate.[24]

The Jamaican population suffers from report fatigue. There is an aversion to, or at least considerable impatience with, any attempt to study the crime problem. There is an understandable demand for action. Studies are in this setting regarded as excuses for inaction on the part of the state. And yet the knowledge gaps are so great that they permit politically convenient constructions of the problem that allow the authorities to evade accountability for non-performance.[25]

The failure to understand the crime problem has very practical negative consequences, as have occurred when mediation and peace-making strategies are applied to conflicts involving organized crime groups. The most obvious example of this was the attempt to negotiate peace between the One Order and Clansman groupings. These negotiations, which occurred in 2005, were brought to public attention when a member of the One Order group was murdered while he was travelling in a motor car with the member of parliament for St Catherine Central, Olivia Grange (*Gleaner*, 7 October 2005). They were both returning from peace negotiations that had the approval of the police.[26] The peace process, and this associated killing in particular, revealed the protective nature of the relationship between the political parties and organized crime, and symbolized the weakness of the police and the power of the organized crime groups.

One outcome of this was that the two members of parliament for the neighbouring constituencies of St Catherine Central and St Catherine South Central, Olivia Grange and Sharon Haye-Webster respectively, who were involved in the peace negotiations (representing the opposing political parties) were forced to justify their involvement in the process. In so doing, the logic of political self-defence led to a misrepresentation of organized crime and the nature of the violence of these groups. The description of the violence tended to converge with the popular narratives which present it as the escalation of interpersonal conflicts and even the outcome of seemingly noble causes such as the defence of their communities. At worst, the violent activities of the new phenomenon of organized crime are interpreted as simply the intensification of old patterns of youth gang and party competitive behaviour. Such representations of organized crime by highly placed members of the political elite may be expected to have the effect of demobilizing the society and law enforcement.

It was not until the mid-1990s, after its transnational character had become evident, that the phenomenon came to be called organized crime by the Jamaican police. In 1997 an Organized Crime Unit was established within the police force (personal correspondence with a senior officer, June 2006). The Jamaica Constabulary Force then began in practice to distinguish more clearly between organized crime and ordinary gangs. Nevertheless, there is still some confusion about the nature of the phenomenon.

Organized Crime Defined

Popular notions of organized crime tend to highlight its *organizational features*, that is, the degree of structural complexity and formalization (Albanese and Das 2003, 4–5; Zhang 1992). There are three aspects to this: the existence of a clear division of labour, that is, specialization by functions and roles; a hierarchical order or command structure that distinguishes operatives from those who make critical decisions; and spatial dispersion, that is, the extent to which the organization or network is distributed across space and thus has to engage in complex coordination. From this perspective, group characteristics, such as the age range of members (extending beyond youth) and their occupations (for example, the inclusion of lawyers, chemists, police officers, financial advisors, politicians and other professionals), may also be regarded as defining features.

Organization and group characteristics are considered to be important as they signify the durability of these networks. The age range of members, for example, suggests that they tend to be involved in life-course–persistent criminal behaviour, and the general organizational characteristics of organized crime groups indicate that, unlike youth gangs, these groups are enduring. These characteristics also determine the scale of operations that are possible; they enable organized crime groups to engage in more lucrative types of crime. The organizational features are thus bound up with the activities of organized crime; the former sets the limits of the latter.

Using these formal organizational features as the defining characteristics, doubt has been cast on whether Jamaican crime groups, including the most successful transnational groups and networks that are engaged in drug-related criminal enterprises, are really organized crime *or* "disorganized crime".[27] Such was the level of confusion among foreign law enforcement officials and researchers in the early 1990s that the Jamaican networks that were operating in the United States were even then described as "organized-disorganized crime".[28] Clearly too much emphasis is placed on formal organizational features as a necessary condition for organized crime. It is simply associative, and may be flexibly associative. Some of the major Jamaican organized crime groups, for example, are highly organized within Jamaica, where they are territorially based, but operate more loosely as networks in foreign territories where they are deprived of community and political protection.

Descriptions of organizational features, including hierarchy, are however important for elaborating policing strategy. If one wishes to destroy a criminal firm, knowing the chain of command, information pathways, and the critical roles within the organization are critically important. The centrality of formal organizational features in this type of thinking is understandable. Some groups have become much more structurally complex since the early 1990s when these characterizations were made, but even if the complexities are grasped, this would nevertheless remain a one-dimensional depiction of organized crime.

Others treat the nature of its *activity*, or rather, activity and organization as the defining features of organized crime (Shigui 1992; Kenney and Finckenauer 1995). Its motivation and activity are seen as being exclusively fixed on material gain. From this perspective, organized crime is enterprise crime. Although ordinary predatory criminal activity is also largely aimed at material gain, it is not enterprise. Ordinary predatory criminality does not have a market orientation and does not engage in the provision of services. Relative to organized crime, it has considerable limitations. Robbery, for example, usually involves great risk in order to access large sums (although some forms, such as computer fraud and corporate crimes, now make access to large sums possible – but these are not street crimes). In contrast, the supply of illicit goods and services tends to yield much higher and recurring returns. This applies to the exploitation of large global markets in illegal drugs, and the provision of protective, sexual and other services. Organized crime groups are able to generate the demand for some of these services. For example, it is well known that by paying in part for transhipment services in the form of addictive drugs, the trafficking groups and networks are able to stimulate the development of a captive local market in hard drugs. More importantly, predatory crime creates the demand for security and protection which the organized crime groups supply. Economists would describe these activities as having good linkages. Moreover, the organized crime groups are able to provide these services (in the local markets) at relatively low risk when compared to the activities of ordinary predatory criminals.

These types of activity tend to stimulate organizational complexity and flexibility. This is especially true for transnational activities operating in international illegal drugs and firearms markets where the criminals are faced with pressures from effective police services and have more limited community support. Even local extortion rackets may require support services, such as bookkeeping, and thus the recruitment of members with the needed competencies.

Legalistic definitions tend to take this tack, that is, highlight the activities and organizational features of organized crime. An example of this is the

INTERPOL definition which was adopted by its General Assembly in 1998. These features are also captured by Albanese (2004, 10) in the following definition: "Organized crime is a continuing criminal enterprise that rationally works to profit from illicit activities that are often in great public demand. Its continuing existence is maintained through the use of force, threats, monopoly control, and/or the corruption of public officials." He specifies the activities and methods of organized crime. This definition of organized crime is, however, too exclusive. As von Lampe (2003, 10) notes, it excludes significant aspects of organized crime, such as predatory activities that have no market orientation, and involvement in "quasi-governmental or parasitic power syndicates". The above definition, while correct in emphasizing the relationship of organized crime to the market, regards it as having one motive, that is, profit making. This is perhaps a generalization from the American experience. However, as will be discussed later, there is also the power motive and strong status strivings, that is, the non-enterprise aspect to organized crime.

Exclusive focus on the profit motive limits understanding of the phenomenon. For example, such an understanding cannot adequately explain the territoriality of Jamaican organized crime. This would have to be regarded as irrationality or a vestige of the pre-enterprise stage of its past when most of these groups and individuals operated as political gunmen or thugs and predatory criminals. It is because of common orientation to power, and particularly its expression in territoriality that organized crime has developed such a close and comfortable relationship with the political system and the parties, not just with individual corrupt politicians with strong pecuniary drives. The power motive also helps to explain why the webs of criminally exploitable ties are so broad and so successfully upward reaching.

Its structural complexity and enterprise character are important aspects of organized crime, but perhaps the most conceptually insightful defining principle is its relationships, especially its relationships with the upper-world. In the Jamaican context, what characterizes organized crime, and clearly distinguishes it from other categories of crime, is the nature of its relationship to power and to key institutions. Organized crime brings the underworld into a mutually beneficial corrupt relationship with powerful upper-world actors and institutions. These webs of criminally exploitable relationships are what make it so corrupting and dangerous.

The relationships that constitute and facilitate the activities of organized crime are governed by implicit and explicit rules. A code of silence is one such rule. In the Jamaican case, as in Italy where organized crime has been grounded in a broad set of relationships and community norms, this rule is accepted, or at least adhered to, in these wider relationships. In other words, in the Jamaican context, some of these codes find reinforcement in a sub-culture where there is considerable alienation from the state. This alienation and subcultural formation in turn explains the expanded political space within which the quasi-governmental activities of organized crime find approval. In its territorial domain, organized crime engages in rule making and rule enforcement. Indeed some territorially based groups have developed elaborate systems of rule enforcement that apply not just to the members of the group, but also to the entire communities in which they operate. These are the "jungle courts" of Kingston's inner-city communities where residents may be tried and punished for various violations.[29] Infractions range from fraudulently presenting themselves as agents of the organized crime groups who are assigned to collect extortion fees, to rape, physical abuse of one's partner and child neglect. The governmental functions that have been usurped by organized crime include policing, justice administration, and the provision of welfare services, such as food aid and early childhood education. While these activities yield considerable benefits to the enterprise and profit-making endeavours of the groups (for example, tales of the recovery of property stolen from a poor market vendor is good advertising for protection racketeering), they also highlight the power motives of these groups.[30]

Cressey's definition of organized crime, although written in 1969, succinctly captures the essential elements of a good conceptual definition of the phenomenon, that is, the activity, organization, relationships and means used. Unlike most of the other definitions, it takes the definiendum as the act rather than the entity that commits the act: "An organized crime is any crime committed by a person occupying, in an established division of labor, a position designed for the commission of crime providing that such division of labor also includes at least one position for a corrupter, one position for a corruptee, and one position for an enforcer" (Cressey 1969, 319, cited in Abadinsky 1990, 3).

Organized crime groups and networks thus contrast with youth gangs and groups of ordinary criminals. These latter groupings, particularly youth gangs, tend to emerge spontaneously from the everyday interaction of young people in conditions of high population density, high levels of youth unemployment, high household density, weak family support systems, and intense street life that plays an important role in the socialization of adolescents. As Thrasher (1994) has pointed out, their "most rudimentary form of collective behaviour is interstimulation", that is, the rehearsal of adventure – including sexual adventure and violent conflicts. In the Jamaican context, these groupings seek to control space (their "corner" or "ends"), develop a group solidarity and identity, and to collectively participate in mainly non-criminal activity. Some of these activities, to the extent that they involve movement outside of their territory (for example, to attend dances) may bring them into conflict with other similar groups. Such conflicts are usually over intangibles, including identity issues and simply being in the territory of another group, but may also be over girls and, at times, over guns. Individual members of these groups may engage in predatory crimes, but the group is not formed for this purpose. Such gangs are usually called "crews" to distinguish them from groups whose *raison d'être* is crime, as is the case with organized crime.[31]

A Typology of Organized Crime

Organized crime is diverse in its forms. It consists of networks that are engaged in enterprise crimes, and the violent entrepreneurs. This distinction turns on the predominant types of activities they are engaged in. Those who are engaged primarily in enterprise crimes, supply goods and services that people more or less willingly purchase under conditions of illegality. The violent entrepreneurs constitute a special variety of organized crime that makes a business of violence, including providing violence-related services to the political parties (such as purging a constituency or smaller territorial unit of persons affiliated to the opposing party, switching an area in terms of its party affiliation, and lesser forms of voter intimidation).

Classifying the types of organized crime by this method may yield useful insights into the patterns of demand for illicit services in the society. For example, the demand for access to the means of violence (resulting in the sale and rental of illegal guns on a commercial scale) and the demand for violence itself (which is met by murder-for-hire "professionals" and protection services). From this, further study of the process of commoditization of violence may tell interesting tales about social and political change.[32] It also permits analysis of how differences in the illegal opportunity structures at the community level may account for the difference in the activities of organized crime networks. For example, groups that are located in communities that are in close proximity to sea and airports may enjoy greater possibilities for involvement in drugs and arms trafficking than other groups that are not so situated. This categorization may therefore be used in useful and analytically productive ways.

Their organizational styles and the nature of their relationships may also be used as categorizing principles. Enterprise crime operates on two models: the corporate model that is typical of those networks that operate on the north coast and in central Jamaica; and the clientelistic model that is typical of those groups that operate in the greater Kingston area.

The different organizational forms signify the differences in the nature of the larger set of relationships in which they are entwined or suffused with. At the risk of overdrawing the distinctions, the corporate model is a pattern of organization that approximates the formal structures of a corporation or firm with clear notions of ownership, a more or less formal hierarchy, and employer-employee type relationships (Abadinsky 1990). The patron-client model, on the other hand, is based on chains of personalized relations, hierarchies ordered on the principle of proximity to the leader (inner circles and outer circles), role and status hierarchies that are derived from this, reciprocities, and overt political relationships that are all formed in the context of a community or some territorial unit. Such organized crime groupings are a part of sets of networks that seek to "convert the state into a source of patronage and material rewards for individuals" (Stone 1980, 92).[33] The influence of the groupings in these criminally exploitable networks have historically been based on their ability to use force and fraud to determine the margins of victory in local electoral contests – usually, but not always, in a context of an already existing majority support for their party.

Those groups that take the corporate form seek to bridge the worlds of formal business and criminal enterprise. Their "business" activity is an extension of their criminal activity. The corporate model may be interpreted as a pathway out of crime, but may simply be a link in a chain of criminality. For example, drug trafficking may be used as a source of capital accumulation. The criminally acquired funds may then be used to acquire heavy equipment and to start up firms that supply various services to the state such as road construction, haulage, solid waste disposal and land fill. Both sets of activities (the overtly criminal and the seemingly legitimate) are integrated and mutually supportive, but appear to be distinct in terms of their legal statuses, and separate in terms of their operations. The reality is however usually not as simple as that. The "legitimate" business firms are usually also directly engaged in criminality; its methods may include defrauding its clients and refusing to pay its workers. Its methods of business are systematically criminal, but its outputs, that is, its products and services, are not defined in law as criminal.

Their network of criminal relationships extends into the professions, particularly the legal profession. For instance, some criminal entrepreneurs in the city of Montego Bay are known to create opportunities for these professionals to participate in drug trafficking as joint financiers of particular deals (personal correspondence with a participant).

This corporate type of organized crime is typically non-territorial. They are not domiciled in the communities of the urban poor. Their capacity to protect their operations and to engage in violence is consequently very limited. Indeed, some of them may become the victims of extortion. They are dependent on external forces to provide protection for their operations. Such services may be outsourced to other organized crime groups that have greater capabilities in the field of protection, or to corrupt police officers. Its leaders therefore tend to enjoy a lower level of visibility, and greater social acceptability than their more violent counterparts.

Those groups that operate on the patron–client model tend to be territorial, are involved in the political administration of the communities, and tend to mimic the methods of building support and organizational style of the political parties. They seek to sustain and strengthen their social support base via patronage and the cultivation of relationships that are based on dependency. A standard method is the use of various welfare projects and even programmes aimed at different target groups within the communities such as the youth and the aged. In addition there are the ad hoc everyday opportunities for extending influence and building social support that may be illustrated by the following case. A prostitute from one of the inner-city communities of Kingston (that is a site for other research project) left her children on their own for a period of some four days so that she could go to work on the north coast of the island. On her return, she was tried in the local jungle court on charges of child neglect (not prostitution). Instead of being punished, the don secured a job for her at one of the more established companies that operate in close proximity to the community. Clearly there was some relationship between the company and the don. It is suspected that the firm was under the protection of the don and that he asked for a favour that could not be refused.

This effort and outcome presents the organized crime firm as a good corporate citizen. The recipient of the favour would be eternally grateful. The story of her treatment would (and did) extend and reinforce the support of the organized crime group as a part of the governance structure of the community.

This type has a tradition of delivering goods to the community as a whole, not just to individuals as individuals. There are benefits that are clearly derived from the mere presence of the organized crime group in the community. These, as will be discussed later, include access to free utilities. The presence of the organized crime group dissuades the providers from attempting to collect for their services. Even privately owned factories that operate within the territorial boundaries of the local organized crime group, and which do not produce electricity, may be unwilling providers of this service. Householders simply illegally connect their homes to the factory as a power supply and the protection of the don ensures that the connections are not removed.

The dynamics of territorial control are such that the groups that operate on the patron–client model do not restrict their activity to enterprise crimes. Their very survival necessitates the development of some capacity to protect their territory. Some elements of this latter type may specialize in the business of violence and businesses that are based on their capacity to deliver violence with impunity such as extortion and protection rackets. They may become violent entrepreneurs.

As a pure type, the violent entrepreneur is predatory. Violent entrepreneurs may emerge in conditions where there are no opportunities for enterprise activity and in some instances their geographic location may even place the lucrative extortion rackets out of their reach. Their major assets become their capacity to deliver violence and their linkages to the political parties. They become very violence prone as they seek to extort other organized crime networks of the enterprise type that are better placed to enjoy high-yield criminally exploitable opportunities and may engage in constant battles with other groups for the opportunity to extort occasional road works projects and to share in the rewards of simply permitting various types of state-related work to take place. The predatory impulses are so strong that they at times even strain the very political relationships that protect them.

The Features of Organized Crime

We may now employ these definitional insights to analyse the nature of organized crime in Jamaica with emphasis on its activities, relationships and means used to achieve its objectives.

Activities

Jamaican organized crime is involved in a widening range of illegal and legal activities. Some of these illegal activities within Jamaica's borders have been noted above and include: enterprise crimes, that is, the supply of illicit goods such as recreational drugs and pornographic productions that involve children, and seemingly licit goods such as sand, but which are illegally acquired; the supply of illicit services such as prostitution and violence related services such as protection rackets and political intimidation. Its seemingly legal activities include construction, trucking, solid-waste disposal and related services, hotel services, entertainment, motor vehicle parking, and financing or informal banking. These lists are far from exhaustive. Josephs (1999) provides a similar description of some of their activities in the United States. There, unlike in Jamaica, most of the activities of Jamaican organized crime are limited to the supply of illegal goods. They have not been able to build the wider political and social networks that would allow them to cross over in any significant ways into legitimate business activity.

As discussed earlier, differences in the activities of organized crime groups indicate a differentiation in group and network types. Developments in the construction sector of the economy illustrate this. Some of the more entrepreneurial groups that are concerned with laundering criminally acquired funds and developing legitimate businesses have formed construction firms and exploit their relationship with state actors to secure contracts, establishing private sector partnerships, and delivering legal goods and services. That they are organized crime affiliated firms gives them advantages. They may avoid extortion charges, and labour problems, such as work stoppages that delay job completion. On the other hand, those groups that are specialists in violence intimidate construction companies to employ affiliates of these crime groups, and force the companies to assign these workers to types of work that are beyond their competence and to award them rates of pay that are commensurate with these fictitious skills. For example, unskilled workers may be employed as masons with obvious consequences for the quality of work done. These organized crime "firms" then "tax" or extort the workers as a return on their "job placement" service. By these means, their reputations for violence, like Midas's touch, are capable of turning things into gold. They may even extend their targets to some of the entrepreneurial organized crime groups, often precipitating violence.

The above differentiation is, however, not always very clear. The older, highly organized, territorially based patron-client groups are becoming increasingly involved in the full range of illegal services, including activities such as north coast prostitution, which, before, were largely left to free individual operators. These are full service providers, or criminal conglomerates, that are able to protect their own enterprise operations and also engage in predatory activity, such as extortion rackets. New and more corporate networks are opening up non-traditional fields, such as real estate rackets, that target victims across the globe via internet marketing. These latter types are vulnerable to the more powerful and more violent predatory groups that may begin by extorting them, but may later take over partially, or in full, some of their businesses.

Drug trafficking to and distribution in the drug retail markets of North America and Europe, however, provided the main impetus for the development of organized crime and gave it a service and market orientation.[34] Penetration of the international drug markets helped to transform territorially based groupings of gangsters and political thugs into organized crime groups. For more than four decades, Jamaica has been a major producer and exporter of cannabis. There has been considerable variation in production levels. If drug seizure by the police is an indicator of the levels of production and export activity, then the years 1989 and 2003 represent high points in production and exportation.[35] Some 440,723 kilograms of prepared cannabis were seized in 1989 and 444,639 hectares of the crop destroyed in 2003 (table 1.1). In 2006, Jamaica was responsible for 51 per cent of all of the cannabis seized in the Caribbean (figure 1.1).

Once entry into the retail trade was established, Jamaican groups sought to diversify their product offerings to include the distribution of Colombian cocaine. American agencies estimate that in the year 2000, some one hundred to one hundred and twenty metric tonnes of cocaine valued at US$4 to US$4.5 billion were trans-shipped to the United States via Jamaica.[36]

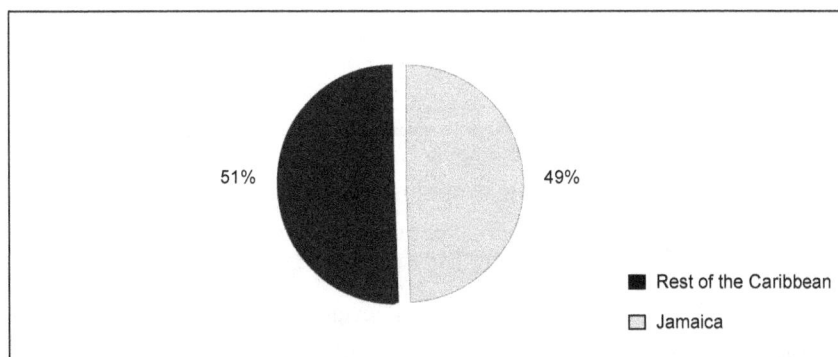

Figure 1.1 Kilograms of ganja seized in the Caribbean, 2004
Source: UNODC 2006.

Table 1.1   Drug Seizures, 1986–2006

Year	Ganja (Kg)	Ganja Production (Ha)	Ganja Products (Kg)	Cocaine (Kg)	Other Hard Drugs (Pieces and Tablets)
2006	37,197	377	128	109	500
2005	19,511	304	5	348	499
2004	20,952	308	229	1,736	136,226
2003	36,604	444,639	1,913	1,619	2,949
2002	27,030	300	509	3,725	2,829
2001	74,432	496	219	2,950	8,181
2000	55,870	10,762	597	1,624	4,790
1999	22,740	1,980	433	2,455	3,543
1998	–	–	–	–	–
1997	31,587	744	451	–	6,296
1996	41,263	497	436	236	2,321
1995	26,807	992	453	571	1,817
1994	32,280	6,406	2,407	124	1,363
1993	49,762	401	123	82	–
1992	41,384	694	120	662	–
1991	3,161	729	–	70	–
1990	26,604	1,540	44	204	–
1989	440,723	2,675	–	13	–
1988	53,080	1,207	–	–	–
1987	216,255	2,565	–	9	–
1986	317,873	2,756	–	547	–

Source: Economic and Social Survey of Jamaica, various years.

Jamaican organized crime groups and networks have become truly transnational. Their international ties and transnational operations tend to track the drug-trafficking routes from the producer countries in Latin America, via the different trade routes into the North American markets. In this regard, they are not exceptional. They are simply one set of actors in a larger global process. As others have argued, the process of globalization has facilitated the transnational activity of organized crime groups (Findlay 1999). Increased movement of goods and people has been accompanied by an increased illicit trade. Illicit goods travel through similar channels as licit goods. Corrupt practices associated with the trade in licit goods, such as the evasion of customs duties, thus provide channels for the smuggling of illicit goods. Jamaica is an open trading economy. Its major trading partner is the United States with its large drug and firearm markets.

Jamaica has a relatively large diaspora that is settled in these countries. The criminal networks have been able to insert themselves into the communities where black and other minority migrant populations are concentrated, and where the social conditions that favour their activities and organizational growth may be found. Bowling and Phillips (2006) provide an excellent analytic description of these conditions in the United Kingdom, and Wilson (1996) and the ethnographies of Anderson (1990) are similarly useful for understanding these conditions as the outcome of enduring racial inequalities in the United States.

As noted elsewhere (Harriott 2006), the violent activities of Jamaican groups involved in organized crime in the United States and the United Kingdom have earned them considerable notoriety and harmed the image of the Jamaican people. This is not peculiar to the Jamaican groups and networks. Other nationalities have been similarly stereotyped as violent and criminal. In the early twentieth century, Italians were described by the American press as "cruel, treacherous, vindictive and violent" (Reppetto 2004, xi), and at the end of the century, Russians were similarly described. American journalistic and academic writings in particular have tended to explain the existence and activity of various organized crime groups in terms of race, ethnicity and nationality (see, for example, Kleinknecht 1996). Given their race perspectives on crime, Jamaican crime thus implicates not just all Jamaicans, but the whole black population. Moreover, in the case of Jamaican crime in the United States, it is foreign and violent and therefore, in the context of strong anti-migration sentiments, would seem to be particularly threatening.[37]

The accumulation of large sums from their activities abroad has facilitated a transformation of the operations of these groups in Jamaica. Their entry into new types of seemingly legitimate businesses and money-laundering agreements with established firms have helped them to set up relationships that make an even wider range of activities possible.

Countermeasures against Jamaican crime networks in the United States and the United Kingdom may have hastened the efforts to develop their business interests and rackets in Jamaica. By the mid-1990s, many of the leaders and operatives in the larger transnational Jamaican networks were either in American prisons or had been deported to Jamaica. Later, there were similar law enforcement efforts in the United Kingdom with similar results. The operation of organized crime in Jamaica seems to have flourished after the mid-1990s with the extortion rackets blossoming towards the end of the 1990s. A national business victimization survey consisting of a sample of four hundred firms revealed that in 2002, approximately 5 per cent of them were regularly paying protection or extortion fees (Francis et al. 2004). The organized crime groups were then beginning to put a stranglehold on urban-based businesses, especially in construction, transportation, the retail trade in haberdashery, and manufacturing. New rackets were emerging and old rackets were being conducted in new ways, on a new scale, and with greater success.

Extortion and protection rackets have become a major source of income and power for the organized crime groups. It is generally understood that there is an important distinction between these two types of crimes. Extortion is essentially a predatory crime and involves the demand for payments in return for protection from the danger presented by the person or group that demands the payments. Protection rackets, on the other hand, are more of an enterprise crime. Payments are demanded in return for the provision of services that protect the victim from others who may present a criminal threat. Unlike extortion, the source of the danger and the source of the protective service are different. Although the contract between the service provider and the victim is an involuntary one, and the price is fixed under the threat of violence, some value is added. Both extortion and protection involve the use of a credible threat of violence, but the seemingly more benign protection racketeer must be able to deliver violence against both his "client" and free agent predators that his clients may encounter. Protection services may therefore easily evolve into extortion rackets.

These rackets have revolutionized crime in Jamaica. Unlike drugs, they produce regular income and at a relatively low risk. Consequently, the dons are able to pay salaries to the members of their groups. Crime has become a regular full-time occupation with a reliable income. These networks are also able to make regular contributions to various community projects and to transform them into programmes that strengthen their support base. There are now two clear features of the more developed criminal networks in the country. These are professionalization and a quasi-governmental engagement. The latter involves the provision of welfare and other services, such as banking, early childhood education and policing. Welfare and protective activity yields strong community support and a benign image. It helps to build the relationships that nurture and empower organized crime, especially the violent predatory variety that is more akin to what is understood as "mafia".[38]

The Relationships and Methods

As discussed above there are basically two models of organized crime. These are the entrepreneurial and the predatory forms that may operate, using corporate and the patron-client methods. Both are useful principles of classification especially when used together.

Entrepreneurial networks that are not territorially based may be expected to evolve in a more corporate direction, while the predatory territorially based groups tend to use patron-client methods to cement their relationships with the communities in which they are based and are more likely to evolve into community gatekeepers.

As noted above, the different organizational forms signify the differences in the nature of their internal and external relationships. The corporate model is proprietary and its relationships tend to take on a business network character while the patron-client model is based on more highly personalized relationships that are formed over a longer period of time in the context of a community.

Most organized crime groups adopt the patron-client model.[39] Its success is based on two sets of relationships: with the communities of the urban poor, and with the main political parties. All other relationships that make both enterprise and high-reward–low-risk predatory crimes possible are built on these two foundational relationships.

Relationship with the Communities of the Urban Poor

Most Jamaican organized crime groups tend to be territorially based and are rooted in the communities of the urban poor in the sense that they belong to these communities, their ties to them being organic and multifaceted. This is where they emerged as street gangs before evolving into units of organized crime. As these communities became politically mobilized and politically homogenous, the resident gangs became party-affiliated actors in this process.

The social conditions in these communities are characterized by high rates of poverty; high rates of youth unemployment; poor housing, including high household density; weak familial relations; over-representation of young people in their population structure; and high levels of violence. Between 1990 and 2002, poverty levels in the country ranged between 28 per cent and 16 per cent.[40] Urban poverty rates have tended to be lower than rural rates. However, the high violence communities of the urban poor all have very high levels of poverty. In some of these communities, such as those of Central Kingston, the estimated level of unemployment is 70 per cent, much of this being long-term or chronic unemployment.[41] In other communities, the levels of unemployment are considerably lower, but the rates of underemployment are high. Anderson et al. (2004) mapped housing conditions in a number of Kingston's inner-city communities. Their research revealed that in some of these communities in western Kingston, while the average household size was not particularly high, household density was very high. In Denham Town, for example, there was an average of 2.64 persons per room, and when the single-person households were excluded from the analysis, the mean number of persons per room was 3.24 (Anderson et al. 2004, 33–35).

Some of the basic demographic characteristics, and particularly the age structure, of these areas are also problematic. National census data shows that the male population is young. In Denham Town and Wilton Gardens, for example, some 73 per cent and 76 per cent respectively of all males are younger than thirty-five years. In neighbouring Rose Town, just over 74 per cent of the population is below age thirty-five years. Some 46 per cent of the population is male, but 86 per cent of all males are under 35 years old. This data contrasts with the national population of which 66.43 per cent of all males are below thirty-five years. It is this age set that is more likely to enter gangs, engage in violence and provide a recruitment pool for the "shottas" of organized crime.

The levels of violence in and between these communities tend to be extraordinarily high. In 2005, the homicide rate for the city of Kingston was approximately 128 incidents per 100,000 citizens.[42] Some of the communities within the western section of Kingston, that is, the sections of the city where lower income households are most concentrated, are sometimes veritable war zones. Table 1.2 provides the homicide rates for selected communities. In 2004, for example, the community of Denham Town had a homicide rate of 611 incidents per 100,000 citizens. These homicides are usually the result of war between groups that reside in the garrison communities.

The Garrisons as "Mafia Republics"?

Inner-city residents face social exclusion and stigmatization. The association of their communities with violence, including violence that is directed at the security forces, has renewed and reinforced old stigmas that predate independence.[43] As communities, their relationship to the law is similar to that of pariah groups in that they are treated as being outside of the law in two senses: being lawless; and not being entitled to protection by the law. Consistent with this, the police either ignore their problems or apply excessive force and disregard their rights as citizens (Harriott 2000).

This reality creates the political space for self-policing and the other quasi-governmental activity of organized crime. If the failure to deliver the needed and expected social goods created the space for these groups to adopt this strategy, their provision of these services have helped to strengthen their social support base in these communities and indeed in the country. They have successfully exploited the alienation from the state and its incapacity to treat the problems of the poor.

Beyond its quasi-governmental activity, organized crime has set up an opportunity structure and offers an alternate or criminal career path to young marginalized males who anticipate social failure were they to persist in seeking conventional opportunities. It is an alternate route to realizing the social goods that they wish to acquire: wealth, power, high status and respect. Acquiring the latter two by criminal means may be somewhat problematic (unless they are very successful and avoid the notoriety that comes from association with violence), but at least they are able to acquire them within the subculture. In inner-city community settings where there are so many living examples of social failure, for young males, organized crime offers opportunities for social success.

The garrison communities are special cases of the relationship of organized crime to these communities and to the political parties.[44] There, these relationships find intensive expression in the quasi-governmental activity of organized crime. The garrison has become a special mode of political administration, whereby powerful criminal groups are a part of the dominant coalition that manages the affairs of the community. Criminal groups are the dominant local power. They negotiate with the political party as active agents and as a political force within it. There is thus constant tension in the relationship between the parties and these groups as the local dominant coalition is usually very different from the dominant national coalition within the parties. The garrison may be considered as a kind of local regime type which is based on the rule of a crime network-political party coalition. This local regime seeks political monopoly and provides a safe haven for criminal groups.

The garrison is a new political creature. It reflects the failure after independence to integrate the urban poor via the mainstream social and economic institutions (school and work); and, in this context, the resort to corrupt methods of incorporating these excluded urban poor into the political system. In this type of community the quasi-governmental functions of organized crime are most evident.

Earlier, the welfare services provided by the dons were described. Its activities, however, extend to what constitutes the core functions of the state, that is, the provision of security services and the administration of justice. Organized crime groups have effectively established a monopoly on the means and use of violence within the garrison communities. In some communities, one is able to hold a personal illegal firearm only with the approval of the don and, even if the permit is granted, the individual is held to account for any armed action taken. On the basis of this monopoly, the crime networks have been able to engage in rule making, the effective policing of these rules and punishment of rule violators. This is expressed in the jungle courts. The power of these networks is institutionalized in rules and administrative structures.

In table 1.2, data are presented on the homicide rates for selected communities in the Kingston Metropolitan Area. It highlights the policing effects of organized crime in the garrisons where its control over criminality is complete. In these areas, the homicides are typically related to the regulation of these communities, and may be the results of sentences that are passed by the jungle courts or directly by the dons. The homicide rates for these areas are usually below the national average and well below the averages for the cities. Indeed, as is the case with Matthew's Lane, Parade Gardens and Tivoli Gardens, the frequency counts tend to zero. This may be contrasted with other selected areas where organized crime groups either do not exist, or have not established a monopoly on the use of violence, their disciplinary power within and control over the given territory is contested, and there is factional fighting between and within communities. In these areas, the homicide rate may even exceed 600 incidents per 100,000 citizens as was the case in Denham Town between 2004 and 2006 and approximately twelve times the national mean. Homicide rates tend to be low within the garrisons, but when the groups within these communities become involved in violent conflicts, these wars may be protracted and the death toll is usually very high.

In the absence of proper state services, the people have come to value the services provided by organized crime (despite the abuses of power they also suffer from these groups). It is not just the welfare services that are valued, but also the violence-related services. For example, the women feel that the "jungle courts" protect them from rapists and other (out-group and otherwise disfavoured) predators. The people tend to regard themselves as stakeholders, or rather, as shareholders in the enterprise with entitlements. Welfare benefits are treated as entitlements; as a return for their tolerance, loyalty and, in some cases, kinship and fictive kinship ties to the leaders of the crime groups. Notions of mythical kinship may be exploited by these groups to build solidarity and a protective shield against the

Table 1.2   Control of Criminals by Organized Crime: Homicide Data from
Selected Communities, 2000–2006

Community	Year			
	2000	2002	2004	2006
Matthew's Lane	0	0	– (1)	– (1)
Parade Gardens	0	0	0	0
Tivoli Gardens	–	0	90 (4)	20 (1)
Fletcher's Land	200 (8)	100 (4)	50 (2)	125 (5)
Trench Town★	113 (8)	55 (4)	155 (11)	126 (9)
Denham Town	383 (32)	503 (42)	611 (51)	681 (57)
Hannah Town★	172 (6)	85 (3)	143 (5)	199 (7)
Tower Hill	0	9.1 (1)	9 (1)	9 (1)
Grant's Pen★	125 (10)	113 (9)	112 (9)	36 (3)

★Community/communities that have had deep and lasting splits into contending factions.

Note: Rates are per 100,000, and the frequency counts are in parentheses.

Sources: Jamaica Constabulary Force Statistics Unit provided the frequency counts, and the population estimates are based on the 2002 census.

authorities.[45] Kinship, however, implies responsibilities and obligations. Naming of the leaders of organized crime as "Father" or "Prime Minister" is thus consistent with this.[46] Bad faith in delivering on his obligations may therefore undermine community support for a particular don (but not the idea of organized crime) and leave him vulnerable to challenges from within the group and pressures from the police.

Gatekeeper and Mediator

The relationship of organized crime with the communities of the urban poor allows the dons to play a gatekeeping role and to regulate access to these communities. External agencies that provide useful services to these communities must seek their approval of projects; non-cooperation on the part of the don may signal the failure of any such project.

The position of gatekeeper may at times present opportunities for a more subtle role as mediator. The following example illustrates how in their gatekeeping position the dons may play a mediating role between entrance-seeking agencies and the communities, in this case, between a small construction firm that wished to do business in the vicinity of a community in which the major organized crime group in the area had considerable influence and power.

This case occurred in Kingston and involved a small but experienced construction firm that had secured a contract to do repairs on roads bordering the community. The dominant political party in the area, the People's National Party (PNP), was also the party in government. The firm did not have well-established links with the ruling party. Indeed, based on its past associations, its owners may have reasonably been viewed as supporters of the JLP, the party in opposition.

As the firm had a subcontract for road construction, it was indirectly doing business with the government. The people in the neighbouring community therefore had a sense of possibilities, and perhaps even entitlement due to their PNP affiliations.

On the first day of operations, some two hundred persons invaded the work-site demanding employment. If the firm had acceded to these demands, the contract would have been unprofitable for it. Only ten workers were needed. The site was therefore closed.

Faced with this difficulty, the firm then made contact with the don of the area who we will call T. The meeting between the principal of the firm and T occurred at the office of the latter and quickly turned to politics as the prominently displayed photographs of the late Michael Manley, former prime minister and leader of the PNP, became the topic of conversation. The contractor expressed his admiration of the popular former party leader and a good rapport was struck with T. He then told T of his difficulties at the work site. In response, T assured him that these were minor problems and that he would send someone to sort them out.

On the agreed date and at the exact time and place, T's representative made himself available to be transported to the site. On their arrival at the construction site, sure enough, the crowd once again descended on it. T's agent asked the contractor how many persons he would be willing to hire. The contractor responded that fifteen would be acceptable (though only ten were needed). The agent then simply selected twelve persons for work and told the other one hundred and ninety to go home. Without complaint they immediately left. There were no further difficulties. The site was now protected.[47]

Mediation services such as the above are highly valued by both parties to the dispute. In this case, the don set the limits on the demands that the citizens, as job-seekers, were able to make on the supplier of services. The contractors were able to function and were well aware that the state did not have the capacity to solve these problems and to provide them with better options. On the part of the community, they too understand that such confrontations had to be resolved as a condition for either or both parties to be able to realize the expected benefits. In this case, they knew that it was impossible for the firm to hire all of them. They had no method of determining who should be selected for employment that would satisfy the requirements for a settlement. They too needed a mediator. The don is therefore also seen by them as having a valued role. Even the apparently arbitrary method of selecting the employees may have been (unwittingly and instinctively) designed to achieve compliance. The twelve appeared to have been chosen on a whim (it was done in a matter of seconds) and in a manner that seemed to emphatically express the unfettered power of the don. With a seemingly arbitrary swiftness, he simply selected individuals who were located in different sections of the crowd. The matter may however have been more complicated than that. In this arbitrariness, a method may have been revealed. The method of selection may have appeared to have been based on chance, or as approximating the random principle. If this was the case, or was believed to be the case, then the selections would therefore have been or appeared to have been unbiased and just. If this interpretation is correct, then this was a brilliant expression of the coupling of power and authority. Compliance was not just a matter of domination or of authority. Power was exercised so that it became authoritative and therefore elicited compliance. There is much sophistication in the enactment of the roles of gatekeeper and mediator and in the manipulation of sources of power and authority. The point here is that there was sufficient ambiguity to allow for this interpretation.[48]

The regulation of access also applies to the political parties, but with important differences. The parties command the support of sections of the population and, depending on the level and intensity of this support, the dons may threaten to lead a defection of the community to the opposing party. This tactic may be used to extract resources from the party or state. In the case of the garrisons, the parties command the overwhelming and easily mobilized support of the people. Here the dons may still leverage their gatekeeping positions, but within tighter limits.

The power and influence of the dons due to their quasi-governmental role, while expressive of the failures of the state, also reflects adaptation to this failure by building partnerships that maintain a measure of party control, albeit weakened and negotiated.

Prefiguring the don of the 1980s was the "rankin" of the 1970s, that is, the gang leader-cum-political militant. He too was a middle man – he represented the urban marginalized to the outside world and would extract from outside agencies the needed goods. Davidson (1997, 94) reports an interview with a gang member as follows: "The major Rankin is the most intelligent person, the man who can go out there and speak on your behalf, stand up for you and demand the things that you need. That is the duty of the Rankin. He looks after his boys."

Like the don of today, he had a duty to provide for the community. He was both client and patron. The rankin' was a master gatekeeper who was able to leverage his position in order to access the resources of the state.

"I Want Proof": Relations with Political Parties and the State

Crime has deep social roots, but Jamaican organized crime is both indirectly and directly a creature of the political process. The rise of organized crime is the unintended outcome of public policies that have sustained, if not intensified, the set of social problems that propel the rate of violent crime – high levels of inequality, high rates of youth unemployment and underemployment.[49] This is an indirect influence. Politics has also had a more direct influence on the rise of organized crime. It is this direct influence that, for example, led the then superintendent of police for the area that includes Spanish Town, Kenneth Wade, to state that "the support of the PNP has helped to fuel the criminality of the Clansman gang" (*Gleaner*, 2 November 2005, 1). A similar thing could be said of the relationship between the One Order group – the main rival of the Clansmen – and the JLP. This is not a problem of a particular party or particular personalities within these parties; it is rather a more systemic problem. The relationship between organized crime and the parties is a partnership of institutional actors that serves to reinforce their respective power.

The relationship with the political parties is a pivotal one for organized crime. This is what exponentially expands their criminally exploitable ties and aids access to other exploitable relationships. It links the street criminal to those in the upper reaches of the power structure, links the "downtown" racketeers to the "uptown" racketeers, or as the Italians would put it, the "low" mafia to the "high" mafia. This relationship multiplies the types and scale of the criminal enterprise. To the members of these criminal groups, the state is like an inexhaustible gold mine and their relationship with the political parties allows them to tap the large veins in these mines (personal correspondence with a member of one of the major networks). Being criminal entrepreneurs allows them to do this in ways that were not possible when they were simply gangsters. One of the more recent networks, one with limited community influence, targeted Jamaica House directly, and when this failed, it targeted a politically ambitious minister (personal correspondence between the author and a former Jamaica House administrator).[50] Affiliated firms have since had access to large government contracts via various devices. An ever-expanding set of relationships has allowed this group to grow, from fulfilling contracts funded by a single ministry, to working for an increasing number of government agencies and handling billions of dollars of state funds, and, more recently, to even having access to private sector contracts (where the contracting firm is involved in partnerships with government or subject to ministerial influences).[51]

Many examples of this kind of corrupt partnership may be found across both developed and developing countries. In the case of the United States, the long history of these links has been documented, especially in New York City and Chicago (Reppetto 2004; Kenney and Finckenauer 1995).

The corruption-ridden Liberal Democratic Party of Japan is notorious for its relationship with organized crime groups in that country (see Hill 2004). Italian politics has been marred by the deep involvement of the mafia and other organized crime groups. Santino notes that some seventy-two city councils were dissolved for "the presence of Mafia members as counselors, mayors" (Santino 2003). The problem was not restricted to local politics. There was also the remarkable case of former prime minister Giulio Andreotti, who was charged with being a member of the Mafia. This case revealed how deep the ties of the mafia were to the Christian Democratic Party and how great was its influence in Italian politics. In Russia, "22 assistants to deputies of the State Duma were arrested (in 1995) for dealings with the criminal world" (Gilinsky 2001 cited in Albanese, Das and Verma 2003, 9). Representatives of organized crime are said to have successfully contested for public office in Taiwan (NIJ 2007, 13), and reportedly "sit in positions of local administration" and "play a key role in parliamentary elections" in Thailand (ibid., 14). In India, the dons of organized crime play a prominent role in the politics of some states. For example, they have been described as "an invisible force behind the continuance of every government in Uttar Pradesh" (S. Mishra, "A Criminal Record", *India Today*, 1 November 2004). Nigeria and Colombia have had similar troubles. For example, Pablo Escobar, one of the most notorious drug lords, was, during the earlier stages of his career, a member of the Colombian senate.

In Jamaica, the linkage between the political parties and organized crime is most evident in the garrisons where, as noted earlier, the dons are integrated into the political administration of the community. The garrison is clearly a creature of public policy. These communities were created by public funds as "social housing". They were designed as party-homogenous areas and constructed as such by a process that began with cleansing the locale of all supporters of the opposing party. Violent means were invariably used to achieve this and involved forced removals by the state security forces, and, in some cases, armed terror by party militants. Having cleared the ground, social housing is constructed and allocated on the basis of party affiliation. Tivoli Gardens and Arnett Gardens, the two major garrisons, were created in this way.[52] The place of violence in the creation and maintenance of these communities led to the valorization of the violent elements and gave them high social status and authoritative roles in the administration of these communities. Criminals and armed militants, the one indistinguishable from the other, thus became a prominent part of a system of tight party control.

The weakening of the state during and after the 1980s and the new drug wealth that was acquired by the organized crime groups since then have had the combined effect of loosening the hold of the parties in the inner-city communities and altering the power relations between the parties and the criminal groups in these localities. This change is now reflected in the quasi-governmental functions of organized crime and the nature of the partnership with the parties. Channelling state funds to the organized crime groups is a manifestation of the partnership. In turn, the dons make handsome contributions to the campaign funds of the candidates of their choice.[53] Money is passed in both directions. They are no longer simply party thugs, but partners. The quasi-governmental functions of organized crime should therefore be seen in this context, that is, as the assisted activity of one of the partners (that benefits both, but alters the power relations between them).

Enforcement is another dimension of this partnership. Organized crime has been involved in a range of enforcement and control functions, and not just as part of the party system, but as partners of the state. In April 1999, pro-government organized crime groups were involved in suppressing Opposition-led demonstrations against anticipated increases in the price of gasoline. During the course of the protests, demonstrators in the downtown area of Kingston were attacked by thugs affiliated to the Spanglers network and were successfully driven from the streets. In recognition of their services to the ruling party, the then prime minister, P.J. Patterson, visited the community base of the Spanglers, reportedly greeted Phipps, the acknowledged leader of the group, and spoke approvingly of his efforts to counter the demonstrations.[54] Considerable reinforcement of the specific type of activity was thus provided, and the general importance of the relationship between organized crime and the political parties underlined.[55] The logic of these types of relationships is such that similar events may be found elsewhere, even in strong liberal democracies with low crime rates, such as Japan. There, in 1988, a prominent leader of the Liberal Democratic Party "personally thanked and praised" a leader of an established organized crime group "for silencing extremist opposition to Takeshita Noboru's bid to become Prime Minister" (Hill 2004, 102).

These types of regulatory activities may be regarded as an extension of the control role that the dons now play in the communities, and which now allows them to become actors on the national stage. Some of the dons have indeed advocated a partnership with the state that would take the form of a more overt and formalized working relationship with the police. As one suggested in a personal interview, "the illegal guns should work with the legal guns". This is exactly what occurred in Guyana at the dawn of the new century. In its effort to control violent crime, the Guyanese government allegedly used the services of Shaheed Khan, a reputed drug kingpin, to set up "phantom" vigilante squads that pursued and killed other criminals. After his arrest by American law enforcement agents, Khan published a statement in which he claimed that "during the crime spree in 2002, I worked closely with the crime-fighting sections of the Guyana Police Force and provided them with assistance and information at my own expense. My participation was instrumental in curbing crime during this period." He also claimed to have provided information to the American Embassy in Guyana which led to "the issuance of an arrest warrant for Shawn Brown", who he alleged was responsible for the kidnapping of an American diplomat (see *Kaieteur News*, 12 May 2006).

In Jamaica, what is proposed, and indeed exists in some localities, is a partnership that involves the state delegating to the dons the right to police and punish within the latter's "jurisdiction". This is already operationalized in the jungle courts. The local jurisdiction of the don is exercised "in conjunction" with the state and police. As Blok has noted, it is precisely this joint exercise of power with the state that distinguishes mafia from other types of criminals (Blok 1974, 94).

Thus collusion between organized crime on the one hand, and the police and the political parties on the other, serves to legitimize the behaviour of organized crime as a power-holder in the inner-city communities. Tilly, approvingly citing Stinchcombe (1968), suggests that legitimacy is not assent to government, not simply the ruled believing that the rulers have the right to rule, but rather "the probability that other authorities (power-holders) will act to confirm the decisions of another authority (power-holder)" (Tilly 2002, 38). Elsewhere (Harriott 2000), this is referred to as a "soft definition" of legitimacy. It is a minimum condition that allows regime maintenance. The suggestion is that the relationship between the power-holders is the critical condition for legitimacy. This may bear a close resemblance to domination, but is a kind of elite consensus, a consensus among authorities. The use of the word "authority" is not immaterial. It suggests that the power-holders are in some measure accepted by the ruled or sub-populations of the ruled. The assent of the ruled is thus brought back in – albeit a passive assent. This point carries added force in the Jamaican context, given its British colonial history of descending authority that is typical of the unbroken monarchical tradition. This is a tradition of difference and compliance that has lost its force in the post-independence period, particularly after the democratic-socialist disruption of the 1970s, but which still remains.

In the case of the garrisons, both sets of power-holders are thus, in some sense, authorities who have an active relationship with the people and constantly seek their support. The don is regarded as a "big-man". He is not necessarily a representative of the marginalized out-group in which he has his origin but someone who is regarded as a social success and an institutional actor in the political system and local power structure. The power-holders in the communities, criminal and conventional, thus tend to reinforce each other in their respective roles.

As a central aspect of its quasi-governmental role and power projection within their jurisdictions, organized crime groups have also become involved in other, more everyday aspects of public order policing. City authorities have used them to coerce, or shall we say "encourage", street vendors to use the markets and arcades – a task that had proved beyond the capability of the police force. Following the lead of the state, private businesses have also contracted the more powerful organized crime groups to discipline the vendors. As partners of the state, elements of these groups were even incorporated into an embryonic parks and markets police service. Unlike the regular state police, they have experienced very little resistance to their efforts, and the usually disagreeable vendors (who for many decades successfully resisted the efforts of colonial authorities and later all administrations since independence) have tended to be most compliant.

More troubling than their involvement in public order policing are instances when the leaders of organized crime are used to broker deals on behalf of the formal justice system in a manner that subverts the attempts of citizens to seek redress for injustices inflicted by agents of the state. Redress implies an ability on the part of the state to self-correct. It symbolizes a commitment to justice and law. Tampering with this is thus particularly problematic, especially when the tampering introduces the agents of organized crime to the citizen-complainant as negotiators on behalf of a state agency. This is exactly what was done in the case of Janice Allen, a child who was accidentally shot by the police (personal correspondence with a member of the human rights group Jamaicans for Justice). An attempt was made to use the local don to negotiate a settlement with her family on behalf of the state. The don symbolizes power that is unrestrained by law. Their involvement as intermediaries introduces intimidation into the process and suggests a reluctance on the part of elements in the state to be restrained by the law. Indeed, this case (while being evidence of state-organized crime collusion in the administration of "justice"), if taken by itself, may be seen as signalling a reinforcement of the marginalization of the inner-city poor by the state. It means that they do not have the protection of the law, and that violations of their rights by state agents may be settled under the threat of further violence by agents who are even less accountable to the law than the initial violators. The inner-city poor are confronted by two sets of institutional power-holders: organized crime, and the police. One illegal and the other holding legal authority, but both occupationally associated with the use of violence and reinforcing its use by each other. As institutional actors, the leaders of these territorially based networks have progressed from being party agents, to being party/state agents that are involved in some of the core (control) functions of the state, albeit in very informal and functionally and spatially limited ways.

The above range of functions and roles highlights a tendency and hints at a system of rule that relies on organized crime in interfacing with the urban poor when *credible force and lawlessness* are required. It highlights the developing relationship between organized crime and the political parties and state as a relationship that rests as much on the opportunities for corruption and material gain as on an increasing demand for violence.

Methods: The Logic of Violence

The high level of violence that is associated with the territorially based organized crime groups is thus integral to their activity and relationships. Their activities create a demand for violence as this is needed to regulate illegal business transactions. A regulatory or enforcement imperative is even greater in conditions of low interpersonal trust within and among the criminal networks and between them and their collaborators in the "upperworld".

These organized crime groups tend to use violence liberally, not just to settle particular disputes, but as power projection. The instances of violent conflict are treated as challenges to their power, as opportunities to project power and to achieve dominance over their competitors and their territory, and as a part of the process of trying to impose their monopoly on the use of violence within an expanding territorial domain.

Organized crime has thus added considerable thrust to Jamaica's homicide rate. In 2005, the homicide rate was 63 incidents per 100,000 citizens, having increased from 19 incidents per 100,000 citizens in 1985.[56] In 2005, it was approximately three times the mean rate for Latin America and the Caribbean, which is the region with the highest rate of ordinary criminal violence in the world.

The violence of organized crime is rooted in the following:

- The type of criminal activity that it engages in, such as extortion rackets which are inherently violent.
- The regulation of criminal transactions, such as drug deals.
- Its quasi-governmental functions, that is, rule making and rule enforcement for whole communities.
- Its relationship to territory. Rule enforcement within communities, the collection of tributes from subordinate criminal groups, and the defence of territory from external enemies are all violence prone.
- Periodic confrontations with the security forces. In the special case of the garrisons-as-safe-havens, this involves using violence to exact a

political and human price on the security forces that is so high that it deters them from entering these communities to effect arrests.

- Involvement in competitive party politics – usually in the more violence-prone communities where it may try to switch the political loyalties by encouraging defections among the community gunmen.

The combination of enterprise and enforcement, the power derived from wealth and control of significant means of violence, along with the ability to use these means freely distinguishes organized crime from common criminality. Groups that operate on the corporate model may enjoy greater wealth and income, but the patron–client territorially based groups tend to enjoy greater power of enforcement. The latter may provide enforcement services for the former, and, as noted earlier, may even extort the former. This has been the source of some of the conflicts between groups. Such problems tend to impel the more corporate-oriented networks to improve their self-protective capabilities. As more actors develop their capabilities to deliver violence, continued increases in the rate of murder may be expected. A sharp separation of the *business enterprises* (suppliers of goods and various services) and the *violence enterprises* (specialist suppliers of violence-related services) has therefore not yet occurred – although at the individual level there are specialists in the use of violence, and some groups have already begun to specialize in violence-related services.[57] Evolution in this direction, that is, of greater specialization in violence, should lead to the more powerful groups establishing monopolies on violence and enterprise criminality within larger territorial zones and thus fewer groups engaging in criminal violence and a consequent reduction in the homicide rate.

Violence is directed at the state authorities and violence is used in defence of the political administration and parties. The first category of violent activity increases the risks and human cost of effective law enforcement, thereby forcing an accommodation or inducing an *entente cordiale* with organized crime. Examples of this are the repeated battles between the security forces and the gunmen of Tivoli Gardens, the last of which was in July 2001 and which was the subject of a major inquiry (WKC 2002). Examples of the second type, such as attacks on protestors, have already been discussed. Some dons have even made known their interest in the newspaper writings of critical commentators and have delivered cautionary notes (personal communication with the author). Violence that is directed to achieve both of these ends erodes the democratic foundations of the state system.

While much of the violence of organized crime is undisputedly instrumental, it is increasingly being delivered in a style that is expressive, indeed performative. For example, beheadings, gouging of eyes, and other forms of body mutilation are now part of the homicidal repertoire. This expressive style should not be surprising, as the violence of organized crime occurs in a context in which violence is widely used in everyday conflicts among ordinary citizens who are not engaged in predatory criminality, and because much of this social violence is increasingly becoming symbolically loaded and thus culturally performative (Harriott 2005).

The Rise of Organized Crime

This section attempts to sketch the outlines of an explanation of the development of organized crime in Jamaica. As the earlier description includes elements of an explanation, in this section only a summary of some of the antecedent processes, "root causes" or preconditions for the development of organized crime are presented. Some of these root causes are shared with other crime phenomena. The challenge is to distinguish the sources of organized crime from more general root causes of violent crime. The more proximate factors or precipitants, such as the growth of the international drug markets and the demand for protection; and the prime facilitators or enabling and permissive factors, such as the social and political practices, attitude sets and patterns of thinking that are supportive of and positively sanction organized crime, are therefore given greater prominence in the analysis. Taken together, these three sets of factors, that is, the antecedent processes, proximate factors, and facilitators, are best treated as elements of a historical process rather than aspects of a schema.[58]

Organized crime is a global phenomenon that takes different forms. It is thus able to develop and thrive in a variety of environments. It is not always easy to distinguish between those conditions that are simply contextual and those that are necessary for the development and continued existence of organized crime. The factors associated with its rise in Jamaica are not completely abstracted from their historical context, but rather are treated as elements of an integrated historical process. Undoubtedly, there are con-textual gaps which, if filled, would better illuminate the rise of the phe-nomenon, but later studies may remedy these weaknesses.

Elsewhere (Harriott 2000), it has been argued that organized crime is socially embedded in the communities of the poor. By this it is meant that the major organized crime groups enjoy protective ties that are grounded in deep, extensive and intricate social and political relationships. This embeddedness even finds expression at the level of popular beliefs that pro-vide justification for the activities of organized crime as a "pro-social" and "pro-poor" actor. It is a degree of permissiveness with regard to this form of criminality that Gurr (with reference to terrorism) calls "social facilita-tion" (cited in Crenshaw 2001).

Acknowledging this social support for organized crime, which is most intense in the communities in which it operates but extends nationally, and understanding its social bases is central to any explanation of it. Probing this aspect of the problem may help to systematize the analysis. Its social basis is constitutive of the social structural roots from which organized crime emerged, of its ties with organized interests, and of its relations with citizens. Underpinning this social basis is the opportunity structure.

Exploring the conditions associated with the origins of organized crime helps us to identify and understand its diverse forms and the processes asso-ciated with its evolution. This accords considerable importance to its ori-gins, but the originating conditions should not be confused with the sustaining conditions. To confuse these two sets of conditions as factors accounting for organized crime is to commit a fallacy of origins. For example, the conditions associated with the origins of the Chinese triads and the Italian mafia included local territorial isolation from the rest of the respective countries and a weak state presence in these localities. Today, the Fujian Province and Sicily are connected to the main centres and institu-tions of the respective countries, and, in conditions of globalization, are strongly connected to the world, and are highly integrated into fairly pow-erful state systems. Organized crime has been able to adapt to these changes, to survive sustained assaults by law enforcement and, in some cases, exploit the opportunities that are associated with increased connection to the world (shipping links, the demand for migration opportunities) to grow even stronger. The fallacy of origins may be avoided by tracking the changes in the evolution of organized crime (for example, to transnational organized crime) and in its main relationships, the changes in the environment, and the forces and processes that account for these changes. The originating forces may not be the sustaining forces. In the case of Jamaica, however, organized crime is a new phenomenon and so there is not much difference in time (and environmental conditions) between origins and the contemporary situation.

The Socio-structural Roots of Organized Crime

The immediate post-independence period was one of high aspirations. Political change was expected to bring meaningful social and economic change and a higher living standard for the people. The colonial legacy of high levels of inequality and the associated obstructions of race and class exclusion were to be ended, and high growth rates and industrialization were expected to reduce unemployment and poverty. Yet this promise contrasted sharply with the realities and capacity of the state to deliver the expected social goods. The mobilization of the people, as reflected in the rate of rural to urban migration, exceeded the capacity of the fledgling industries to absorb them, resulting in the even higher rates of unemployment, especially youth unemployment and the growth of shanty towns in the vicinity of the industrial belt of the capital city. Mobilization was quickly followed by the economic and political crises of the 1970s. Thus, the first two decades after independence, the 1960s and 1970s, were periods of social dislocation and the strain associated with the high but unmet aspirations of the urban mobilized poor. These were conditions that were conducive to high rates of violent crime. These were, however, insufficient conditions for the emergence of organized crime.

The enduring and intensely concentrated social disadvantage that is encountered in the urban inner-city communities and which has already been described earlier, corrupt state and political institutions, illegal market opportunities of a certain scale and type, and a low risk environment tend to provide fertile conditions for organized crime to emerge and flourish. The major organized crime groups in Jamaica have evolved from ordinary urban gangs that emerged in the harsh conditions of the communities of the marginalized urban poor. What is common to this evolution is their relationship to politics. If the social conditions in urban Jamaica have been conducive to the development of violent crime, the formation of gangs and the emergence of a protective subculture marked by a code of silence, that is, conditions that constitute a good incubator for the emergence of organized crime, then politics has been the midwife that delivered it.

The career and evolution of Group 69 illustrates the role of the political parties in the emergence of organized crime. Group 69 was an affiliate of the PNP which was active in the period after the general elections of 1944 and which later spawned the Spanglers as a group of politically affiliated gangsters.[59] The Spanglers evolved into what may be called "Spanglers International", a transnational network involved in drug trafficking and drug dealing in the United States. Later, it became a major local player in a more diverse set of illegal enterprises in Jamaica. It has not yet become the "Spanglers Conglomerate", but its behaviour suggests that it may have these aspirations. Other organized crime groups have already achieved conglomerate status by setting up a wide range of businesses that provide licit goods and services funded by criminal wealth and by giving a more corporate shape to their structure.

There have thus been four clear phases in the development of this group. It is not necessary to discuss here all four phases, since much of this has already been done earlier as stages in the evolution of organized crime. In the first phase, Group 69 provided protection for the PNP by supplying it with its street fighters. The early career of the group or, more specifically, its role in the general elections of 1949 is discussed in Sives (2003). A similarly violent competitiveness among the party-affiliated trade unions, which was an extension of the political competitiveness, increased the demand for protection and meant that gangsters and toughs on both sides were welcomed and their contributions valued as a defence of the democratic rights of the party and trade union competitors. Later, in the 1960s, Group 69 also played an important role in the violent competition between the political parties in the impoverished constituency of Western

Kingston.[60] With the consolidation of Western Kingston as a JLP dominant zone, Group 69 (in its different forms) has retained its importance to the PNP by containing the JLP and limiting its further expansion in the area.

Party competitiveness intensified in the mid-1970s through to the early 1980s when there were sharp programmatic and ideological differences between the two major political parties. After the mid-1970s, these political conflicts became violent, with most of this violence being concentrated in the communities of the urban poor where the level of ordinary criminal violence was already high. During this period, the party-affiliated gangs became virtual party militias, thereby consolidating the relationships with their respective parties. There was an unbroken line in the relationships and in the violence, especially in western Kingston (meaning now the southwestern section of the city rather than the constituency designated Western Kingston), with the Spanglers playing a prominent role in this period as well.

The construction of Tivoli Gardens as a garrison community served to consolidate the constituency of Western Kingston for the JLP and to provide favourable conditions for the rise of what later became known as the Shower Posse, which is arguably the most powerful organized crime group in Jamaica and a long-standing enemy of the Spanglers. The fortunes of the latter may have been very different had the PNP been in power in the 1960s. Empowered by state support, they would probably have become a much more important force in party politics and in organized crime. Instead, the Shower group, which was the beneficiary of the first garrison in Tivoli Gardens, emerged more quickly as a superpower in organized crime.

The career of Group 69 highlights the role of the political parties and successive political administrations in the evolution of organized crime in Jamaica. More generally, it is a story of how the connections to powerful and critical institutions were made and the importance of this for the development of organized crime. As important a condition as this was and is, it is however not sufficient. As outlined above, Jamaican politics had created a demand for violence and the thugs of the time supplied it behind the powerful protective shield that politics provided. The leaders of these gangs acquired reputations as ruthless men of violence, reputations which were later used to provide protection and to extort private businesses. This history of militant political activism propelled these groups along a trajectory of providing violence-related services. Their ties to politics did not, however, give the Spanglers an enterprise or market orientation – the international illicit drug economy would provide this.

Illegal Entrepreneurial Opportunities

International Drug Markets

"Enterprise theory" argues that the demand for illicit goods and services is a necessary condition for the emergence of organized crime (Smith 1978). This demand must be sustained and the profits must be sufficiently high in order to attract the criminal entrepreneur. In the context of globalization, the demand for illicit goods need not be local. Thus, in the 1980s, as was the case with the Spanglers, other Jamaican crime groups and less well-organized networks that were involved in the drug trade also became transnational. Since the 1960s, the demand for illicit drugs had been rising in the United States, but in the 1980s, this was further stimulated by the crack revolution. Supplier groups from the producer countries sought to cash in on this by entering the retail market in the United States.

Jamaican groups were well positioned to exploit these opportunities. Geographically, Jamaica is advantageously situated to facilitate the transshipment of South American cocaine to the United States. The relationships between Jamaican groups and international drug traffickers were well established as Jamaicans have been major suppliers of cannabis from as early as the 1960s. In the 1970s, the poor political relationship between the Jamaican and American governments and the consequent weakening of law enforcement cooperation were exploited by the traffickers.[61] Large quantities of drugs were airlifted by private aircraft from the many illegal air strips across the island. At the end of the 1970s, Jamaican networks were fully involved in the export of cannabis. The challenge in the 1980s was to diversify the product line (adding processed or valued-added cannabis products, and cocaine and cocaine products) and to get into the retail trade in the United States, either as direct suppliers or as supplier-dealers.

In these conditions, a range of independent criminal entrepreneurs emerged, including a rural-based type. Their relationship to territory is quite different from that of the urban organized crime groups, but the community opportunity structures were also important in their emergence. For example, proximity to illegal airstrips created jobs as loaders of ganja airplanes and protectors of drug warehouses. These jobs facilitated contact with international traffickers (pilots and dealers) that could be used to launch international criminal careers. As was the case in the urban areas, political activism assisted this process by facilitating contact with corrupt party-affiliated police officers, and helped to forge protective relationships with the communities.

The political influence of these rural criminals rests less on their ability to intimidate the Opposition and to directly deliver votes for their party and more on their money. Their ties to politics tend to track their entrepreneurial accomplishments. Unlike their urban counterparts, they have not acquired national notoriety from persistent involvement in violence and garrison politics. They are thus better able to participate in legitimate businesses and to form corrupt partnerships with professionals, legitimate business persons and selected politicians.

For this type and, more generally, those of entrepreneurial origin, institutional factors (money, status and respect as social values) may carry greater weight in the explanation of their rise than the social structural factors (inequality, youth unemployment and social exclusion), although the former are best understood in their relationship to the latter.

This type of criminal is non-territorial in origin and typically has a limited independent capacity to deliver violence. Some will take losses due to theft and other forms of bad faith by their associates and business partners without killing and tend to rely on corrupt police officers for protection. However, with their growth, some may be expected to become more violent, especially if they try to claim territory, overtly engage in politics, and supply labour-intensive services to the state (like their urban entrepreneurial counterparts). Territorial attachment brings new challenges, including the independent capacity to deliver violence. This may be subcontracted to other groups that are more competent in this field and which tend to be of the same political affiliation, but this outsourcing of violence fuels tensions between the two types of groups (violent entrepreneurs versus drug-enterprise criminals). The former may, for example, try to extort the latter (that is, the drug entrepreneurs). These tensions explain some of the violence between groupings affiliated with the same party that occurred in the late 1990s and which continued up to the time of writing.

This territorialization may be a pattern that develops in the areas that have been experiencing rapid urbanization, such as along the south coast conurban corridor from Kingston to May Pen, and perhaps on to Mandeville, and in the north coast city of Montego Bay. With this, a more national spread of violence must be expected. Some groups and networks have, however, not followed this pattern and remain entrepreneurial, corporate and fixed on the American drug market.

The migration of the gangs that later became organized crime groups was not only influenced by the pull of the American drug markets, but also by a push out of Jamaica that was partly influenced by the political process. In the 1970s, non-cooperation between the parties led to a breakdown in the old arrangements that allowed for the allocation of some state benefits to the supporters of the Opposition. The pro-JLP gangsters looked outward. After the general elections of 1980 which resulted in the defeat of the PNP administration, many of that party's gangster-militants fled to the United States for fear of being eliminated by special squads in the police force.

External accumulation has enabled those groups that became truly transnational to consolidate their influence and power in Jamaica. Organized crime has been able to use its new-found wealth, influence and power to alter its relationships with the political parties. Instead of always being the recipient of state contracts at the behest of the political leadership, the organized crime groups are now able to fund party candidates. Funding successful candidates increases their influence in the legislature which must pass laws concerning organized crime. It strengthens their influence in the parties and better positions them for partnerships with the high mafia that exploit the resources of the state.

Severely constrained or even blocked legitimate opportunities are not sufficient conditions for the emergence of organized crime. As indicated above, the expansion of illegal opportunities is also necessary. In the case of

Jamaica, these illegal opportunities were not limited to drug trafficking and drug dealing in Jamaica and abroad. Beginning in the 1970s, a wider range of activity that was closer to the mainstream of society and economy and which also coincided with the growth in ganja trafficking was created. Funds accumulated from drug trafficking could therefore quite easily find its way into the mainstream of economic activity.

Public policy has helped to create (as unintended consequences) some of these more mainstream illegal opportunities. For example, in response to the crisis conditions of the 1970s, the government imposed foreign exchange controls which, predictably, precipitated a thriving black market in American dollars. The demand for foreign exchange led to its supply by traffickers and developing interdependencies between traffickers and legitimate businesses. In the 1980s, even the Bank of Jamaica sought to channel much of this tainted money into the banking system.[62] This situation produced a number of middle men who operated in the grey area connecting the criminal underworld to legitimate business. Similarly, import restrictions as an adjustment to the foreign exchange crisis led to a black market in ordinary consumer goods. These goods were smuggled into the country and sold on the streets. Criminal groups provided some of these traders with dollar loans. If there are distortions in the formal system and policy constraints on the ability to legitimately satisfy the demand for goods and services, then the consequent growth of the informal sector may be associated with the growth of organized crime.

This pattern shows similarities with Colombia and other countries that now have severe organized crime problems. In 1968, the government of Colombia imposed foreign exchange controls and restrictions on external trade (Schulte-Bockholt 2006, 99). The outcomes were quite similar to those that occurred in Jamaica in the 1970s. High taxes on cigarettes in China created the opportunity for Hong Kong triads to smuggle cigarettes into China at profits of more than US$1 billion per year during the period 1987–93 (McWalters 1999). Alcohol prohibition policies in the United States have had similar effects. These policies and activities typically give added impulse to corruption and, more broadly, the social facilitation of organized crime.

Corruption and the Facilitating Conditions

Social and political facilitation involves the social and political habits or patterns of behaviour and thinking that positively sanction crime. It contributes to the climate of permissiveness, or a social milieu, in which organized crime is able to thrive. This includes the indirect facilitation of patterns of thinking that, in their more developed forms, are apologetics for crime. These ideas find popular expression in everyday life and in popular culture where they may even serve to romanticize organized crime. The following report on the appeal to the court for bail by Phipps illustrates this. His lawyer argued that he was a "good protector" of his community and that, during the period of his imprisonment on charges of murder, the crime rate in the downtown area of Kingston had increased. It was therefore in the interest of the country that he be released on bail – presumably so that he could return to his business of running the protection racket in the downtown area and thereby reduce the crime rate.[63] The lawyer's words were approvingly reported in a highly respected national newspaper ("Zeeks' Trial Postponed", *Gleaner*, 7 December 2005, A5). Similarly, in a television interview, a then minister of government described a particular organized crime-affiliated firm as one of the most "efficient" contractors to the government and its owner as his "friend".[64] Both the lawyer and the minister regard organized crime as "efficiently" delivering valued services and indeed, in some cases, delivering primary public goods, such as public security. These are the more indirect aspects of social facilitation. Those that are expressed in patterns of thinking that take a more coherent, near ideological form are more fully explored elsewhere.[65] Here, the focus is on the more direct behavioural forms of facilitation of which corruption is the most pernicious.

State corruption has played a critical role in the consolidation of organized crime in Jamaica (that is, in the current phase of the relationship between criminal networks and the political parties). In 2005, Jamaica's ranking on the corruption perception index was sixty-fourth of the 159 countries surveyed and its score was 3.6 out of 10, where 1 represents the highest level of corruption (Transparency International Corruption Perception Index 2005).

State corruption in the contemporary period must be understood in the context of the passing of the idealism of the early post-independence era and a shift from programmatic mobilization to the professionalization of politics and greater reliance on patronage as a tool for political mobilization. In recent years, there have been charges of maladministration in a number of state agencies, including the National Housing Development Cooperation and the National Solid Waste Management Authority.[66] Organized crime has been able to access state contracts on a new scale, contracts that are cumulatively valued at billions of dollars. Elements in the state have become partners in enterprise crime.

In their apologetics for corrupt practices, public officials promote a benign view of organized crime as normal business. Some officials, as noted above, have, for example, claimed that the firms that receive state contracts are "efficient", high performance companies. There may be some truth in this as these firms are not confronted with labour and extortion problems. The difficulty is that they also efficiently undermine the core principles of good governance as the systems of accountability are corruptly subverted in order to favour them. An outcome of this process is that institutions vital to the proper functioning of the state are corrupted and actually become contributors to the crime problem. This unfortunately also applies to the police.

A Weak Criminal Justice System: Immunity and the Waiving of Negative Sanctions

Where there are high levels of corruption within law enforcement agencies, wealth and influence easily immunizes high-end criminals against police action. This is certainly the case in Jamaica. Moreover, the criminal justice system is, in some respects, antiquated and overloaded and thus unable to effectively respond to the more sophisticated criminal groups. Associated institutions, including the existing body of laws, are also, in some respects, inadequate for dealing with organized crime. For example, in responding to extortion rackets, the police must rely on the Larceny Act of 1943 and, more specifically, a subsection of this act on "Demanding money, etc. with menaces". In order to disable the criminal firms that run these rackets, the police must be able to connect the lower level operatives to the leaders of these firms, but the laws have not been crafted with sufficient attention to this issue.[67] Consequently, since 2000, the number of arrests for this crime have not been significant enough for the police to record it as a separate category of crime and to report it in the annual police crime statistics. This type of crime is therefore still statistically invisible. Legislation designed to better control organized crime such as the Proceeds of Crime, Money Laundering, and Corruption Prevention Acts (most of which are responses to external pressures) have only recently been passed or have been tabled as a part of the legislative agenda of the parliament.

The case-load of the investigative units of the police is a good indicator of the degree of immunity from law enforcement (not crime-fighting) that is enjoyed by criminals. For effectiveness, the number of investigators should be greater than the number of cases to be investigated. Instead, a single divisional homicide investigator is, for example, burdened with a case-load of twelve to fifteen homicides, and this was in 2000 (PERF 2001, 49). Not surprisingly, in 2004, the clear-up rate for murder (the number of arrests as a percentage of all reported murders) was 44.8 per cent, and the clear-up rate of violent crimes, that is, the most serious offences against the person (murder, shootings, rape and robbery aggregated) was 39.8 per cent (PIOJ 2005, 24.3). For serious crimes, the clear-up rates are poor, and given the case-load ratios, the conviction rates are unsurprisingly low. In the case of murder, the conviction rate is estimated at less than 20 per cent.[68]

The clearance rates of the courts may also be taken as an indicator of immunity. It may indicate problems with the investigative process, as well as incapacities and managerial difficulties in having the cases adjudicated. Given the sheer number of new cases at the known clearance rate, each year, some cases will be terminated due to administrative failure. Consistent with the pattern of criminal offences in Jamaica, whereby a high proportion of all crimes are violent, while the lower courts report satisfactory clearance rates, the higher courts are overloaded and suffer from low clearance rates. The clearance rate in the Supreme Court approximates 30 per cent and the situation in the Gun Court is similarly problematic (CGCED 2000, 47).

Moreover, as noted earlier, there is considerable social support for the territorially based organized crime groups. This is a significant source of their immunity to police action. Communities support and protect these groups because it is difficult for them to see their quasi-governmental functions and partnerships with the political parties as solely serving criminal goals and as a means of entrenching their power. On the contrary, the activities of these groups are perceived as a kind of social banditry or "Robin Hood" criminality that serves the poor. The relationship between the groups and the political parties, which is an important piece in their protective armour, is in turn conditioned by this social support for the dons. The benefits gained from organized crime at both the community and national levels (such as foreign exchange inflows) creates an ambivalent space for the dons. This ambivalence saps the civic and political will to respond effectively to organized crime and explains why, despite the high levels of violence associated with the activities of organized crime, there has not been any sustained civic action and movement against it.

Most dons therefore have either a clean criminal record in Jamaica or one that is sullied only by minor crimes. Some have been arrested on serious charges, but have not been convicted. An analysis of twenty-seven selected leaders of organized crime groups in Jamaica revealed that eleven (41 per cent) of them had criminal careers that extended beyond thirty years and 70 per cent (cumulatively) had careers that lasted from more than twenty years. During their long careers, only three were ever convicted for serious offences that were related to their organized crime activities (one was also in prison on a minor conviction). Five were extradited to the United States to face serious charges. Nine were killed. Interestingly the risk of being killed by other criminals was greater than the risk of being killed by the police. The remaining nine (33 per cent) were at liberty and actively continuing their careers.[69] Thus, for example, at the time of his conviction for murder in 2006, Phipps had no prior conviction for any serious crime committed in Jamaica during his reign as the leader of the Spanglers and don of Matthew's Lane (although he had been repeatedly charged with serious crimes). At his sentencing hearing, character witnesses could therefore be called to speak of his "kindness" and "good works" on behalf of the poor (Howard Campbell, "Life without Zekes Is Tough",

Sunday Gleaner, 4 June 2006, A6). Prior to his conviction on a charge of shooting with intent to kill, Joel Andem, a former leader of the notoriously violent Gideon Warriors gang, had been convicted of only petty crimes which occurred in the early stage of his criminal career. The existing leaders of the major organized crime groups are not wanted by the police for any crimes. At the time of writing this study, none were on the publicly announced "Most Wanted" lists of the police. They remain free to cultivate exploitable relationships that extend into the political administration and the state bureaucracy – relationships that further empower and protect them from law enforcement and even public exposure.

Approaches to Controlling Organized Crime

There are different perspectives on how the society should respond to organized crime. These include peacemaking, co-option, and suppression by unconventional crime-fighting and conventional law enforcement.

Organized crime ought not to be treated like regular criminality. Any attempt to elaborate an effective strategy to deal with it must begin with recognition of its power and influence and their sources. Peacemaking reflects recognition of its power, but suggests a misunderstanding of the sources of this power and of its nature. Peacemaking is useful when applied to conflict groups. Organized crime may be involved in conflicts that are named inter-community conflicts and political conflicts, but it is quite different from, and should not be treated as, a conflict group.

At times, there is considerable community pressure to pursue the peacemaking approach, that is, to find a non-policing resolution of the violence between the gangs. The success of this strategy rests, to a large measure, on the power of the people in the localities, and their ability to resolve the disputes and to impose a measure of informal social control over the youth gangs that are involved in these conflicts. However, even when applied in those circumstances, the efforts of the community will remain largely ineffective if law enforcement is ineffective. Given the hold of organized crime on the communities in which they operate, the prospect of informal community control over its activities does not arise. In such conditions, when peacemaking is extended to treating organized crime, it effectively becomes a discourse of decriminalization that leaves their businesses and methods intact. Indeed, for organized crime groups, peacemaking that involves the police as a party to the negotiations entails amnesty and freedom from police action.

If peacemaking is an inappropriate response to organized crime, so too is state administrative co-option. This involves formally incorporating the dons as part of the system of state control. As discussed earlier, this is already a shadowy reality. The idea has appeal because it is understood to mean that they would help to police the inner-city communities and be accountable to the police force. Such a policy would provide state recognition of the current reality, thereby taking it out of the shadows and, it is believed, would add a measure of accountability.[70]

As described previously, a partnership for political control already exists between the political administration or political parties and organized crime. Converting this to co-option by the state for law enforcement seems to overestimate the power of the state to successfully co-opt these groups. Any attempt at co-option by an enfeebled state under which organized crime has flourished, may not only open the door to a return to the politicization of policing and politically selective criminal enforcement (in the sense of targeting the less influential criminals), but may also more deeply mire the police in criminality. Unless there are consequences for non-compliance with the rules governing such a process, efforts by the state to co-opt elements within the organized crime groups are unlikely to be successful. And if the state could enforce its rules governing the incorporation of the leaders of organized crime into its law enforcement machinery, then perhaps it would be able to successfully repress organized crime by other means anyway. This seems to be a self-defeating strategy.

Crime-fighting methods have been used against organized crime and the more violent gangs. The results have not been good, as is evidenced by the tendency for the rate of violent crimes to increase and for the organized crime groups to grow. Indeed, crime-fighting methods, such as the elimination of the leaders of these groups, have only precipitated more violence over leadership succession and efforts to alter the balance of power between competing groups.

Despite its limitations, effective law enforcement is a more appropriate response to organized crime. The more successful law enforcement strategies against organized crime that have been distilled from international experiences are generally known. Effective law enforcement requires actions that, at a minimum, end the ability of the organized crime groups to act with impunity and, even better, put the firms, not just their individual members, out of business. Such measures typically target their wealth and income, and in the Jamaican context, would also need to target the relationships that protect and sustain their activities, including the relationships with the communities, parties, state and businesses.

Their wealth and income streams are important sources of their power, including their referent power. Removal of the main symbols of success, that is, their wealth and money, diminishes their power and social support. In this regard, various nations have made good use of legislation on forfeiture of assets. After first passing a feeble bill (at the time of writing), the Jamaican legislature was considering a revised bill. Legislative "modernization" is useful, but should also be accompanied by police and justice system modernization that would improve the investigative competency of the police, control corruption, and modernize its relationship with and service to the people. This has been extensively discussed elsewhere (see Harriott 2000).

Confiscating the wealth of organized crime may prove difficult if the relationships that empower and protect them are not broken or, at least, weakened. This means, most of all, cutting the links between the political parties and organized crime. One of the best ways of doing this is to ensure that state contracts are not awarded to firms that are affiliated with the organized crime groups. This would cut the flow of funds in one direction, that is, from the state to organized crime. A legally acceptable method of operationalizing this suggestion presents some challenge. One seemingly simple enough solution may be to impose the requirement that all contractors satisfy the standard of being "fit and proper".[71] This device is used in the granting of licenses to stock-brokers and there is no obvious reason why it should not be applied in granting of state contracts to all service providers. Regulating political party funding in a manner that forces transparency regarding contributions to the parties and accountability for all funds that are spent may cut the flow of funds from the other direction, that is, from organized crime to the parties, thereby reducing the direct political influence of the dons. Such measures would rupture the relationship between the parties and organized crime by weakening its material underpinning.

Supporting legislation, such as conspiracy laws, that would allow public officials who assist the flow of state funds to organized crime enterprises to be charged as criminal co-conspirators would assist the realization of these objectives. For example, when a government minister or mayor of a city signs documentation awarding a contract to a firm that is a front for organized crime, this should be sufficient grounds on which to charge the official for being a part of a criminal conspiracy. Such legal provisions should be accompanied by supporting measures, such as requiring the police to list all criminal enterprises and to make these lists available to all contract-granting authorities.

State agencies that have established a pattern of corrupt practices and which repeatedly conduct business with firms affiliated to organized crime groups should be placed under a special trusteeship that is given the authority to re-engineer their systems of accountability and to purge their managerial staff of incompetent and corrupt facilitators of organized crime. Where necessary, the trustees should be enabled to terminate or pass "death sentences" on these agencies. The United States has used trusteeships that are empowered by their courts under the Civil RICO laws to sanitize such organizations. It is a largely unannounced and unnoticed aspect of the celebrated decline in crime in the city of New York (see Jacobs 1999).[72] In Jamaica, the contractor general should be empowered to initiate a systems review of such organizations and to apply to the courts for such offending agencies to be placed under trusteeships.

"Yardie" networks and "Posses" were weakened in the United States and United Kingdom because they did not enjoy protective relationships in those countries. They may benefit from the indifference and alienation in some immigrant communities, but they have no political influence, institutional support and relations with conventional businesses. By rupturing the key relationships, and seizing their assets, law enforcement ought to be able to put the criminal firms out of business. On this foundation, prevention measures that are aimed at the root causes of crime and at weakening the relationship of organized crime with the communities of the poor may be more effectively undertaken.[73]

As the crime-party nexus is strongest in the garrison communities, severing this relationship must involve dismantling the garrison communities. This would help to remove the immunity that organized crime now enjoys.[74]

The problem is, however, not restricted to the garrisons. The relationship between the crime groups and the inner-city communities may be weakened by better integrating these communities into mainstream society. Strengthening the institutional linkages to the mainstream of the society (via schools, voting, the provision of effective rights regarding police services, tax-paying) is one way of doing this. Successful integration involves the provision of quality services that truly equip these citizens for participation in the labour force, in business, in politics, and in all aspects of life. On this basis, a transformation of these communities may be effected by tackling youth unemployment, housing, infrastructure, the nature of their encounters with politics and relationship to the political institutions and the state, and their responsibilities as citizens. It is not just the physical environment that ought to be transformed, but also the social environment, including the relationship of inner-city communities to the society and its key institutions. The relationship to work is critical, as status, notions of self-worth, identity (especially male identity) and dignity are bound up with it. Apart from its other benefits, such a programme would undermine the social support base of organized crime. Forced out of the communities of the poor, they may adapt and become more corporate, but would nevertheless become more vulnerable to police action.

These are not comprehensive measures. The intent here was simply to sketch the approaches that have been found appealing in sections of the political elite and the mass publics, and to suggest an approach or direction that may show some promise.

Conclusion

Organized crime emerged in Jamaica after a long period of gestation. Socio-economic conditions that favoured high rates of violent crime, international market opportunities, ineffective law enforcement, and thus increased demand for protection and other services locally (at the community level and with firms), and competitive party politics that stimulated the demand for violence all provided the conditions that fostered its development. Official corruption and community support have allowed it to flourish.

In this situation, controlling organized crime presents challenges for the society. There are problems of civic and political will and different political coalitions may seek to resolve their relations with organized crime in different ways (with some coalitions relying more on it as a player in the political process and others relying on it less). Beyond this are also real problems of resource limitations, problems of institutional capacity and capability.

There are a number of conditions for the success of any sustained effort to reply to organized crime. These include solving the problem of ambivalence toward organized crime that exists in the society and which extends into the political elite, and developing a societal consensus about the direction of the response. Civic resistance to organized crime is thus important in achieving these political conditions. However, as the Bulbie demonstrations have hinted, organized crime is an active player in these power struggles. Public opinion and a more active citizenry will have to weigh in. In the next chapter, some of these and other issues related to the prevention and control of organized crime will be explored further.

2

Controlling Organized Crime
Elements of a Strategy

IN THE PREVIOUS CHAPTER, an analysis of the nature of organized crime, an explanation of its emergence and spectacular rise, and its impact on different aspects of national life and critical institutions of state and society were elaborated on. In this chapter, the elements of a strategy for responding to it are presented. This is an ambitious project, and, perhaps in attempting it, one runs the risk of overextension.

Academic researchers tend to be quite comfortable with providing explanations of phenomena that are objects of study within their disciplines. Such explanations may be treated as a technical or scientific process of causal discovery or as interpretive insights (based on systematic observation) into the meanings that people attach to these phenomena. To prescribe, however, is more value-laden and always seems to involve a degree of certainty that is beyond the state of the discipline and, for this reason, may justifiably be regarded as displays of egotism and even arrogance. The word "arrogance" is used to capture the idea that one knows what is correct and right for the country and that all should therefore yield to the superior wisdom and moral judgement of such a person. It is not that the Jamaican professional middle-strata are exactly deficient in these qualities. Indeed, after centuries of colonial battering at their self-worth, the post-independence generation may have needed these qualities in order to accomplish anything worthwhile as individuals, although these qualities remain somewhat of a hindrance to greater collective accomplishments. In the present context, however, this brand of arrogance may not only be an expression of unjustifiable certainty, but perhaps of plain stupidity. After all, it involves exhibiting one individual's limited understanding and experience.

The elaboration of any policy or strategy for dealing with major national problems requires a method or process that is not overreliant on lone researchers, but rather one that ensures the incorporation of various types of knowledge of the problem including the experiential knowledge that resides in various institutions. Public policy that affects the lives of all and instructs the expenditure of significant national resources ought to involve a truly national effort. Sometimes, however, national conditions (and social pressures) urge individuals to throw caution to the wind in the hope that their work may contribute to further clarification and to a larger effort that is beyond their own capacity. As the work of a single individual (albeit with the benefit of exchanges with others), the following is limited by the knowledge deficits, disciplinary boundaries and life experiences of the author. The concern is not with operational law enforcement issues, but rather with the development of a more overarching strategic perspective.

The purpose of this chapter is to elaborate on and justify the elements of a strategy for preventing and controlling organized crime and to discuss the prospects and prerequisites for its success. First, the critical elements of the problem, that is, the features of organized crime that are relevant to any strategy for its prevention and control, are briefly described. Second, some of the obstacles to the development of an effective state-adopted strategy are identified. The elements of the proffered strategy are then sketched. Finally, some conditions for success are discussed (lessons from international and local experience are presented), including the need for a broad anti-crime and anti-violence movement that would provide a driving force for a sustained programme of action and which may find expression within the political administration. Many of the specific suggestions and ideas presented here are not new, but an attempt is made to present a perspective on the prevention and control of organized crime that extends beyond the limits of law enforcement and is consistent with how the problem is understood. The primary purpose is to encourage systematic thinking about how the problem may be tackled.

In sketching an approach to the problem, the customary categories of long term and short term are avoided as these categories are more useful for detailed planning and are better introduced after an understanding of the response as a coherent integrated process, that is, the response as strategy, or elements of a strategy.[1] Moreover, the use of these categories tends to have the effect of taking the long term off the agenda for action. In conditions of scarce resources, pressing immediate demands, and a politicized environment in which short-term political returns are not inconsequential considerations, only the short term is considered worthwhile. The long term simply becomes tomorrow's short term. Consequently, only limited strategic advances are made.

Critical Elements of the Problem

If it is to have a fair chance of succeeding, a strategy to effectively control organized crime must rest on an understanding of the nature of organized crime and the processes that nurture, facilitate, and serve to consolidate it in Jamaica.

The most important features of Jamaican organized crime and ideas that are of relevance to a control strategy are (1) understanding the demand for the services that it provides to its various clients and partners, especially the supply of drugs to external markets and the provision of protection locally; and (2) its relationships to the communities and to powerful actors and institutions in the society. These features of organized crime, which have already been elaborated on in the previous chapter, may be listed with greater detail as follows:

- It responds to the demand for illicit goods and services such as drugs.
- It provides protective services to local businesses and communities in areas that are underpoliced and/or improperly policed.

- It is attached to local territory but is also transnational.
- It is rooted in a special type of territorial and protective community relationship that is most intensely manifested in the garrisons.
- There is a developing differentiation between entrepreneurial elements and specialists in violence. Differentiation may be a response to the extended range of illegal opportunities in conditions where, with some exceptions, this wide range of opportunities is not available to each group.
- It has penetrated the political parties and established special interdependent relationships with elements within their leadership structures.
- It has established plain parasitic as well as mutually supportive relationships with legitimate business.
- It operates in a climate that is socially facilitating.

Measures of Success

The features highlighted above specify aspects of the problem that may be treated as targets for action and elements that may be used to shape a strategic response to the challenges presented by organized crime. Dissecting the problem in this way also helps to clarify the appropriate measures of success or the desired outcomes of the prevention and control processes. For example, dismantling the garrisons, that is, removing the protective shield that is provided by the relationship of organized crime with the communities would be one measure of problem-solving success. Weakening, or severing its links with the political parties would be another. The seizure of the assets and closing of the businesses of the leaders of the major organized crime groups, and severing their supply lines to the local communities, that is, the remittance of drug money and the provision of guns, are other ways to measure success. Reducing the demand for illegal guns and drugs and for protection (through more effective state policing) and creating a less permissive social environment would be other important indicators of sustainable success.

The above measures include, but are not limited to, the arrests and conviction of the leaders of organized crime. Convictions are an important measure of success in dealing with particular groups, but should not be treated as such in dealing with organized crime as a general phenomenon. For example, the conviction of the leaders of a particular group may lead to the strengthening of a competitor group or the formation of a number of splinter groups from the remnants of the original group. Convictions are thus *means* of achieving the outcomes listed above, not ends in themselves. To treat arrests and convictions as measures of success in responding to organized crime would be similar to treating the number of traffic tickets issued by the police as a measure of success in regulating traffic. As means, this type of police action is important but should not (as is often done) be mistaken for the ends being pursued.[2]

Even short-term changes in crime rates may not be true measures of success. Lower robbery rates, for example, may be the outcome of successful protection and extortion rackets. Extortion and protection rackets must be expected to have a substitution and displacement effect on robbery and other crimes against businesses such as breaking and entering. And if the territorial control of organized crime is extensive enough, it may even have a control effect on these types of crime. Lower robbery rates may therefore indicate the increasing power of organized crime groups, not improved public safety. Since 1995, Jamaica's official or reported robbery rates have been declining and have dropped precipitously after 1996. Between 1995 and 2006, the number of incidents per 100,000 citizens declined from 178 to 75.3.[3] This is the period of the rise in extortion and protection rackets. And yet these crimes do not yet appear as a category in the annual reports of the police and in the official reports of the state agencies.[4] A downward trend in the true crime rate is normally a clear measure of success. Even this, however, may be problematic when dealing with organized crime. Jamaica's aggregate crime rate has been declining since the late 1990s, and yet the country has become more dangerous and people more fearful of criminal victimization.[5] In a high violence society such as Jamaica, the homicide rate is generally the best indicator of the state of public safety, but a downward tendency (not trend) in homicide rates may not necessarily indicate a safer society. A reduction in homicide rates may indicate organized crime monopolies on the use of violence and their successful control of amateur criminals and youth gangs that operate in their jurisdictions. A more dangerous situation would thus find expression as reduced true rates of violent crimes. Such is the impact of organized crime that the traditional measures of safety and crime control may be losing their validity. For these reasons, it is important to focus on the more fundamental, qualitative measures of success: the outcomes listed earlier that would indicate a weakening of organized crime.

Despite this cautionary note, it must be understood that law enforcement nevertheless remains the main means used to control organized crime. Law enforcement approaches tend to be based on tactics that target the activities and organizational features of the crime groups with a view to decapitating and disrupting them case by case and group by group. For example, law enforcement tends to hone in on the structure of these groups and to dedicate considerable effort to mapping their hierarchies with a view to targeting the individuals who occupy key positions in the top tier or who play critical roles. They may track the patterns of communication within and by the group in order to implicate the top leadership and thereby try to cripple the organization. This may be described as "head-hunting" when it is done without sufficient regard for law and as "targeting-up" when is more lawfully executed. Some of the methods of targeting-up famously include plea-bargaining (which is not legally permitted in Jamaica) and prosecution for tax violations (the pursuit of which may trigger anxieties throughout the society as tax compliance is notoriously low).

When applied to the more flexible ("organized-disorganized") Jamaican organized crime groups, especially those with a highly organized core and a flexible and extensive outer network, and which are not based on the corporate model of organization, head-hunting and targeting-up are unlikely to be as effective. Mapping the patterns of communication may reveal the roles of persons in the group and their proximity to the leader, thus allowing law enforcement to target and remove the leaders of the group, but is unlikely to lead to the arrest of large numbers as co-conspirators and to thereby disable the group or firm or prevent its recrudescence (if there is some success in disrupting its activities). All of these techniques of targeting-up are useful and important. However, the Jamaican experience suggests that the leaders are easily replaced and that, despite their occasional removal by death, arrests and convictions, the organizations persist and may even multiply. Their relationship to territory as sites of the social conditions and the political relationships that reproduce the phenomenon explain this.

The resilience of organized crime rests on its deeply rooted relationships, especially its relationship to the urban communities and to the political parties. Police killings of the leaders of the groups tend to reinforce the commitment of members to the group and to solidify the relationships with the communities and the political parties (especially if the killing is successfully named as an act of political targeting). This is evident in the very public displays of collective grieving, such as draping utility poles with black flags, lining the streets with candles that are lit after dark, and especially the organization of the funeral as a show of solidarity. There have been many examples of this, including the funerals of Donovan Bennett ("Bulbie") and Andrew Stevens ("Andrew Pang"), both of whom were territorially based dons.[6] The process may even continue after the funeral when ways may be found to memorialize the fallen don as a heroic figure. Convictions in the courts do not tend to produce such solidarity. Trials usually reveal damaging information about the leaders and their groups, but the major groups have been able to survive these assaults and remain active.

Law enforcement approaches have yielded good results elsewhere, such as in the anti-mafia prosecutions in Italy and with the triads in Hong Kong. The effectiveness of these strategies and tactics is, however, dependent on the environment in which organized crime operates. For example, Jamaican transnational organized crime in the United Kingdom and the United States has been successfully tackled using law enforcement measures only. This has been possible because in those countries they are not as embedded in protective relationships as they are in Jamaica. The groups have tried, but were unable to reproduce the garrisons there. In those countries, they have no political protection, little community protection, and encounter lower levels of law enforcement corruption.[7] In Jamaica, where there is considerable social and political support for organized crime, a broader strategy is required.

Elements of a Strategy

Any strategy attempted should be informed by an understanding of the phenomenon in the national and local or community contexts or social environment in which it operates, its critical features, the processes that sustain it, its vulnerabilities, and the strengths and vulnerabilities of the response agencies.

Jamaican organized crime is still evolving; it has not yet reached a mature stage. It is more vulnerable now than it is likely to be in the near future. The high level of violence associated with it, including violent clashes with the security forces, gives it considerable visibility in the press and keeps it on the political and state-administrative agendas. Quick and frequent resort to violence suggests that there are problems of internal control within the groups, challenges from other groups, and that the authority of some of the leaders may be somewhat limited. Its influence in the institutions of the state travels with, and is thus still largely limited by, its party ties. The nature of the relationships of organized crime with the state agencies indicates a developing interdependence and even local co-ruling with the state, which are signs of a measure of maturity, but beyond the garrisons, co-ruling is not yet consolidated and would require changes in the character of the political administration. Its transnational character is both a source of strength and of vulnerability. Transnational operations are a prime source of wealth, but the consequence is that they attract the attention of external law enforcement operations that are beyond the influence of the Jamaican groups.

The idea, then, is to disrupt the processes that empower organized crime and thereby make it more vulnerable to law enforcement, in other words, to target its sources of power and influence, that is, its proximate roots. This approach allows us to distinguish the sources of organized crime from the more general sources of violent crime and to give the former a more focused treatment.

A useful way of thinking about strategy might use the following categories as organizing principles:

- The relationships of organized crime
- Its functions and activities

- The socio-political processes in which it is embedded
- Its methods

Law enforcement focuses on the activities and methods of organized crime in order to effect *case solving*. While not ignoring the activities and methods of organized crime, special attention is given here to the relationships and processes, as these latter aspects take us beyond the scope of law enforcement and tend to be ignored, yet are critical to prevention and *problem solving*. As noted earlier, the perspective proffered is thus partial.

Disrupting and Severing Relationships

Relationships are the main sources of the success of organized crime. These relationships provide it with opportunities, give it the degrees of freedom needed to be able to successfully adapt to changes in the security environment, and nurture the process of maturation. Organized crime spans both the criminal and the conventional worlds. The political parties also operate in both worlds. For example, they pass laws to strengthen the integrity of the electoral system, but organize voter fraud. Some business firms similarly span both legitimate activity and the grey area of the informal sector, for example, selling or processing unaccustomed goods. This seeming duality (which, in reality, is integrated behaviour patterns that are regarded as evidence of a mastery of the respective games) makes for enduring partnerships of various combinations between organized crime networks, politicians and private businesses.

Corrupt politics facilitates organized crime, and organized crime assists corrupt politics in ways that have already been noted in chapter 1, such as by constructing and sustaining local single-party monopolies in the form of garrisons, organizing voting fraud, and by funding party candidates. Severing, or at least weakening, this relationship therefore ought to be a key element of any effective strategy to control organized crime.

Cutting Relationships with Private Businesses

The partnerships with private business firms and relationships with the formal economic institutions that are crime reproducing should also be (and indeed are) targets of any control strategy. National economic dependency on the enterprise activity of organized crime may be observed in some of the micro-states of the region and is already problematic in Jamaica. This dependency saps the will to forego the benefits of crime and to face the economic adjustments that would follow from a more robust crime-control strategy that targets high-end enterprise crimes.

However, obstructing the entry of organized crime into legitimate business activities and its access to formal banking means that the leaders of organized crime must constantly hold large sums of cash and thus will tend to spend it on consumption thereby further advertising and glamorizing the criminal lifestyle. Cash-holding increases the incidence of robbery, which in turn may trigger chains of retaliatory face-saving and indeed business-saving violence. Moreover, if there is no incentive or hope of incorporation into legitimate business and conventional society, then there are no incentives to get out of crime (with the associated criminally acquired wealth) and to act in more conventional status-seeking ways.

Often, entry and acceptance in conventional society is not possible for those who criminally acquire their wealth, but they may seek to position their children for a conventional life of wealth. Directing the flow of already acquired criminal wealth into legitimate business firms, if this could be done without criminalizing these businesses (that is, importing criminal methods into legitimate businesses), may provide an exit route for those wishing to enter conventional society. Italy and Colombia have tried to construct exit routes but with very limited success. Weak systems that are faced with extraordinary problems may try to find ways of doing this. As weak systems, they act in this way to take the heat out of the crime problem, but as weak systems, they are unable to force those who take the exit option to make a clean break with criminality. This approach thus runs the risk of spreading criminal methods into mainstream business and politics. However, if the criminal groups are forced to remain on the outside as disreputable outlaws, then they must be expected to challenge the state authorities from the outside (if they are able to find a political partner that is willing and able so to do). Taking the direction of blocking their access to legitimate business firms may thus lead to greater violence and disruptions, unless there is effective law enforcement that is able to execute this policy and to put the organized crime groups out of business, or at least considerably weaken them.

Cutting Relationships with Law Enforcement

The ability to cut relationships assumes a capable and effective system of law enforcement and criminal justice. If this does not exist, as is the case in Jamaica, then developing such a system ought to be an essential part of the process. As organized crime thrives on its opportunity-seeking and protective relationships with the political parties, a condition for law enforcement and criminal justice effectiveness is their independence and insulation from inappropriate political influences. Methods of appointment to the top positions in the system, such as that of commissioner of police and chief justice, the appointments to boards that have the power to promote senior personnel, and the general systems of accountability ought to be improved with a view to further minimizing undue influence by the political administration. The legal authority to appoint should be structured to ensure that these are appointments by consensus and consensus only.

Political interference in the affairs of the police that subverts the merit principle and rewards party loyalty and incompetence usually results in system ineffectiveness. Alliances and shared party affiliations that include powerful organized crime groups that do business with the state give all of the actors involved immunity. The relationships are, however, also more direct and more complicated. There are active members of organized crime groups within the police force (personal correspondence with members of the Professional Standards Branch of the Jamaican Constabulary Force). Some constables collaboratively engage in high-end crimes with these groups. The police and organized crime groups co-police some of the high violence communities. Severing the relationships between organized crime and law enforcement, that is, a thoroughgoing anti-corruption programme, is therefore a condition for greater effectiveness of the police. The relationships of organized crime with business, law enforcement, political parties and communities are thus important targets of any anti-corruption effort, but consistent with the main thrust of the analysis. Here the focus is on the latter two.

Cutting Relationships with Political Parties

Cutting relationships with political parties and politicians ought to involve cutting off the flow of money in both directions, that is, from the party in power (at the national and local government levels) to organized crime as state contracts and subcontracts, and from organized crime to the parties as campaign financing and community programmes. As suggested in the previous chapter, facilitating the access of organized crime firms to state contracts and subcontracts ought to be defined as a crime of conspiracy. It is corrupt facilitation that seeks to avoid detection. This would put colluding state bureaucrats and politicians at risk.

Law enforcement measures are not sufficiently preventative. If there were greater political disincentives for partnerships with organized crime, these partnerships would be pursued with less enthusiasm. The political parties must be made to pay a political price for their association with organized crime. Presently, this association yields political dividends in the form of campaign financing and the mobilization of votes. Exposure of these activities to a less permissive (and less politically tribalized) public would exact a political price and thus have some deterrent effect.[8] Documentation now exists on contracts between various state agencies and organized crime front companies. These firms are not veiled in burkas. Greater exposure of the activity and linkages of these firms would make successive political administrations politically accountable, even if they are able to avoid legal accountability.

The case of Donald Phipps illustrates the vulnerabilities of organized crime once the political support that they enjoy is lost. The effects of the change in political support for this nationally known leader of organized crime may be highlighted by contrasting the Phipps of the 1998 riot that violently protested his arrest with the convicted Phipps of 2006. In 1998, he was arrested for attempted murder and other charges that were derived from a case of his unsuccessful imposition of "community justice". His arrest precipitated a riot in the centre of the city. The security forces were the prime targets of the protestors. Four persons were killed and a few police vehicles torched. The people of the community marched to the police station where Phipps was being held and demanded that he be freed. Faced with a hostile crowd that had encircled the police station, the officers allowed the don to address the crowd and to reassure the protestors that he would be released. Although under arrest, Phipps was clearly in charge and enjoyed a robust support that extended beyond his immediate community.[9] He was later released by the police and, predictably, the accused were unsuccessfully prosecuted.

In 2006, the situation was very different. Phipps was charged with the murder of two of his business associates and party colleagues from another section of the city. They were from another section of the party machinery and their political influence was independent of Phipps. The victims and the offender were partners in a racket involving service provisioning contracts with a state agency.

By 2006, Phipps had already acquired a reputation for the excessive and unjust use of violence against the members of his own group and for increasing unpredictability in his behaviour (personal correspondence between the author and selected members of the community). The murders for which he was charged were taken as evidence that he was out of control and erratic in his judgements, especially those judgements related to the use of lethal violence for control purposes. Many of his own thus felt threatened by his power. This behaviour was, in part, popularly explained in terms of the belief that he was terminally ill.[10] The people of his community were familiar with this pattern of behaviour: his whimsical displays of absolutely unchecked power and the internal power struggles that it tended to precipitate. For example, this pattern had been observed in the final stages of the career of Carl Mitchell ("Byah"), a former leader of the Shower Posse (see Blake 2002, 135–38).

A second factor in Phipps's demise was the seizure of large sums of money from him by the police (Glenroy Sinclair, "Zeeks Charged with Murder", *Gleaner*, 31 May 2005, 1). The large sums in cash were interpreted to mean that he was taking more than the lion's share of the income from the extortion and protection rackets while his operatives in the community were underpaid. This helped to change opinions of him, from that of a kind of social bandit and benevolent leader of the community who provided a highly structured pre-school programme for the children and welfare for the aged, to that of a self-seeking predator who exploited his own. These developments considerably weakened the intensity of community support for him.

Having been weakened, his leadership was challenged by splinter factions. One such challenge came from a former lieutenant. In the context of the difficulties outlined above, this faction was able to secure the support of elements within the Spanglers (Phipps's group) and that of the Mathew's Lane community in which it operates. And this support was secured despite the alliance of this challenging faction with the Shower, a group that has been a historical enemy of the Spanglers and which is aligned to the opposing political party. This situation was seen as threatening to the interests of the PNP. Continued support for an unpopular Phipps became risky. Stability required his removal. The murder of his two business partners noted previously was the last straw. He had lost social and political support locally and in his party nationally. The protective shield that his relationships with the community and the party provided was considerably weakened. Police action was thus more successful than on previous occasions.

Other dons have also become vulnerable after falling out of political favour. Bennett lost his life shortly after a code-violating armed attack by members of his group on a car in which a member of parliament was travelling (see chapter 1). Attacks on the members of political elite are always consequential.[11] Political protection, or even indifference, is the mother's milk of organized crime.

The Need for an Anti-corruption Programme

An anti-corruption programme is essential to severing the relationship between organized crime and the political administration and reducing illegal opportunities in the supply of services to the state and to development projects. These ought to be the two main goals of an anti-corruption strategy that is supportive of efforts to control organized crime. While anti- corruption programmes have other goals, these are the two of greatest relevance here.

Corruption lubricates the relationship between organized crime and the state agencies. It aids the evolution from a simple parasitism of the extortionist type to a symbiotic parasitism between corrupter and corruptee. In the latter, they become business partners. Customs evasion, intimidating business competitors and drug trafficking are, for example, activities that are mutually beneficial. And once symbiotic, it then becomes more entrenched and protected by power. Hong Kong had one of the more successful campaigns against organized crime because it was accompanied by a strong anti-corruption strategy aimed at sanitizing law enforcement.[12] A police service that is unimpeded by corruption may then target the criminal activity of the powerful and is likely to be more effective in doing so.

Prevention is as important as enforcement. Good anti-corruption programmes tend to promote opportunity reduction as a prevention strategy. This typically involves reducing the scope for rackets, simplifying state bureaucratic procedures thereby narrowing the possibilities for system circumventing services, and ensuring the effective delivery of services. Protection rackets, drug trafficking, drug dealing and state contracts for services are the major opportunities for organized crime. The first may be weakened by the delivery of more responsive and effective policing services. With regard to the second, the decriminalization of drugs would remove the most lucrative opportunities for organized crime. However, it is not politically feasible for Jamaica to act unilaterally in decriminalizing drug use. And even if the Government of Jamaica were to act unilaterally, it would not resolve the problem as the main opportunities are in trafficking to other countries. This, therefore, has to be settled as an international issue. The third set of opportunities, that is, the supply of services to the state, has already been discussed.

Corruption is reinforced by supporting ideas. For example, the idea that, as an instrument of public policy, corrupt practices may be a useful means of effecting structural transformation that ends the dominance of racial minorities in important sectors of the economy. Such outcomes, even if they were not designed, may also be taken as *post hoc* justification for the corrupt practices that animated this process.[13] The idea here is that this is at worst a kind of noble cause corruption. It may also be argued that some benefits are filtered to the poor via organized crime, and that facilitating organized crime is a redistributive strategy in favour of the poor. There is no evidence in support of this, but that hardly matters. What matters are the beliefs about the functionality of corruption related to organized crime. Such apologetics arise from the experiences of social exclusion and the desire to end it. An element of strategy, therefore, should be a programme that better integrates the society, and which could begin by strengthening the main integrative institutions. On the basis of such a programme, public education that contests these beliefs and the behaviour sets that are socially facilitative of organized crime may enjoy some success.

Such public education efforts will be ineffective if the bases of these beliefs are not eroded by a legitimate programme of constructive social change that integrates and creates opportunities for the excluded urban poor. Organized crime is appealing because it seems to succeed in circumnavigating the blockages to social success, albeit with the assistance of the political administration.

Cutting Relationships with the Communities

This involves relieving the organized crime groups of their wealth, or at least cutting off the transnational transfers of money and, consequently, its security and welfare provisioning to group members in the communities. It also means having the state provide these services more effectively, and, in the process, better integrate these marginalized communities. As has been emphasized in this work, providing more effective police protection to the communities of the urban poor is perhaps the most important way of reducing the power and influence of organized crime in these communities.

If the state provided the services now offered by organized crime groups, its legitimacy might be re-established and the hold of organized crime on the communities weakened. This is not a project that can be easily executed. The administrative capacity and resources of the state are limited. Moreover, even if these problems of state incapacity were solved and state services effectively provided, the influence of organized crime would remain, but to a lesser degree.

Given the present reality in the communities, the state agencies, including the police, now operate in a competitive environment in which there are observable differences between the style of services delivery of organized crime and that of the state. As is generally understood, personalized help by the state must satisfy norms of legality and bureaucracy. Police protection, unemployment assistance, school fee and other welfare support are subject to procedural rules. The police officer cannot legally punish an offender, and the criminal justice system cannot punish simply on a report from a victim. The police officer cannot instantly seize and return stolen goods. These goods must first be held as evidence and released at the end of a long legal process. The don, on the other hand, provides these services in a different style. This style is that of a patron, "big man" or "father" who does not require that forms be filled out, the signatures of officials be secured, long hours be spent waiting at various offices, and that the recipients of assistance risk humiliation at the hands of power-conscious petty officials who will pry into their personal lives. The don, like a good father, simply helps. Thus, the thief is speedily caught and the stolen goods speedily returned to the eternally grateful street vendor or poor slum dweller who is made to believe that they now have a responsive and powerful protector.

There are understood reciprocities associated with this type of service. The people keep silent and, at times, protect their benefactors. The people who seek assistance thus have some power in this type of relationship (they may, for example, withhold or suspend their protection of the don). In contrast, state provisioning seems to magnify the powerlessness of the people and, even at times, rob them of their dignity (as, for example, at times with the reporting of rape cases to the local police station).[14] There will thus remain, as Robert Merton notes, a "struggle between alternate structures for fulfilling the nominally same functions" (Merton 1967).[15]

Functional Displacement

The relationship of the organized crime groups to the communities of the urban poor rests, to some degree, on its functionality. The marginalization of these communities, which, in some cases, has existed since they were founded as squatter settlements, has had consequences. Organized crime tries, in self-serving and power-enhancing ways, to meet the material and security needs of the marginalized communities. Importantly, it provides avenues for mobility, including geographic mobility, across national borders in search of legal and illegal opportunities, and upward social mobility, via services such as informal banking support for micro-business ventures and by coercing employers to hire members of their communities. It is also a source of respect and other intangible but important goods even if these are achieved by criminal accumulation and gun-holding. Respect must not be confused with deference to disreputable power-holders. In the relationship between the organized crime groups and their communities, the two are discernible. True respect matters and this shapes conduct within the communities. Organized crime has built an alternate opportunity structure in these communities. This is why it is so deeply embedded.

An aspect of the response to this entrenchment of organized crime ought to be its functional displacement and the integration of these communities. Integration entails a resolution, or at least negotiation, of the fundamental conflict issues such as the just allocation of state resources and the nature of the opportunity structures, access to criminal justice and the just treatment of citizens by the system. In general, issues of opportunity, justice, equality and citizens' rights. This requires a more robust response by the integrative institutions of the state, such as those institutions that are involved in education, skills training (technical and social) for job readiness, and the delivery of basic social services. This idea has already been introduced; here the focus will be restricted to the problem of security provisioning.

The protective function is vital. It is difficult to break the power of the organized crime groups if they are believed to be the most reliable security providers in these communities, rather than sources of their insecurity. Given the high levels of violence in these communities, and the power of organized crime within some of them, an intensive policing presence is required initially. A period of pacification may be necessary before greater integration and community transformation is able to proceed.

Pacification seeks to bring peace to the high violence communities. This may be achieved by different methods and has the greatest chance of success and sustainability if these methods are pursued in mutually supportive ways. Systematic peace-building is one element. This is necessary to defuse the decades of hostilities between some of the communities and between the gangs (excluding the organized crime groups). Intensive interactive policing of these communities coupled with the mobilization and empowerment of the citizenry are additional elements. Taken in combination, the peace option becomes more attractive. Pacification would remove the demand for protection by organized crime and hasten an end to the immunity of these groups. This would remove the justifications for the possession of weapons and for the code of silence that supports armed "protective" activity. Given the current conditions in the high violence communities, the demand for protection and the acceptance of its supply by the criminal groups will soften only if the state security forces develop a system that truly protects the residents of these communities. This means an active, permanent and initially high-density presence by the police in these communities. Attending this project is the risk of abuses of power by the police. Such an approach is likely to succeed if, and only if, there is an agreement between the ruling party and the Opposition and a system of accountability that minimizes the abuse of power and allows adequate and speedy redress whenever these abuses occur.

The long-term success of pacification rests on shifting the power relationships within these communities so that the people are not intimidated by the armed capacity and activity of these criminal groups (and by degrading this capacity). In the absence of any significant progress in transforming the Jamaica Constabulary Force, this may necessitate giving policing powers to disciplined and accountable units of citizens who reside in these communities. As a bridging measure, this type of citizen involvement in policing would be necessary until the establishment of normal professional policing services that enjoy the confidence of the people. Indeed, voluntary avocational policing units that monitor their own communities could mediate between the communities and the national professional police in helping to bring this about. This is a very risky project with real dangers of the political manipulation of these groups and new expressions of the abuse of police powers, but systems of accountability may be devised to minimize the risks.

Other countries have attempted such measures. In Haiti, MINUSTAH (the United Nations Stabilization Mission) appears to be attempting an experiment in pacification that has some of the elements noted above. In

2007, over seven hundred members of the more violent "gangs" were arrested.[16] This, in combination with successful peace negotiations that involved groups from different communities that were in conflict and welfare support for the most vulnerable members of the communities, has reduced the level of violence in some of the slums. However, in the absence of investigative work and convictions in court, states are faced with the choice of disregarding the democratic rights of their citizen-suspects or releasing them. If they choose the former, the evidence suggests that any gains are only temporary and hardly worth the damage done to the criminal justice and political systems by the initial mass arrests. Jamaica's experience with such measures is that, once they are applied for a prolonged period, they lead to abuses of power and to a rot in the police force. In Italy, during the period 1986 to 1987, some five hundred mafia suspects were arrested and put before the courts in what became known as the "maxi-trials". They were arrested, tried and convicted en masse. This was preceded by a diligent, carefully orchestrated investigative process (see Stille 1995). Mass arrests usually have the effect of severely disrupting the activity of the group and may put it into disarray. It also increases the chances of convicting the more important actors. Such successes may energize a dispirited public and prompt people to come forward as witnesses, yielding further convictions and may thereby further increase the chances of closing the particular criminal firms.

This approach has also been sharply criticized as being abusive of basic citizens' rights, such as the right to avoid self-incrimination and the use of mafia informants who were themselves facing serious criminal charges.[17] Any process that involves mass arrests and mass trials tends to put these rights at risk. These international experiences, in their positive and negative aspects, are nevertheless all useful and may be distilled and used to inform new projects. If there is an understanding of the limitations of each experience and of each aspect of the response to the problem, then perhaps Jamaica as a learning jurisdiction may be able to score new successes with fewer negative effects.

The limitations on functional displacement have already been discussed. Given these limitations, as long as the acute social problems remain, organized crime will continue to have a social base. Community transformation entails changing the social relationships and mentalities which are firmly anchored in the material conditions of everyday life in these communities. As youth unemployment is a major determinant of violent crime, this means most of all creating meaningful employment opportunities.[18] This cannot be done by local action only or by encouraging micro-enterprises and small scale projects in these communities. It has to be done on a scale such that the national impact would be of some significance. This must involve the creation of opportunities in the mainstream of society and building pathways to these opportunities for the marginalized urban youth. Greater social integration is thus a condition for community transformation.

Improving the built environment is also an important aspect of community transformation, but the poor physical conditions are expressions or outcomes of the harsh socio-economic realities. Integration is a condition for access to the opportunities for change at the level of the individual and the basic social unit to which he or she belongs, that is, the family. With greater integration and opportunities for individual success, the next challenge involves getting the successful people of a community to invest in it, for example, to upgrade their existing homes rather than move out of the community. Upward mobility is coupled with spatial mobility. It is expressed in movement to higher status neighbourhoods. If the inner-city problems are to be solved, social mobility must be de-coupled from spatial mobility. This is a difficult proposition, as people wish a better social environment in which to live and to bring up their children, and it is easier to move to such an environment than to construct it. The state may assist the process of change and encourage citizens to break this pattern of mobility by reducing public poverty in the inner city, by getting the roads fixed, the garbage collected and school performance improved. Retaining those citizens who have achieved social success by conventional methods means reinforcing the institutionally charted pathways to the mainstream, strengthening those institutions and ensuring easier access to them. Transformation is possible if this is done.

Interrupting Processes

The rise of organized crime in Jamaica is related to the social exclusion of large sub-populations, the weaknesses of the state which are grounded in its incapacities and poor relationship with the people, and to the methods of political mobilization, that is, to deep processes in the polity and socio-economic structures of the society. These conditions provide the fuel for the rise of organized crime. Along with corruption, which oxygenates the process, they give organized crime the thrust that it exhibits. Interrupting the processes that have given rise to organized crime involves the difficult challenges of changing the social conditions and style of politics that fuels it.

Since independence, public policy has contributed to shifts in power away from the old elites to new emergent groups. These changes have not been properly mapped, but wider access to secondary and tertiary education has contributed to higher rates of social mobility and changes in the race and colour composition of the middle strata (see Gordon 1987). Stone argues that, since the 1970s, there has been a shift in economic power in favour of previously excluded groups (Stone 1988). State agencies that facilitate access to business information and loans have contributed to the growth of a stratum of upwardly mobile owners of small and medium businesses.[19] Traditional businesses that have heavily relied on state contracts in housing and infrastructure have thus had to yield some ground to new firms led by new entrants to the world of business. Robotham (2000) has named this the "Black Bourgeoisie" project which has been sponsored by successive political administrations since 1993. There is a powerful, morally compelling and developmental case for such a policy. Properly administered, such a project would promote greater social cohesion and perhaps even greater economic dynamism. However, some organized crime front firms that are able to project themselves as the successful efforts of the enterprising poor have been able to exploit these opportunities and to gain support as deserving clients of the state. State assistance to these firms may then be treated as a noble programme for redressing historical injustices. This may simply be justificatory rhetoric, but it resonates among the excluded and previously excluded. Corruption may integrate, but there are better and more open merit-based ways to achieve such an integration project.

The above are opportunity-producing processes that are external to organized crime, but related to these are other distinct processes that are internal to organized crime and which are of relevance to a control strategy. This is the process of evolution or maturation of organized crime. Once this process is understood, then the disruption and termination of it becomes the challenge. The process of maturation is best understood in relation to changes in the environment, changes in the demand for illegal goods and services (illegal opportunities), changes in the nature of the critical relationships, and in the methods of organized crime.

Maturing involves successfully responding to the changing demand for illegal goods and services that are generated by changes in the environment. For example, the global demand for illegal drugs has stimulated the transnationalization of the local groups. The demand for protection by local commercial interests has been met by protection rackets. The demand for sexual services is likely to increase with the growth of mass tourism, and organized crime may respond to this by better organizing and exploiting the prostitution business. These opportunities allow the organized crime groups to diversify their funding streams, thereby making them less vulnerable. It also gives them the resources to develop new methods of doing business and to cultivate new types of relationships. They are now able to foster truly symbiotic relationships based on the demand for illegal services.

Maturing means greater penetration of the formal economy. It also involves the consolidation of the hold of organized crime on the communities by a process of increasingly taking on quasi-governmental functions and forcing co-administration with the state. Extending and deepening its influence in politics is another element in the process of the maturity of organized crime, and an even greater indicator of its maturity is when its political influence is not treated as problematic.

This last point is the critical one. It means that the relationship between the political institutions and organized crime groups are accepted as normal business and the role of organized crime in politics as normal politics. Its methods and practices are taken for granted. Normalization may be achieved by equating the predatory activity of organized crime with corrupt practices involving the old elites, and by claiming that, in their substance, these practices have always been a part of the political process. The association between organized crime and politics, and its corrupt practices, is in this way cynically naturalized.

In general, maturation refers to the process associated with the empowerment of organized crime, its increased connection to the centres of power and the increasing acceptance of this process as normal. Its methods are thus extended to the mainstream: in business, community administration and national politics. Politics is criminalized and criminality politicized. Maturation, in its methods, involves reduced resort to violence and greater and more effective use of corruption and political influence to achieve its goals. Maturation is a process of increasing acceptance of organized crime in the society and its increasing capacity to mask its true characteristics.

In Jamaica, three phases may be discerned in the process of maturation of organized crime. The first is the formative stage where it is geographically restricted to garrison communities and is generally politically subordinated as clients of the parties. During this phase, it enjoys the protection of the community and party but does not wield administrative power within the communities. It has some disciplinary power, but this is largely restricted to disciplining its members. They become involved in the drug trade as predators who rob drug entrepreneurs and, later, as traffickers and dealers.

The second phase of maturity is the growth phase. During this phase, organized crime largely remains tied to territory but spreads across the capital city of Kingston and migrates to other cities and towns, establishing its hold on new localities as predatory organized crime with each group being somewhat limited by the political geography and the patron-client model that relies on face-to-face relationships and interpersonal trust.

There is further spatial extension beyond the national boundaries, engaging in drug trafficking and distribution primarily as enterprise activity. The main income streams are illegal, but formalized legal businesses that thrive on state contracts, and whose existence is based on a symbiotic relationship with state bureaucratic and political actors, are constructed.

These firms serve as bridges, or meeting points, where old predatory relationships with conventional actors in business and politics may be reconstructed along more mutually beneficial lines. This reconstruction begins but remains incomplete.

There is considerable violence that is generated by the competitiveness between groups, the need for internal discipline, predatory victimization, and conflicts with the state security forces. Enterprise groups that are vulnerable to the predatory behaviour of other groups are forced to develop their independent violent capability. Specialization among organized crime groups begins to emerge during this phase but is limited.

The leaders of the organized crime groups become community gate-keepers who regulate access to the communities and negotiate the flow of resources into the communities. They begin to take on quasi-governmental administrative and functional activity. This is the current stage in Jamaica.

The mature phase, which is a logical projection of the tendencies discerned from observation in the earlier stages, is marked by reduced use of violence as more developed symbiotic relationships are established with businesses and state actors and as the more powerful organized crime groups secure local monopolies on the means and use of violence. There is greater involvement of organized crime in legitimate businesses. This, along with the reduced use of violence, lowers the visibility of the organized crime groups and makes them less vulnerable to police action. Interdependencies are further developed that may be measured in terms of the relative contribution of the criminal economy at city and national levels. On this basis, the influence of organized crime in politics is amplified. Its control of the inner-city communities is consolidated via the exercise of quasi-governmental functions in the communities (this is different from the old garrison relationship when the party had sole, undivided control).

At this phase of maturity and consolidation of local power, breaking the hold of the organized crime groups on the communities may lead to some instability in these communities. At this point, a further flagging of the political and civic will to deal with organized crime may be expected. Elements of maturity are already being exhibited.

These are *phases* rather then *stages* in the development of organized

Table 2.1 The Level of Maturity of Organized Crime Groups

Structure
- Flexible, adaptable, durable — M
- Hierarchical relationships within groups accepted — H
- Leadership changes without violence — M
- Composition of membership and associates (lawyers, law enforcement personnel, chemists, other professionals included) — L–M

Activities
- Range of enterprise crimes and services — M–H

Extent of Transnational Activity
- Number of countries and cities in which operations are conducted — H
- Nature of relationships with foreign transnational organized groups (superordinate, subordinate, independent) — –

Penetration of the Legitimate Economy
- Size of the underground economy as a percentage of the formal — U
- Range of sectors penetrated — M
- Number, size, of organized crime affiliated firms established — –
- Local dependence on drug money — M–H
- Dependencies at the macro level (e.g., foreign currency supply) — –

Relationships
Political Influence
- Community influence/community administration (inner city) — H
- In local government – cities — H
- Individual candidates and party representatives — –
- National influence in the parties as institutions — M
- In the national state agencies — –

Social Embeddedness
- Number of garrison communities established — –
- Dependency on OC ratios for OC dominated communities — –
- Extent of job access via organized crime groups — –

Table 2.1 continues

Table 2.1 The Level of Maturity of Organized Crime Groups (*cont'd*)

Tolerance of Organized Crime

– Organized crime accepted as a useful supplier of valued social goods	H
– Accepted as helping the poor	H
– Coherent apologetics that have wide appeal	M
– Front firm activities accepted as normal; business with state agencies unquestioned/officially treated as being unquestionable	M
– Activities not socially defined as crimes	M

Methods

Level of Violence

– Local monopolies on violence established	M
– Capacity to repel the state police/security services	M

Use of Corruption

– Systematic use of corruption	H
– Law enforcement systematically corrupted at the local level	H
– At the national level = immunity bought	M–H
– Corruption essential to its "legitimate" activity = state contracts	H

L = low
M = medium
H = high
U = unknown

Note: This table was inspired by similar ideas that are presented in UNODC 2002, 24. It is incomplete because there are still data gaps in the research.

crime. Elements of each phase may be found in all three, but nevertheless, one may see distinct changes in the main markers of the maturity of organized crime. An impressionistic rating of the level of maturity of organized crime on these markers is presented below in table 2.1. Response strategies that are preventatively focused on these markers may be elaborated upon. For example, they may seek to make the shift from ordinary parasitic to difficult symbiotic relationships and thereby prevent interdependencies from developing. Disrupting the processes and methods that are described above means uncoupling the crime–politics link, that is, depoliticizing crime and decriminalizing politics. This must entail further reduction of party political influence within the police and criminal justice system, and the reduction of the impact of other forms of corruption.

Countering the Methods of Organized Crime

Corruption, violence and intimidation are the standard practices of organized crime. These methods are applied separately or in combination to ensure goal achievement and to secure immunity against law enforcement. The scale of the corruption and credibility of the threat of violence guarantees the effectiveness of these methods. Both sets of methods, that is, corruption and violence, may be countered with adequate law enforcement instruments and more resilient systems in the public and private sectors. The latter measures of the preventive type may, for example, involve improved systems that make it more difficult to secure subcontracts, inflate invoices and give shoddy work by corrupting or intimidating a few officials. With regard to the more reactive measures, it is generally argued that Jamaica has adequate laws and that the problem lies in ineffective enforcement. This may be a general truth, but it does not apply to organized crime. Organized crime requires new legal instruments and the legislature has been considering some of these.

Jamaica does have legislation specifically designed to deal with organized crime. The following conventions and agreements have been signed and/or ratified by the Government of Jamaica:

1.   The United Nations Convention Against the Illicit Traffic in Narcotic Drugs and Psychotropic Substances 1988
2.   The Barbados Plan of Action 1996
3.   Anti-Drug Hemispheric Strategy 1996
4.   The Bridgetown Plan of Action 1997
5.   Guiding Principles of Drug Demand Reduction and Measures to Enhance International Cooperation to Counter the World Drug

Problem 1998 (Twentieth Special Session of the United Nations General Assembl)

6. The Caribbean Regional Maritime Counter-drug Agreement 1995

7. The Jamaica Maritime Counter-narcotics Cooperation Agreement 1997 updated in 2004 (the Ship-Rider Agreement)

8. The US-Jamaica Mutual Legal Assistance Treaty (MLAT)

9. The Inter-American Convention on Mutual Legal Assistance in Criminal Matters

10. The Cooperating Nation Information Exchange System

11. The agreement on money laundering and the formation of the Financial Action Task Force (FATF)

12. The United Nations Convention Against Transnational Organized Crime 2003

13. The Declaration of Santo Domingo 2007

Most of these conventions and agreements are instruments of international governance. They seek to promote international law enforcement cooperation, extradition, confiscation of criminal assets, eradication of drug-producing crops, and the criminalization of money laundering among other objectives. If taken seriously, then these conventions must find expression in national legislation and the institutional capacity to enforce such legislation. Thus, in recent times, the Jamaican legislature has passed the Money Laundering Act (1996; amended in 1997), the Maritime Drug Trafficking Suppression Act (1998), the Corruption (Prevention) Act (2000), the Proceeds of Crime Act (2007), the Interception of Communication Act which was amended in 2006, and the Terrorism Prevention Act (2005). All have provisions under which organized crime may be controlled.

There is, however, a need for additional legislation that specifically targets neglected aspects of organized crime. For example, there is the need for legislation that criminalizes any conspiracy between the criminal groups and their upper-world partners so that the actors may be discovered and brought before the courts as organized crime collaborators. Similarly, there may be a case for defining membership of an organized crime group as a crime. Some criteria for determining membership may include systematic ties to the group, decision-making influence, and involvement in a pattern of criminal-offending with the group. Thus, state officials who repeatedly breach procurement guidelines to award contracts to organized crime groups may be considered conspirators with or members of these groups (elements in an outer network of contacts). Both crimes would be defined by observable patterns of behaviour.

Any legislative agenda that is aimed at the methods of organized crime and is intended to improve the tools that are available to law enforcement should consider the following:

- Placing limits on the use of cash in business transactions. Exceeding this limit would trigger an investigation, possibly resulting in a cash-defined crime. Violations of such a law could be easily detected by investigators.[20]

- Making the use of intimidation to secure contracts and to prevent proper accountability with respect to goods and services delivered under contract an activity warranting police use of wire-tapping and other legally accepted techniques for dealing with organized crime.[21]

- Legislation targeting firms that act as fronts for organized crime.

- Making provisions to deal with organized crime interference with the right to vote that extends the existing prohibitions under the Representation of the People's Act. These provisions should make it a *serious crime* to intimidate or bribe voters, and to promise to mobilize votes for a politician in exchange for money, or a promise of monetary rewards if their electoral efforts are successful.

New legislation is almost pointless and may even bring the law into greater disrepute unless there is an accompanying capability to enforce it. The Jamaican police force has been in a process of reform since 1994 with mixed results (Harriott 2000, 2007a). If there is an inability to make the entire Jamaican Constabulary Force more effective as an instrument of crime control then more dedicated effort should be directed at devising a unit that is able to deal with high-end transnational crime and crimes that involve powerful individuals and groups. The kernel of such a group already exists within the police force.[22] However, laws that would increase the powers of the police may be abused by both the police and political administrators who may exercise undue influence over and within the police force. Protective devices based on international experience and an understanding of the Jamaican environment should therefore be built into the legal provisions.

Having anchored the discussion of strategy in an understanding of organized crime and of the local environment, the lessons from selected international experiences may be re-examined. The exportable value of these experiences is in the principles that guide the broad strategic approaches taken and the general lessons that may be drawn from them, not in promoting imitation of the forms that have been adopted elsewhere.

Lessons from International Experience

Italy, Hong Kong and, more contentiously, the United States (which remains the largest drug market) may claim to have had some success in controlling organized crime. These countries are included in the set of states that have also had the longest histories of organized crime. The United States has had over a hundred and twenty years of experience with organized crime since the presence of mafia activity among Italian migrants was first detected in New Orleans in 1880 (Reppetto 2004, 8).[23] Italy and Hong Kong have some two hundred and one hundred and sixty years of experience respectively in controlling organized crime since its emergence in Palermo in the early nineteenth century (Blok 1974, 10–12) and since gaining visibility in Hong Kong just prior to 1842 when the latter became a British colony.[24] Gambetta (1993, 136) notes that the word "mafia" was first used in official documentation in 1865. This is not inconsistent with Blok's claims regarding the earlier emergence of the phenomenon. The dates that are noted above refer to the recorded observations of the behaviour set that later came to be associated with identifiable groups.

In all of these cases, while countries have had some success in controlling organized crime, they have had great difficulty in eliminating it. Organized crime has proved to be highly adaptable and resilient in different socio-economic and political environments, having survived the relentless onslaughts against it by fascism in Italy, communism in China, the efforts of the British colonial administration in Hong Kong, and those of American democracy with its periods of corrupt politics but legally empowered, multilayered, and relatively well-resourced criminal justice system.

The American Experience

The American experience has been well documented in English and therefore is most available. America has had a long and intensive experience with organized crime. Its control performance has been mixed. Criminal justice in the United States is highly politicized. Judges who preside at the state level Courts of Appeal, for example, are usually appointed by the governors, and judges of the Lower Courts are directly elected by the citizenry.[25] Mayors have direct control over the city police forces, and political and law enforcement careers may hinge on crime-control outcomes. Premature and exaggerated claims of success are therefore not infrequent. However, despite these problems and the mixed outcomes, the American experience is worth examining.

According to Abadinsky and other authorities, such as Kenney and Finckenauer, the main elements of action taken in the United States have been

- to increase the risks to organized crime activity by expanding the powers of the police and increasing resources to law enforcement;
- to decrease the opportunities for organized crime by legalizing some of its activities;
- to reduce the attractiveness of organized crime by providing alternate legitimate opportunities; and
- to educate and mobilize the public against organized crime. (Abadinsky 1990, 481–500; Kenney and Finckenauer 1995, 342–71)

These are observations of the historical experience of the United States. They do not represent a coherent and consistent policy observed at any particular time. For example, with respect to decreasing the opportunities available to organized crime, after the negative effects of the prohibition of alcohol (1920–1933) became apparent, the production and consumption of alcohol was legalized.[26] This aspect of the strategy has not been consistently adopted and has not been applied to the current situation with recreational drugs. Drug trafficking and drug dealing is the main business of organized crime. It sustains not just American organized crime, but the transnational organized crime groups in producer and transit countries such as Jamaica. The market in illegal drugs in the United States is estimated to be some $100 to $120 billion (Naylor 2003, 262). Thus, although the risks associated with participation in the trade may be increased by greater investments in law enforcement, the rewards for drug dealing are great and tend to increase in direct relation to the risks. Manipulating risk as an element of deterrence only makes sense in relation to the potential rewards. Logical consistency would seem to dictate that drug use should be decriminalized, but its decriminalization is opposed by powerful interest groups and moral entrepreneurs within American society.[27]

Reflecting on the problems of policing the drug trade, August Vollmer, one of the most accomplished American police chiefs turned academic, wrote in 1936: "Stringent laws, spectacular police drives, vigorous prosecution, and imprisonment of addicts and peddlers have proved not only useless and enormously expensive as a means of correcting this evil, but they are also unjustifiably cruel in their application to the unfortunate drug victims. Repression has driven this vice underground and produced the narcotics smugglers and supply agents, who have grown wealthy out of this evil practice" (Vollmer 1936, 99–118, cited in Woodiwiss 2003,11).

Well-intentioned and moralistic but overreaching and ineffective crime-control policies may compound the crime problem. An appropriate application of the opportunity reduction principle to the drug problem surely cannot be beyond the collective wisdom of the international regulatory bodies and the nations that are the major actors in the trade as consumers, producers or transit countries. The American approach is grounded in a mix of deterrence and opportunity theory and is informed by a studied understanding of the features and activities of organized crime. Deterrence theory is essentially about manipulating risk, and opportunity theory is about reducing the opportunities for crime. Although the approach is theoretically informed, there is still quite a bit of muddling through.

Woodiwiss (2003) argues that the effort to control organized crime in the 1930s was the most instructive period in the American experience. This was the period when policy was most coherent and thus most effective. He states that during this period "government action not only ensured the conviction of large numbers of gangsters and at least some of their political protectors, but more significantly, it also reduced the opportunity for successful organised criminal activity". In 1933, Prohibition was ended and the New Deal was announced (Woodiwiss 2003, 32).

The Experiences of Other Countries

Since then, despite the racketeer-influenced corrupt organizations (RICO) laws and assets forfeiture, the sites of innovation in dealing with organized crime have shifted from the United States. There have been interesting approaches to anti-Mafia legislation in Italy. It is interesting because it "targets up" in a different way from the Americans, allowing powerful sponsors and facilitators of organized crime within the political elites to be successfully targeted. In this regard, the most well known case is that of former Prime Minister Giulio Andreotti, who was charged and put on trial for his involvement with the Mafia. Japanese laws are similarly interesting for their precision in targeting organized crime. Their "anti-Boryokudan" or anti-organized crime law of 1991 uses the categories "designated Boryokudan" and "designated Boryokudan members". Among other crimes, it prohibits them from the following:

- acts of unreasonably demanding subcontract jobs
- acts of demanding protection money
- acts of unfairly intervening in out-of-court settlement arrangements (Uchiyama 2003, 274)

Another set of laws was passed in 1999 in Japan that was more typical of anti-organized crime legislation. These laws gave the police highly regulated powers and distinguished crimes committed in furtherance of the interests of a criminal organization (Hill 2003, 259).

The Boryokudan Eradication Centres (Hill 2003, 231) provide a range of services to the public and former members of organized crime groups, including public education regarding the practices of organized crime, resilience training for officials and operatives most exposed to demands by organized crime (such as contract granting officials), and assistance to members of organized crime groups who wish to be rehabilitated and to re-enter conventional society.

In the Netherlands, a fairly coherent and consistent strategy has been pursued. Their drug policy is well known (see Blom 2001). But more interesting is the idea of "phenomenon research". This seems to be a promising approach that involves research-oriented scanning and problem solving. It is promising because, unlike the American approach, it makes a shift from an exclusive focus by law enforcement on case solving to problem solving in dealing with organized crime.[28] Phenomenon research begins with an analysis of the "structural opportunities open to organized crime" then seeks to reduce these opportunities. Oon van der Heijden (2003) provides a good illustration of how this works. He cites the case of an analysis of the currency exchange transactions by tourists in Amsterdam. These exchanges, he writes, could be done at a number of poorly regulated exchange offices in the city. Analysis of their activity revealed that several offices were owned by a small number of families and that in some cases the turnover of the offices "exceeded the sum of the transactions by tourists by a factor of 10". The upshot of this was better regulation and a reduction in organized crime activity in this field (see van der Heijden 2003, 124). There is a strong case for such an approach. This chapter argues for the incorporation of these elements in dealing with a wider range of problems and as a part of a strategy that is even more comprehensive than the approach that is taken in the Netherlands.

In most developed countries, the responses to organized crime have been led by law enforcement, but with a measure of political mobilization for action. Parties that are implicated as collaborators and protectors of organized crime may be made to pay a political price for their conduct.

In the developing and newly developed countries there are fewer success stories. As noted earlier, Hong Kong has been one such case. India, it may be argued, has also had some success, but these have been less sustainable and more restricted to the city level. For example, exposure of extortion rackets in their film industry attracted public attention and forced the state to act against the groups involved. In most of the successful cases there was popular mobilization and political action. This triggered pressures for more effective law enforcement and anti-corruption measures. In some cases, the latter was a condition for the former, especially in instances where there was a single national police service, as was the case in Hong Kong and is the case in Jamaica. In the United States and Italy there are national police services that may be deployed where the local police services are compromised.

The general lessons gleaned from these experiences and observations may be highlighted as follows:

- Competitive political systems should provide scope for their parliaments and the opposition parties to hold the government and law enforcement to account in organizing effective responses to organized crime. Political competition in a mature polity may be made to work for crime control and the national interest. The experiences of some countries suggest the importance of national institutions such as crime commissions with appropriate powers to investigate and expose organized crime. They help to inform public opinion and to force political action. These are entities that may be set up by parliaments.
- Public opinion and civic mobilizations are very important, as seen in the examples of the United States, Italy and India).
- The problem of corruption, especially corruption in law enforcement, cannot be avoided if organized crime is to be successfully controlled.
- International cooperation is critical. This is perhaps even more important for small states with limited capacity to deal with transnational crime and whose national identities are at risk of being tarnished by the external activities of organized crime and the political responses of the more powerful states.
- There is a need for an adequate legal framework that specifically targets organized crime, but which typically includes less precise but useful laws that, for example, prevent the abuse of banking secrecy, that provide for forfeiture of assets and which regulate the methods employed by law enforcement.
- Such laws are not to be treated symbolically but rather as elements in a larger campaign against organized crime. Legal symbolism tends to be

employed in times of crisis events and panics as knee-jerk responses. The announcement of incapacitated or otherwise unfit police special units may be regarded as a similar symbolic manipulation.
• Response overreach creates political divisions on key law enforcement issues and makes the efforts ineffective.

Conclusion

Elsewhere, an argument has been made for understanding organized crime as part of the system of power (see Harriott 2007a). This, along with other features, is what places organized crime at the centre of the Jamaican crime problem. Consistent with this analysis, an approach to the prevention and control of organized crime that is informed by its key characteristics and which extends beyond the limits of law enforcement is advocated. This involves looking beyond the immediate organized crime actors to their support and enabling systems. It means touching the powerful in the society, including members of the political elite and the business classes and placing institutions that lie at the heart of the state under critical scrutiny. There is not likely to be much enthusiasm for this approach.

There is thus the need for a social movement against high-end criminality and violence which would put pressure on the political administration and the law enforcement agencies for systematic action against organized crime and which would educate the public on these matters. To the extent that it would do this, such a movement would, in effect, challenge the methods of political organization and mobilization (vote buying, intimidation), that is, contend with a system of power for its transformation without such a movement itself being power oriented. This would be very challenging.

More immediately, there is a need for capable, independent and effective law enforcement that would end the immunity of organized crime. They need the necessary legal tools. It has been suggested that there is a need for even more comprehensive legislation to treat with the specific problems presented by organized crime. However, excesses in the form of draconian laws, and especially policing measures that are illegal, ought to be avoided. Such excesses tend to precipitate resistance by the communities that are most affected by the crime problem, a backlash of public opinion, and an opening-up of the social and political divisions in the society. The ultimate outcome of this is operational ineffectiveness and policy failure.

The prevention and control of organized crime should not be allowed to follow the general (failed) pattern of crime control. This pattern may be described as a cycle that begins with reactions to a wave of violence or some outrageous boundary-breaching crime that attracts media and public attention. This is followed by an emergency reaction that involves intensive policing of the high violence communities by the police and military and the formation of special squads. In such a climate, there are often human rights violations and suspicious killings by the police, followed by anti-police demonstrations and a falling-off of public support for the efforts of the state. The campaign ends without success and a new accommodation and higher threshold of tolerance of violence and organized crime activities is established. Sustainability, including political sustainability, must be anchored in more measured responses, more robust institutions with capable dedicated staff treating with both prevention and control, and in an informed public.

An attempt has been made to sketch the broad outlines of an approach to the problems presented by organized crime. The intent is simply to open up the discussion – with the understanding that the effective control of organized crime does not rest solely on having a good strategy. There are many obstacles to success. These include real material interests that find expression in the nexus with politics. The real challenge is in getting the policy process to work for larger, more national interests.

3

Political Corruption and Organized Crime

LLOYD WALLER AND ANTHONY HARRIOTT

POLITICAL CORRUPTION (HENCEFORTH "CORRUPTION") has been described as the handmaiden of organized crime (Shelley 1998; McWalters 1999; Buscaglia and van Dijk 2003; Donais 2003; Lotspeich 2002). Together they form a nexus. In this chapter we examine this nexus in Jamaica. In so doing, it is intended that the analysis will help to expand the range of alternatives available to the policy- and decision-making machinery in Jamaica for effectively controlling and preventing both corruption and organized crime, whether collectively or independently. The approach of this paper is not a moralistic one. Rather, the central concern here is with understanding the problems and their configurations with a view to correcting them.

Framing the Nexus

The popularization of the connection between good governance and development, highlighted in the 2002 United Nations Development Programme Human Development Report, *Deepening Democracy in a Fragmented World*, brought to the forefront the long-standing issue of corruption.[1] For the purpose of this study we define corruption as the misuse of entrusted power by a politician, a party, an institution or public servant for private benefit[2] – to enrich, or in various ways advance, their interests or the interests of others.

Although people have been writing on corruption since Plato (Wilson 1989; Warren 2004), it was Leff (1964), Leys (1965), Bayley (1966), Nye (1967) and Huntington (1968) who, as far back as the 1960s, drew attention to the existence, prevalence, causes and consequences of corruption in many different types of societies, ranging from pre-industrial to post-industrial. Their narratives brought the discourse of corruption to the contemporary scholarly and policy podium. Since then, there have been many other studies conducted to either deepen or expand our knowledge of corruption. (See, for example, Mason 1978; Johnston 1982, 2005; Theobald 1990; World Bank 1997; Charap and Harm 1999; Rose-Ackerman 1999; Warren 2004; Steligson 2006; Transparency International 1999–2007.)

Throughout these decades of talking about corruption, many have helped to put a face on corruption, leading to the emergence of a more sophisticated spectrum of discourses which range from creating a taxonomy of the forms of corruption (Transparency International 1999–2007) through to deconstructing the causes and consequences of corruption (Rose-Ackerman 1999; Warren 2004; Johnston 1982; Steligson 2006; see also Wei 2000; Nice 1986). One dimension of the corruption problematic which has emerged during the 1980s is the connection between corruption and organized crime.

Since the mid-1980s there has been an exploration of the connection between corruption and organized crime (Kelly 1986; Lupsha 1988; Beare 1997; McFarlane 1998; Minnaar 1999; Donais 2003; Shelley 2005). Through these scholars, we have discovered much regarding the connection between corruption and organized crime in many parts of the developed and developing world.

❖

Dedicated research on the connection between organized crime and political corruption in Jamaica, however, is wholly lacking. Both issues, corruption and organized crime (both major problems in Jamaica), have largely been treated separately. Recent global literature on both organized crime and corruption has, however, suggested that the two should be treated interdependently in order to understand the configuration of each and devise strategies to reduce them (Beare 1997; McFarlane 1998; Minnaar 1999; McWalters 1999; Shelley 2000, 2001, 2003; Buscaglia and van Dijk 2003; Donais 2003; Lotspeich 2002).

What we know from the global literature regarding these problems is that when the political machinery connects with criminal enterprises, the nexus undermines the proper functioning of political and legal institutions, challenges the integrity of the state, and threatens the very fabric of democratic or good governance. This can occur in instances where the widely recognized norms, legal arrangements and standards which govern economic transactions are violated. It also occurs in instances where the functioning of a nation and the ability of institutions in society to attain stated objectives are hijacked. Among these, the administrative system, political institutions, and the judiciary are of key concern. In such a space, merit-based mobility, innovation and creativity are stifled. In essence, then, the nexus both undermines the culture and shrinks the domains of democracy.

Beyond these threats to good governance, but linked to them, are also economic consequences. The nexus distorts private and public investment (for example, the channelling of funds into highly corrupt sectors such as construction). It subverts the merit principle and rewards those who do not play by the rules (thereby reducing competition), weakens the authority of the rules and laws and the methods and processes that lie at the heart of the democratic process. The livelihoods of the poor are particularly at risk. Resources required to address their needs are siphoned off to meet the needs of an individual, a political party or another group. This essentially means that corruption may, in some instances, help to perpetuate the status quo by providing those who seek to protect their own interests with the power to do so. According to Shelley (2006, 1), for example, in 1996 the International Monetary Fund stated that "2 per cent of global GDP [gross domestic product] was related to drug crime and the laundered sums associated with corruption". Unarguably, this suggests that the link between corruption and organized crime has even deeper implications for the developmental possibilities of a state.

Peter Lupsha (1988), in his anthology of organized crime at the global level, argues that the nexus, while threatening good governance and development generally, benefits both the corrupt political machinery and the criminal enterprise. According to him, political systems "support the existence of organized crime through collusive support of criminal groups as extra governmental tools for sanctioning opponents" (Lupsha 1988, 2). Looking at the history of organized crime in the United States, he draws our attention to the fact that "the use of criminal gangs by political machines to harass the opposition was a commonplace" practice in the urban areas of the United States. He then goes on to highlight similar practices around the world:

> Chiang Kai Shek and the Kuomintang used the organized Triads of Shanghai as enforcers to massacre communist party members in 1972. The French government used the Corsican organized crime groups of Marseilles as informal security agents against both French communist and right-wing military terrorists. The US military occupation forces and Army intelligence, G-2, in Japan made similar tacit agreements with Japanese organized crime, the Yakuza, and helped established [*sic*] their primacy in post-war Japan. (Ibid.)

Beare (1997), in extending the work of Lupsha (1988), also sees this form of corruption as being beneficial to both corrupt political officials and the organized criminals. Based on her study of organized crime and political corruption in the United States, she explains that the political machinery "chose to collude with organized crime in order to stay in power, eliminate opposition, or fund-raise through the involvement in illegal commodities, i.e., drugs" – minimizing risk through the use of organized crime.

Criminal enterprises, on the other hand, view the corrupt political authority as a "unique powerful instrument for organized crime" (Reuter, cited in Beare 1997, 158). Corruption minimizes risk. According to Kelly (1986, 15), each "crime network attempts to build a coercive monopoly and to implement that system of control through . . . [the] corruption of public and private officials". Criminal agents are able to buy protection from enforcement, and from the rule of law of a state. Similar articulations can be found in the writings of Donais (2003) as well as Shelley (2006).

Criminal groups, Beare further argues, in time political corruption and organized crime normalize and even legitimize their criminality as they become more integrated in the political machinery, through business relations, political alignments, or the judicial space facilitated by corrupt decision-makers. This, it is argued, is possible as the "ability to corrupt enables one to control the definition of what is or is not defined as corrupt" (Beare 1997, 158). Indeed, the powerful have the ability to call their corrupt activity something else. It is possible to argue that contentions over corrupt activity easily become political battles over the power to define the activity rather than issues of accountability to the laws and established rules. Shelley gives us an example of this in Russia when she states that during "the Yeltsin era there were also close links between the Kremlin and leading crime figures who had direct access to the levers of power" (Shelley 2005, 3). The "levers of power", she argues, through power and influence, helped to normalize the illegal practices of leading crime figures.

Johnson and Soeters, in a comparative analysis of organized crime in Jamaica and Italy, have similar arguments. They have observed that criminal enterprises in these countries have extraordinary influence on the use of public resources through their connections with the political machinery. This nexus is so strong that the criminals become "active participants in public life and hegemonic power holders within the civil sphere" (Johnson and Soeters 2008). The end result, they argue, is that it becomes almost impossible to tell where the legitimate state leaves off and these illegitimate criminal enterprises begin. Based on the literature reviewed, similar circumstances exist in countries such as Bosnia, Colombia, Mexico and parts of Africa, to name a few, where, for example, political parties are now inseparable from criminal organizations (Shelley 2005; McWalters 1999). Such circumstances aid criminal enterprises in building their empires.

Criminal networks, operating through legitimate spaces facilitated by corrupt mechanisms, build their empires, as mentioned earlier, not only through protection from law enforcement and by escaping the rule of law, but also through the facilitation of corrupt mechanisms in terms of the provision of information regarding criminal countermeasures by governments, contract distributions (both international and local), offered to them through legitimate state bodies, and, in some instances, through tax evasion. They are effectively able to "eliminate competition and amass capital" (Reuter, cited in Beare 1997, 158; see also McFarlane 1998). Lupsha (1988) refers to these activities as the "maximization of profits through attempts at cartelization or monopolization of markets, enterprises and crime matrices" (Lupsha, cited in Kelly 1986, 33). They are, in many ways, aspects of "new capitalism" as discussed by Jessop (2000).

Lupsha (1988) further argues that these criminal syndicates or networks are not only able to protect their enterprises through legitimate means, but they are also able to spread their influences both horizontally and vertically and may even become national in scope. Shelley, for instance, notes how corrupt mechanisms have also assisted criminal enterprises in the massive transfers of assets from countries in the South, like Nigeria, to countries in the North (Shelley 2006, 3). Unarguably, such practices have severe implications for the advancement of developing nations, as the perception of a nexus, not only by locals but by global actors, undermines the trust in government.

Research Design

This study explores both actual corruption and perceptions of the nexus between corruption and organized crime, but with an emphasis on the latter. It is understood that perceptions, among other factors, may be distorted by an already existing lack of confidence in the institutions of state. However, as an object of study, perception is a fair proxy for actual corruption as some of its effects are quite similar to the effects of actual corruption.

This research design is located in the space where objectivism and interpretivism connect – a dialectic space. Based on this, the methodology employed was both the survey research (a quantitative approach) and narrative analysis methodology (a qualitative approach).

Two different sets of samples were used for this research project to ensure both reliability and validity (the trustworthiness of the findings). A national survey was conducted using the multistage sampling technique which included fifteen hundred persons taken from all fourteen parishes in

Jamaica. In addition to the survey, a focus group as well as fifteen elite interviews (that is, interviews with policymakers and persons in positions of authority) were conducted. The focus group and interviews were conducted with personnel from various key government agencies usually viewed as corrupt, but with an emphasis on those agencies associated with the Jamaican construction industry. These include the customs department and the police force. Also, eight elite interviews were conducted with key non-government organizations which have been involved in monitoring either corruption or crime in Jamaica. Lastly, interviews were also conducted with key members of both political parties in Jamaica as well as community area leaders (and dons) who work with these individuals. Informal discussions were held with various persons in the Jamaican underworld, that is, those involved in illegal activities.

An instrument was developed and deployed to gain insights from the Jamaican people about the perception of a link between organized crime and corruption. The survey was only able to show what we *think* we know. The in-depth elite interviews were therefore needed to provide information regarding actual instances of the political machinery colluding with criminal enterprises, that is, what we *do* know.

As noted earlier, use was also made of two data sets relevant to the present study. The first was based on a survey by the Centre for Leadership and Governance[3] – a centre operating out of the Department of Government, University of the West Indies at Mona. This survey explored, among other things, issues of trust, crime and criminality. The second was also based on a survey of the Jamaican economy by another centre operating out of the university's Department of Government, the Caribbean Policy Research Institute (CAPRI). The survey is popularly referred to as the "Taking Responsibility Survey". CAPRI is an independent think-tank committed to evidence-based research to inform public debate and influence policy in order to enhance the development of the region. This survey explored, among other things, corruption – its prevalence, causes and consequences.

Unpacking the Nexus in Jamaica

We begin our analysis of the links between political corruption and organized crime in Jamaica by providing a descriptive picture of the landscape of corruption in Jamaica. The data were drawn from the CAPRI survey which was conducted between November and December 2006. Several aspects of this survey were of interest to us as they provide an understanding of

- how Jamaicans defined corruption
- the perception of corruption in Jamaica
- actual experiences with corruption
- the level of corruption in Jamaican institutions
- the level of corruption in Jamaican government institutions specifically
- the main causes of corruption in Jamaica

Regarding the definition of corruption by Jamaicans, the following question was posed in the survey instrument used to collect the data: "Which of the following statements matches closest your understanding of what 'corruption' is?" Several possible answers were presented, all of which are outlined in table 3.1 below.

These findings revealed that most Jamaicans define corruption as "The misuse of public office for private gain". From the data presented in table

Table 3.1   How Jamaicans Define Corruption

	Frequency (n)	Per cent (%)
Misuse of public office for private gain	515	45.0
Mismanagement of government funds	217	19.0
Cost over-runs	95	8.0
Poor management practices	164	7.0
Other	69	7.0
No answer	80	7.0
Total	1,140	100

3.1, it is also clear that some persons are able to decode the euphemistic language that is often used to mask the problem, such as "cost over-runs".[4]

With this in mind, we looked for perceptions regarding the level of corruption in the Jamaican public sector. Based on the data analysed, 7 per cent believed that there was no corruption in the Jamaican public sector, 8 per cent believed that there was very little, 23 per cent stated that they believed that there was some amount of corruption, and a large majority of 62 per cent believed that there was a great deal of corruption in this sector. This is depicted below in figure 3.1.

In addition to this, we also sought to compare these results (the perception of corruption in Jamaica) with actual exposure to corrupt acts. Based on the results of bivariate descriptive analysis (BDS), more specifically through the use of the chi-square (^{2}) test, it was found that a statistical relationship exists between "actual exposure to corrupt acts" and "perception of corruption" in Jamaica [^{2} (6) = 46.33, P_{value} 0.000 <0.05].

The CAPRI survey also sought to identify the perceived level of corruption in several critical public sector agencies and offices. Respondents were given a list of these government agencies and asked to indicate how corrupt they felt that these agencies were. These agencies included: customs, immigration, inland revenue, public works, police, parish councils,

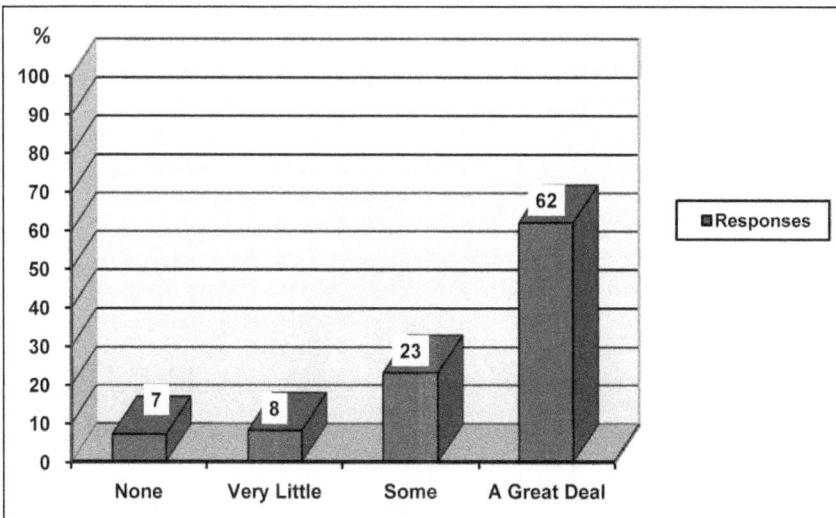

Figure 3.1 Corruption in the political administration

central ministries, executive agencies, and statutory organizations. The findings are presented in figure 3.2.

The findings indicated that the police force, the parish councils and the customs department are perceived to be the most corrupt government agencies in Jamaica. More specifically, the majority of the respondents (52 per cent) indicated that they felt the police to be "very corrupt", with 29 per cent noting that they are "corrupt" and 14 per cent saying "somewhat corrupt", compared to 6 per cent who noted that they were "not at all corrupt". With regard to the parish councils, in excess of 92 per cent of the respondents noted that the parish councils in Jamaica are at different degrees of corruption. For instance, 27 per cent stated that the parish councils are "somewhat corrupt", 32 per cent indicated that those organizations are "corrupt", with some 31 per cent stating that they are "very corrupt". In terms of customs, it was found that less than 5 per cent of the respondents reported that Jamaica's customs department was "not at all corrupt", with 36 per cent indicating that it was "very corrupt", 34 per

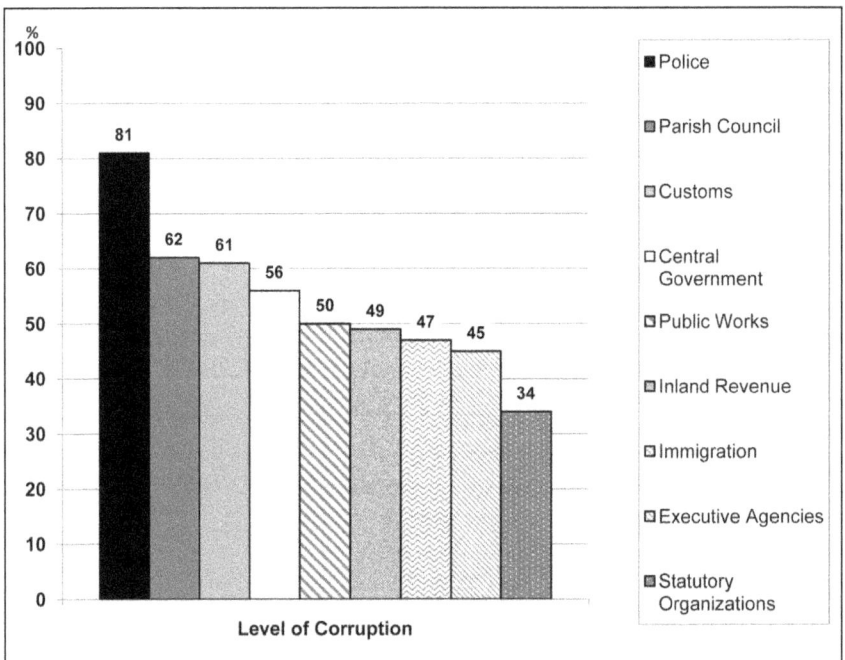

Figure 3.2 Corruption in the state bureaucracy

cent remarking that it was "somewhat corrupt" and 26 per cent noting that it was "corrupt".

Most of the persons interviewed for the CAPRI survey (85 per cent) also seemed to believe that it was very easy to corrupt a public official in these public sector agencies.

Respondents were further asked to state the causes of corruption in Jamaica. They were given a list of possible answers. These included: low salaries (income as a proxy for access to resources); personal graft and greed; many available opportunities for corrupt practices; low risk of detection; high reward for corruption; low risk of punishment; political patronage; absence of an ethical framework in the individual; low levels of transparency; low levels of public accountability; weak management systems and powerful networks of "secret" organizations (cronyism). These are depicted in figure 3.3 below which captures the "very important" causes of corruption in Jamaica.

Respondents tended to favour explanations that are grounded in free individual choice and problems of individual immorality over more structural explanations that implicate the opportunity-generating systems of state allocations of goods, the opportunity-grasping methods of politics

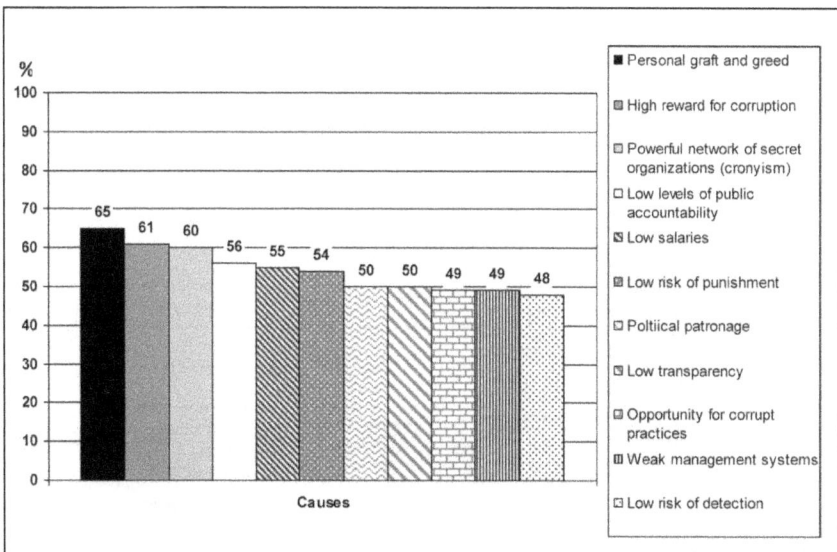

Figure 3.3 Perceived causes of corruption

and poor systems of accountability. Policy responses and programmes that are designed to bring about changes in values and attitudes at the individual level, without reference to the value system of the society and its opportunity structure, thus resonate well with sections of the population.

Interestingly, and directly related to this research on organized crime and political corruption, "powerful network of secret organizations" or cronyism was identified as the third "Very Important" cause of corruption. It is interesting because the findings from the CAPRI survey are in many ways similar to those of the Centre for Leadership and Governance's Values and Attitudes Survey. For instance, respondents were asked: "Do you believe that some politicians help criminals to access government contracts?" Based on the data analysed, it was found that 52 per cent strongly agreed with this statement and 36 per cent somewhat agreed, while 6 per cent somewhat disagreed, 3 per cent strongly disagreed, and the remaining 3 per cent either did not answer the question or claimed not to know the answer. This is represented below in figure 3.4.

More specifically, the persons interviewed for the Centre for Leadership and Governance survey were also asked: "Do you believe that some politicians are involved in criminal activities such as drug trafficking?" Some 57

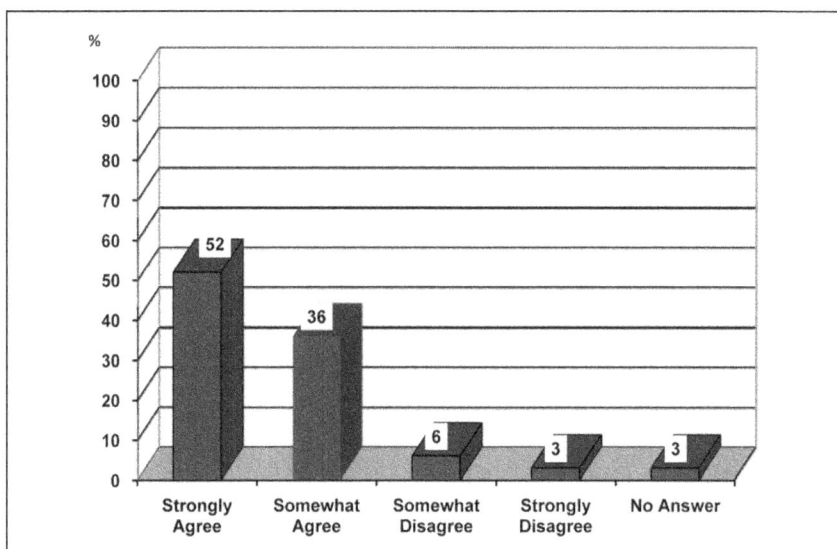

Figure 3.4 Procurement contracts and criminality

per cent strongly agreed with this statement and 28 per cent somewhat agreed, while 10 per cent somewhat disagreed and 2 per cent strongly disagreed, and the remaining 3 per cent either did not answer the question or claimed not to know the answer. An almost similar response was found when the respondents were further asked: "Do you believe that some politicians are involved in criminal activities such as gun trafficking?" Of these, 52 per cent strongly agreed with the statement, 29 per cent somewhat agreed, 10 per cent somewhat disagreed, 3 per cent strongly disagreed, and 6 per cent either did not answer the question or claimed not to know the answer. Both findings are depicted below in figure 3.5.

The findings from the Centre for Leadership and Governance survey do indeed suggest that Jamaicans believe that there is a link between the political machinery and criminal enterprises.

Generally speaking, what these findings suggest is that corruption involves elements within all social groups and among the critical power-holders in Jamaica, but, as may be expected, is believed to be highly concentrated in the institutions of the state, that is, in the sites where political influence and power are strongest, most invisible, and most unrestrained. What is believed to vary are the natures of the opportunities for corrup-

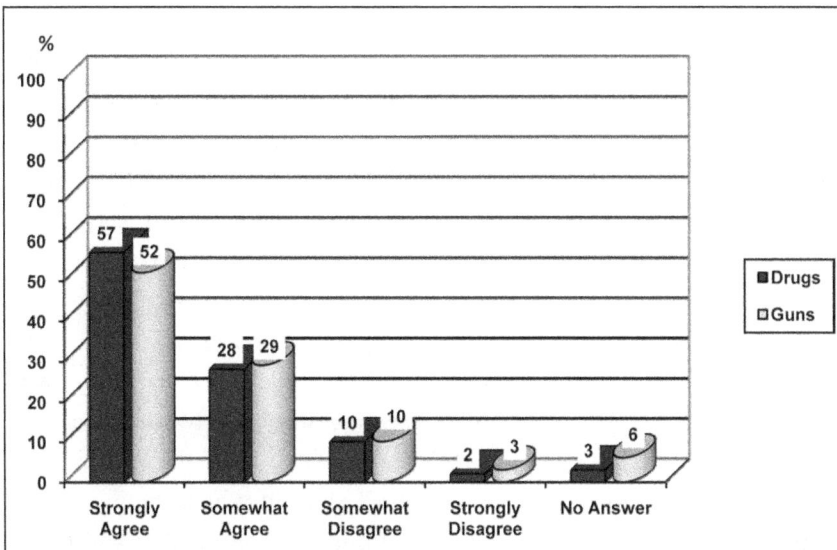

Figure 3.5 Involvement of politicians in serious crimes

tion, the level of risk of exposure and criminal conviction, and the degree and type of impact of corrupt activity.

These findings were not surprising, particularly the statistical relationship between "actual exposure to corrupt acts" and "perception of corruption". It merely empirically validates what can be referred to as a popular belief among many Jamaicans, a belief that has been represented on many talk show programmes, in the media, in the shops and on the street corners of the fourteen parishes in Jamaica. As a matter of fact, it is so much an entrenched vision in the minds of many Jamaicans that it is represented in popular culture – in the lyrics of many reggae and dancehall artists.

To better appreciate the prevalence of corruption in Jamaica, on the 2005 Corruption Perceptions Index of Transparency International – which measures corruption among public officials and politicians within countries around the world – Jamaica received a score of 3.6 out of 10. A score of 10 designates an almost corruption-free environment while 0 signifies a highly corrupt country. Jamaica's score of 3.6 placed the country sixty-fourth among the 158 countries surveyed. Within the Caribbean, Jamaica was fourth, behind Barbados (which scored 6.9), and Trinidad and Tobago and Cuba (which both scored 3.8). The island was, however, ranked higher – meaning less corrupt – than other Caribbean countries such as the Dominican Republic (3.0) and Haiti (1.8).

Similar conclusions have been drawn by many others exploring corruption in Jamaica (see, for example, Carter Centre 1999; Waller et al. 2007). Such conclusions have also been drawn by Jamaican scholars (see, for example, Munroe 1999; Harriott 2000; Collier 2000; Charles 2003). It may also be possible to argue that this has also been the view of the Jamaican business sector and civil society, evidenced by the formulation of a number of state-constituted commissions of inquiry over the years.

According to Collier (2000), for example, corruption in Jamaica stems from a system of political patronage that emerged from the bitter two-party competitive system. For others, it emerges from the Westminster parliamentary system inherited from Britain, which operates as a form of "authoritarian-democratic" rule, that is, a system in which there is a high degree of concentration of power and limited accountability and transparency (see, for example, Onuf 2001). In other words, corruption is an overworked tool of politics. Corruption in Jamaica represents an enduring phenomenon that is partly rooted in the methodology of political mobilization (patron-client) and facilitated by weak systems of accountability and system capability.

While a colonial society, Jamaica was marked by foreign and ethnic minority ownership and control of the economy. After independence, democratic politics became a source of challenge to the old order for the post-colonial restructuring of opportunity. During the 1960s, in the first decade after independence, this found expression in the policy of Jamaicanization, but later, in the 1970s, took a more radical form as democratic socialism, which aspired to state control of the "commanding heights" of the economy. Later, the privatization of state assets, the scaling down of the state's involvement and its outsourcing of services to the private sector presented considerable opportunities for new entrepreneurs, but access was somewhat regulated by political connections and lubricated by corruption. New structures of illegal and grey opportunity were therefore constructed, structures that allowed members of the emergent business classes to realize their goals. Prior to this, access to conventional business opportunities was highly restricted. The latter, that is, the blockages to conventional opportunities, pushed highly motivated aspirants deprived of the enabling resources out of the conventional avenues; and the former, the grey opportunity structure, helped them to innovatively, and often illegally, realize their goals. In this context, corrupt, rent-seeking politics, like drug trafficking and other enterprise activities of organized crime, are all alternative avenues to material success.

Consequently, in every general election campaign since 1967, corruption has been identified as a major threat to good governance and development in Jamaica by either the prime minister, or the leader of the Opposition, or both.

The Nexus at Work in Jamaica: Contracts, Construction and Corruption

One common thread which stretches through many of the aforementioned studies is the prevalence of corruption in local government, and more specifically, corruption in the distribution of government contracts. Collier, in his research on political corruption, explains the fascination with this topic:

> The manipulation of the awarding and financing of state contracts is the single greatest source of political corruption in Jamaica. The funds received from these illicit acts are then made available to the ruling party and its candidates for national campaigns. These funds are converted to votes, not only through advertising and candidate stumping, but also through the dispersal of funds to voters as either benefits (housing, etc.) or direct cash for payments. (2000, 14)

Based on the findings of this research, this is usually the case for the Jamaican construction industry where contracts are given out to build roads, houses, schools, community centres, commercial spaces, retaining walls, play fields, and bridges as well as sanitary related activities. The distribution of contracts has been popularized in Jamaica as the most frequently used way in which the political machinery facilitates and empowers organized crime.

At the global level, corruption in the construction industry has been a main issue in the policy discourse of corruption (Transparency International 2005). Much of the research in this area has highlighted and drawn attention to the important role that the construction industry plays as a space to facilitate criminal enterprises through the intervention of the political machinery. In Jamaica, speculation and allegations suggest that the construction industry operates in a similar fashion. Little research, however, has been done on corruption in the Jamaican construction industry to validate such arguments. This research also seeks to address this gap.

According to one senior government official who works with an agency that monitors and regulates the distribution of government contracts in Jamaica, "the construction industry in Jamaica is perhaps one of the fastest and largest growing local industries" (PIOJ 2005, 14.1). Data from the 2005 *Economic and Social Survey of Jamaica*, an annual publication of the Planning Institute of Jamaica, seems to support his argument. According to this report, the contribution of the construction industry to overall gross domestic product has trended upwards during the period 2000 to 2005. This is depicted in figure 3.6.

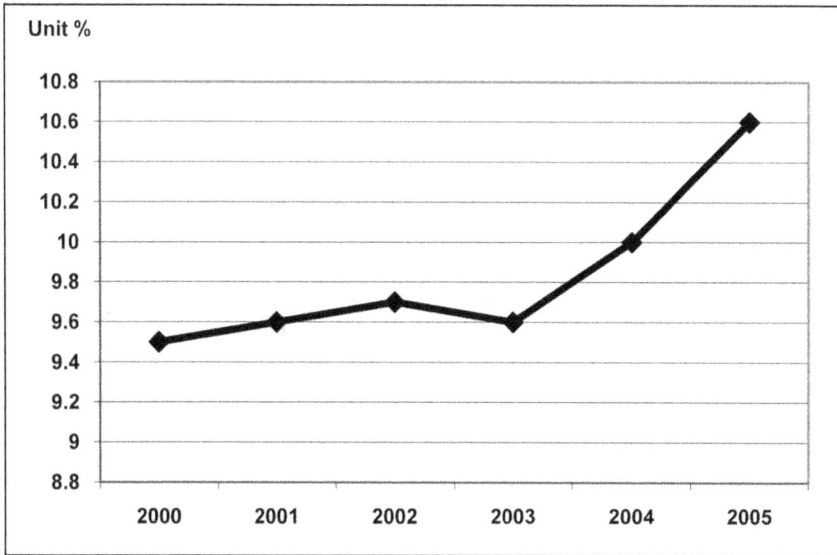

Figure 3.6 Contribution of construction to gross domestic product

According to the Planning Institute of Jamaica, the upward trend is a result of "reconstruction activities associated with the passage of Hurricane Ivan (September 2004), Dennis (July 2005), Emily (July 2005) and Tropical Storm Wilma (October 2005)" (PIOJ 2005, 14.1). The report also highlighted "increases in non-residential activities, mainly due to hotel construction and increased expenditure on the Northern Coastal Highway Improvement Project" as well as the "growth in residential activities" (PIOJ 2005, 14.1). These activities continue even today. In essence, the construction industry is, as one interviewee represents it, "a cash cow in every sense of the term". Similar arguments have been put forward by international organizations, such as Transparency International which, in its 2005 Global Corruption Report, "Corruption in Construction and Post-conflict Reconstruction", stated that "Construction projects are big and complex and, most important, they involve lots of money" (Transparency International 2005, xii). The report further stated "construction projects usually involve a large number of participants in a complex contractual structure" (Transparency International 2005, 36). Certainly this is the case for Jamaica. Figure 3.7 demonstrates this.

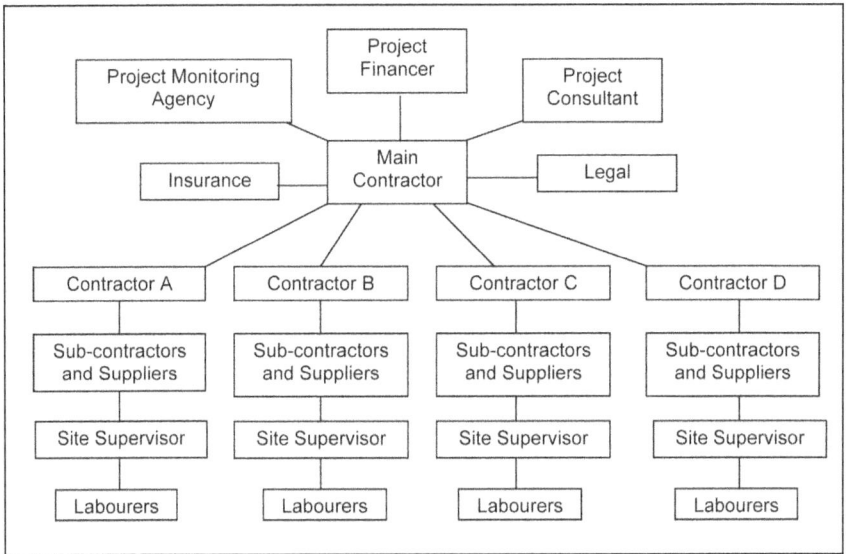

Figure 3.7 Structure of the construction sector

Transparency International notes that, in such an environment, the contractual cascade, which in many ways resembles the configuration of the Jamaican construction industry,

> could easily have more than a thousand links, each depending on other contractual links in the chain. Every single link provides an opportunity for someone to pay a bribe in exchange for the award of a contract. In addition, work and services are exchanged for payments in relation to every contractual link. Every item of work and every payment provides further opportunities for bribes to be paid in return either for certifying too much work, certifying defective work, certifying extensions of time or paying more expeditiously. (Transparency International 2005, 38)

Transparency International further notes that corruption is made easy by several other factors:

> Most components in construction end up being concealed by other components. Structural steel may be concealed by concrete, brickwork by plaster, engineering components in casings, and roof structures by cladding. The industry places an enormous dependence on the individuals who certify the correctness of the work done before it is concealed; once an item is concealed, it can be very costly or

difficult to check if it was completed to the required standard. This cost and difficulty creates an incentive for contractors to do defective work or use inferior
materials, and to bribe the relevant official to certify that the work was done
according to specifications. (Transparency International 2005, 38)

The report of the senior official, who we will refer to as "Bill" (who
works closely with one government agency responsible for the distribution
of government contracts for the refurbishing of schools and roads), seems
to be similar to those of Transparency International's description of the
multidimensional configurations of the construction industry. Bill's
responses are very similar to the view of Transparency International regarding the possibilities of the industry for illegal financial transactions. For Bill,
this is no secret, as many Jamaicans are also aware of these ways of acting
and organizing, and the possibilities and uses of the construction industry
in doing so. For these reasons, he notes: "Everybody is now a contractor, if
you drive a truck you are a contractor, if you own a backhoe you are a contractor, or if you own two machetes you are a contractor; everybody is a
contractor because the construction business can allow you to move from
riding a bicycle today to driving a Bimma [Jamaican term for the BMW
car] tomorrow. Everybody knows that" (personal interview, May 2007).
Bill further argues:

> It's one of those industries in which cash is still used significantly. This is because
> of the nature of the industry and the type of people you have to deal with.
> Contractors often employ people without proper documents and with little or no
> education as labourers. Many of the labourers do not have bank accounts, some-
> times contractors have bad administrative practices, especially the shady ones, the
> ones who do not pay their taxes or those whose money is tied up with other peo-
> ple. There is no structure to it, at least at that level. As a result of this it is easy for
> money to be passed around from here to there, from the politician to the contrac-
> tor to the labourer and back to the politician to be used to fund his election cam-
> paign. A lot of corruption takes place there, man, a lot; and this has always been the
> case. Some of the more organized upfront and honest ones do not use cash. They
> require that their workers open a bank account and get a debit card so money can
> be transferred to their account, while others use cheques. (Ibid.)

The construction sector is therefore a perfect space for laundering, racketeering and brokering illegal deals and arrangements. Based on the focus

group discussion, the construction industry has been a space where the criminal enterprise in particular, along with the help of the political machinery, benefits the most. The provision of contracts to criminal entrepreneurs also ensures a level of security for these politicians as well as the political parties with which they are associated. This is done in many different ways, ranging from: securing votes from the citizens who are controlled by the dons; protecting the interest of the politician in their constituency or parts of their constituency and, by extension, the politician's party; and securing finances for the politician's political campaign.

These dons have established front firms through which they secure these contracts. As one respondent noted during a focus group discussion, "sometimes they [the dons] have more than one business, trucking business, haulage business, all sorts of businesses, and so they are able to bid on multiple contracts and, in most instances, they get these contracts irrespective of the fact that we know these people are involved in illegal activities and perhaps even use the money to do so". Another focus group participant had been a procurement officer at a government agency once funded by several international development agencies. He expressed the opinion that the construction contractual system remains lax despite recent efforts to improve on transparency and equitability in the awarding of contracts in the development of an ironclad government procurement procedure. His views were shared by several other persons interviewed for this research.

These efforts at transparency and equitability have only been implemented in the last two years or so. This ironclad government procurement procedure works as follows: Contracts under J$4 million are normally advertised on community notice boards. All contracts over J$4 million are advertised nationally. Bidders are normally required to purchase bid documents. Once the bid documents are returned to the relevant government agency, the bids are normally opened and the figures are read out in a public forum. The name of the contractor, the figure submitted by the contractor, as well as other documents, such as bills of quantity, tender or bid bonds, and certain required tax certifications are read out in a transparent atmosphere. Thereafter, bids are evaluated by various internal procurement committees in government agencies to ascertain the most eligible candidate. A report of the evaluation process and results is submitted to various external committees, along with a letter from the permanent secretary of the ministry under which the agency falls, for endorsement. Bids of J$15 million and above, however, are then sent to the Jamaican cabinet for approval.

In some instances, however, direct contracting or sole sourcing (going to one person and asking them to submit a bid) or limited tender (where more than one person is asked to bid) may occur. In both instances, prior approval is sought by the National Contracts Commission – the government body that endorses the awarding of contracts valued at J$4 million or above.

According to the focus group participants, circumventing the system is more difficult today than it was a year ago as several new mechanisms have been put in place to ensure that "contractors and government agencies follow the procurement procedures". That being said, however, most of the participants believed that, although a great level of difficulty exists, it is not impossible to beat the system. As a matter of fact, one participant stated that senior government officials still facilitate their cronies in obtaining access to government contracts.

Two focus group participants who are employed with government agencies linked to the distribution and monitoring of construction contracts explained that direct contracting (and, to a certain extent, limited tender) and leaking bid information are two common methods used by the political machinery to facilitate the criminal enterprise in the awarding of contracts.

Getting Around the System

Direct contracting under the instructions of the minister occurs if an agency or a ministry is strapped for time, lacks the technical expertise to undertake a project, or is facing a national crisis caused by some disaster which requires massive reconstruction projects to put the productive sector back on track (roads, electricity and water). According to one interviewee, a good example of this was a recent case where direct contracting was used by a particular senior government official, nearing retirement, who expedited a road project before he retired. According to the interviewee, "this is an example of how simple it is to justify direct contracting".

According to another interviewee, there have been other instances where this method has been used, where politicians have used their power for direct contracting. "Sometimes," the interviewee said, "there are certain volatile areas where only a don can work because the don controls the area; everybody else is afraid to work in that area." "It is easy to justify direct contracting," she notes, "particularly when it comes to situations such as these or others such as the construction of a bridge, dams, or complex water projects." She also reported that there are several contractors who are reputedly sole-sourced and "have been overpricing". "These people," she argues, "get these contracts because of their affiliation with party politics and for that reason only"; they are "not experts and that is no secret", and "should not be used for complex projects" as the "quality of their work is extremely poor". According to her, the consequences of direct contracting using party contractors are, "timelines are generally off, the defects are numerous and many of them do not adhere to basic construction principles and these often lead to cost over-runs that the tax payers feel". Adding to this, another focus group participant further stated:

> The outcome is almost always some disaster or another. That is why we have roads with pot holes caused by bad drainage and the use of inferior aggregate material that is used as a sub-base. That is why the bridge in St. Thomas collapsed, why buildings have structural cracks. Because these people fail to do their work well, they have no capacity. Contractors are building on water-table and loose soil; they build and don't test the soil. These contractors are doing this and some government agencies are reputedly using them through the direct contracting system. One good example is "a Don" who changed the course of the Rio Cobre River because of improper sand mining. This is true; if you don't believe me, check the JLP website; you will see reference to this there, go ahead and check. This is all corruption. (Focus group participant, May 2007)

The general consensus from the focus group sessions, as well as from the in-depth interviews conducted, was that the only winners in such a system are the contractor, who is usually (but not always) the crony (the criminal entrepreneur operating his or her front or laundering business), the politician with whom he or she is working and, in the end, the party to which they both belong. One of these interviewees gave a brilliant example of this network of benefits when he recalled how, at the annual conference of one of the major political parties (just prior to the general elections of 2002), and in the presence of the national media houses and thousands of Jamaicans, a well-known criminal entrepreneur and favoured government contractor took a scandal bag (the Jamaican term for a plastic shopping bag) with a large sum of money and openly placed it on the platform before his party leaders as a donation.

Getting Around the System by Leaking Procurement Criteria

Very often, requests for bids which require specific financial, skill and technical resource requirements are advertised. Usually, the government agency which advertises these bids is more likely to award to the bidder who fits within these specific configurations. The criminal enterprise, with the assistance of the political machinery, is able to get inside knowledge and confidential information regarding the specific requirements which government ministries are looking for in the awarding of contracts. This is a common practice in many parts of the world (Transparency International 2005). As mentioned earlier, both the works of McFarlane (1998) as well as Beare (1997) seem to suggest that this significantly contributes to the elimination of competition and has helped criminal enterprises around the world to amass capital to, among other things, sustain their illegal businesses and, as McWalters (1999) points out, build their empires. This has particularly been the case when it comes to transnational organized crime (Shelley 2005).

One respondent gives an example of how this can be done, based on her own experience. She first explained that most construction projects require a specific amount of civil work which is usually calculated by a quantity surveyor employed by the government ministry setting out to undertake a project. This is referred to as the quantity surveyor estimate: it is the budget for the civil work. Although the estimate is not the only criterion for the selection of a contractor, it is a critical component in the process. The norm for the selection of government contractors is that, once all quality requirements are met, "the most cost effective contractor is usually selected. One can understand this, given the financial problems the country faces". The quantity surveyor and the management of the agency are usually privy to the quantity surveyor estimate, which is not made known until the day of the bid opening when all the bids are read out. After this, the ministry agent reads out the estimate.

The same respondent recalls that in several instances in a particular government agency from which she recently resigned, this information was usually leaked to "well known unscrupulous politically connected individuals" through the management. A management, which she claims, was itself politically appointed because of its "political connections". By leaking out the quantity surveyor estimate, they allowed the bidder to price "their bid proposal in a particular way to be awarded the contract". One of the interviewees spoke of a case regarding a contract which was valued at J$10 million (roughly US$148,000). According to this interviewee, after the tender was advertised, a technical officer working for a company bidding for the contract (who she claimed she knew and who she also claimed was a subsidiary of a parent company which was owned by an alleged well-known, politically connected don), contacted her, claiming that he had received the quantity surveyor's estimate for the project and was seeking her advice about how to price the bid. She claims to have seen the document which, based on her discussions with the technical officer, was allegedly given to the subsidiary company by a senior member of the political machinery. According to other persons interviewed for this research project, this happens frequently, as many of the persons working at the management levels of most government agencies in Jamaica are politically appointed or friends of the party.

Explaining the Nexus

The prevalence of this corruption in Jamaica, including the corrupt facilitation of organized crime, represented above as "getting around the system" may be explained by three intricately intertwined factors. These factors are a high personal motivation to achieve material success (popularly termed greed, but not to be confused with it); high rewards and low risk for engaging corruption; and cronyism. In essence, they represent an environment, captured in the work of Lipset and Lenz (in Harrison and Huntington 2000), regarding one particularly powerful cause of corruption which we wish to extend to the Jamaican case. Even though Lipset and Lenz were focusing expressly on corruption, their arguments could also be extended to include the way in which organized crime has been integrated into the political system. At another level, we also argue that the main themes present in their work can easily be used to describe the Jamaican realities.

Expanding on Merton's work on deviance in the United States and drawing on global cross-national socio-economic data and models, Lipset and Lenz suggest that "corruption is motivated behaviour stemming from social pressures that result in norm violations" (Lipset and Lenz 2000, 116). According to the authors, many societies have social goals which people aspire to within the realm of institutionalized norms. Not all persons have the knowledge, skills or opportunities to attain these goals legally, as many societies either directly or indirectly restrict access to resources (what they refer to as the "opportunity structure"). This is largely as a result of class, race, ethnicity, gender, lack of capital, skills and so on. In such instances, many people seek alternative, often illegal, means to achieve their goals. Lipset and Lenz posit that in societies that "stress economic success as an important goal but nevertheless strongly restrict access to opportunities" (Lipset and Lenz 2000, 117), people will "reject the rules of the game and try to succeed by unconventional (innovative or criminal) means". This would explain some of the variation in the levels of corruption within and across regime types.

They tested this hypothesis using data from the cross- national 1990–1993 World Values Survey and found that "the less affluent countries with high achievement motivation" were found to be the "most corrupt" (Lipset and Lenz 2000, 117). These included countries such as Russia, South Korea and Turkey, which were at that time deemed the most corrupt. By contrast, those societies with low achievement motivation and high access to resources such as Denmark, Norway and Sweden had lower levels of corruption. Lipset and Lenz also undertook a multiple regression analysis using data from the 1990 World Values Survey. From the findings they concluded that "as noted, Merton's theoretical analysis implies that serious corruption will plague countries with high levels of achievement orientation and low access to means", and also that "the availability of institutionalized means to achieve desired ends lowers levels of corruption" (Lipset and Lenz 2000, 118).

Similar conclusions were also drawn by Waller et al. (2007), based on an empirical study conducted in Jamaica. The CAPRI survey concluded that in Jamaica, raised material expectations in the last fifty years and economic decline coupled with an increasingly politicized security establishment and the normalization of corrupt practices in the public sector have led many citizens to resort to corrupt practices. Such practices, it is possible to argue, have negative consequences for good governance and, by extension, development.

Based on the evidence collected for this chapter, we further argue that in such an environment it is easier for criminal networks to thrive. They offer an alternative avenue for those wishing to "innovate" and actively secure the assistance of corrupt public sector workers who assist them to get around the system.

Conclusion

Generally speaking, despite the many shortcomings of the procedure for the procurement of government contracts in Jamaica, all persons interviewed for this study agreed that improvements had been made to the system, particularly in the methods of procurement. As illustrated earlier, however, corrupt behaviour remains as problematic as before. Loopholes remain which allow the political machinery to facilitate criminal enterprise in Jamaica. Party permeation of the state by long-serving administrations allows for the development of backstage informal networks and informal decision making that subverts the front-stage formal arrangements.

These realities, and the associated perceptions, may diminish confidence in the leadership of the most affected institutions of state, and, in some cases, in the institutions themselves. Institutions are vital to any development project. The main institutions of the state, those that focus on governance, development planning, health care, housing, employment opportunities and education, play a direct role in creating the conditions of development and improving the quality of life of the people. Developmental goals are compromised to the extent that these institutions are brought into disrepute. This consequence is of far greater importance than the actual monetary sums that are lost to corrupt activity. Furthermore, it may be argued that it also gives added importance to popular perceptions and patterns of belief about corruption and the consequences of these beliefs with regard to confidence in the institutions, including the legal system. Where these patterns are negative, that is, where confidence in the institutions is low, then development may be expected to be problematic. Unarguably, there is a need to develop effective strategies to correct this problem if Jamaica is to make any significant strides in development. Some suggestions are outlined further in this text.

4

Who Pays the Piper Calls the Tune?
Party Financing, Political Debts and
Organized Crime Networks

THE COMPETITIVE PARTY SYSTEM is a central feature of Jamaican democracy, and financing is vital to the electoral viability of the parties. Parties compete for limited legitimate funding, mainly from businesses that may have common as well as competing interests. Depending on the prospects of the party, fund-raising from legitimate business sources may involve some negotiation about firm, sector, and perhaps even national interests. Funding dependence on legitimate sources thus tends to incur debts and constrain political action. Illegal funding sources, on the other hand, tend to be less organized, less representative of group interests (but more expressive of narrow and very specific self-interest), and more eager to court political power on the terms of the office holders. It is therefore, in general, less politically constraining. Power seeks money (especially during electoral contests) and money seeks power. That money seeks power applies to both legitimate and criminal funds, but with the latter, especially in the form of organized crime, money tends to more aggressively seek political influence and sponsorship. Thus, in response to allegations that he had taken money from Colombian drug traffickers, Ernesto Samper, former president of Colombia, said in an interview with Charles Krause (20 March 1996), "All the mafias in the world, those which have operated in the USA, in Italy, or in Colombia, seek ways to buy political powers." Being a major exporter of ganja for some forty years, and a trans-shipment point for cocaine, Jamaica has large sums of criminally acquired wealth. Criminal entrepreneurs seek influence and power as a means of protecting, laundering and increasing that wealth, and, perhaps in some instances, political power may even be sought and purchased as a means of status elevation and as a good-in-itself.

For any competitive democracy, the issue of party funding, even when restricted to "clean money", remains problematic, as money may buy undue political influence and thereby distort the policy process in favour of special interests. The use of "tainted money", or corruptly acquired funds, is even more problematic. This, for example, includes kickbacks from con-tractors who have preferential access to state contracts. Most troubling is the use of "dirty money" or criminally acquired funds. Concern with the first, that is, with the undue influence of clean money, is a specific expres-sion of the more general concern with the disproportionate political influ-ence of economic elites in democratic societies. Concern with the second and third categories, that is, with the impact of dirty and tainted money, is similarly an expression of concern regarding the influence of another elite group, that is, the criminal elites, at the apex of which are the leaders of organized crime.[1] Unlike the economic elites, however, the latter represent distinctly anti-social interests.

Illicit funds tend to have the effect of magnetizing activity and interests that undermine good governance and destroy confidence in the critical and foundational institutions of the society. This is what makes the funding relationship between organized crime and the political parties particularly troubling. Concerns regarding the political influence of dirty money have been publicly articulated in Colombia, Guatemala, Honduras, Haiti, and Jamaica, that is, in the countries of the region where organized crime net-works are well established and are fairly powerful.

The extant literature on party financing in the region, or even party regulation more generally, is sparse. We are therefore heavily indebted to Professor Selwyn Ryan for his efforts (see Ryan 2005). This chapter highlights the role of organized crime in party financing, by examining the two-way flow of funds between the actors. By tracking the direction of the flow of funds we are able to map the interdependencies between the actors and thus the nature of the power relations.

As so little data have been made available on this matter of the financing of political parties by organized crime, this excursus takes the form of a set of theses. Any conclusions that are drawn from them are tentative. This is perhaps an oblique way of inviting disagreement as a method of advancing our understanding of the problem. The use of tainted funds in party financing is however best understood by placing it in the larger political context.

The Problem in Context

Jamaica now has one of the better electoral systems in the hemisphere. It has largely solved the earlier problems of gerrymandering, multiple voting and other forms of electoral fraud on a national scale. Much of the issue of subpopulations not being allowed to freely cast their votes has been dealt with as ex-convicts are allowed to vote and there are no excluded racial and ethnic minorities. The remaining problems here are limited to the use of intimidatory violence in some constituencies and the garrison problem. As indicated above, the problem of party financing has, however, been neglected. Despite the earlier problems and remaining imperfections of the system, the leaders of the contesting parties have a more or less unblemished history of accepting the outcomes. This is perhaps the most important indicator of the quality and stability of the system.

Jamaica's competitive multi-party system has at its core two broad-based and highly organized parties with relatively long histories. Both were established prior to the first elections under self-government by universal adult suffrage in 1944. Both were constituted as national coalitions.[2] Both have their origins in profound social movements, that is, the labour movement, and the different streams of the broad anti-colonial movement (see Bogues 2002; Stone 1980; Nettleford 1971).

Being broad coalitions of organically linked mass parties with programmatic appeal, they could rely on the volunteerism of their members and supporters, party dues and multiple funding sources. Elite influences based on funding had to contend with the close relationship of the parties to the unions, and the influence of the poor, which was routed via the structures of the parties.

In the post–1980s and post–Cold War context of policy convergence between the parties, the current politics has de-emphasized programmatic mobilization. There have been significant post-independence advances in access to education, health care, and housing, and in Jamaica's rating on the Human Development Index and other quality of life indicators (see JEP 2006; Stone 1989; Nettleford 1989). However, despite these advances, the failure of politics to deliver on its promises to solve the basic problems of poverty, high unemployment, and violent crime, and to transform the society to a more just and meritocratic order has led to a dramatic decline in the status of politicians and in confidence in the political parties and the institutions of state that are most closely associated with the political administration.[3] Clearly, more is expected of the political parties than they can possibly deliver. This may partly explain the decline in their programmatic appeal, but the corruption, violence, and association with criminal networks have accelerated this decline in confidence.

Professionalization of politics at the leadership level has been accompanied by a decline in voluntarism and a corresponding professionalization at the so-called grass roots level among party activists. With leaders and active party members making a "profession" and even a business of politics, supporters seem to be increasingly following suit. This decline of voluntarism is not restricted to party activism, but is more generalized throughout the society and affects all sorts of organizations that rely on the voluntary citizen activist (see Robotham 1998). In this environment, during election campaigns, party-citizen encounters have become more transactional. This, along with costly media campaigns, increases the pressure for funding.

As the community activists and the rank and file members professionalize their services to the parties (and their communities), they tend to lose their direct political influence within these parties. The problems associated with party financing are thus usually framed as party capture by special interests. Indeed, very recent experience suggests that the votes of party delegates may be bought by criminal groups. Where cash profoundly influences electoral outcomes, the role of the parties and the nature of their relationships to the people are likely to become distorted, that is, "marke-tized" or become more transactional. Party leaders are more likely to become advocates for special interests rather than servants of a larger national purpose. Political debts incurred via financial donations to the electoral effort of the party may distort policy and deprive the more vulnerable in the society of the protection that the policymakers ought to give them.

Thus there has been some public concern with regard to the influence of dirty money in representational politics. This issue was recently brought to public attention by the then leader of the Opposition, Edward Seaga, who in 2003 charged that dirty money had helped to determine the out-come of the electoral contest for the position of vice president of his party, the JLP. Later, in 2006, the issue was again raised by the "Trafigura affair" which implicated the ruling PNP.[4]

The Cost of Elections

The backdrop to these events and their exposure is the high and increasing cost of electoral politics. At the time of writing, an unofficial election cam-paign had already begun. It is roughly estimated that, during the official campaign, each party will spend some US$8 per Jamaican citizen.[5] This represents a 60 per cent increase over the cost (to each party) of the previ-ous election in 2002 which was estimated (or underestimated) at approxi-mately US$4.80 per citizen.

Put into regional and international contexts, the above represents a high rate of spending on an election campaign. Using data on eight Caribbean countries as reported in Ryan (2005), campaign expenditure per person ranged from an extraordinary high of US$30 per person in Antigua to a low of US$1.50 in Trinidad and Tobago. These data are presented in figure 4.1.[6] Jamaica falls at the lower end of the high expenditure group with Antigua, the Bahamas and Dominica. This group contrasts with Trinidad and Tobago, Barbados, and Guyana, among whom the methods of political mobilization tend to be somewhat different.

The high and increasing costs are also driven by changes in the methods of work of the parties, methods that have been made possible by techno-

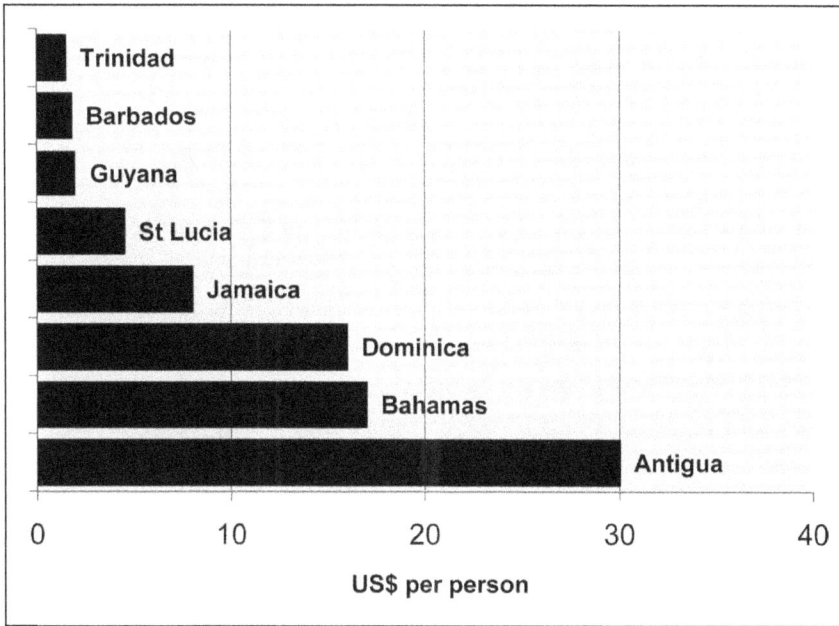

Figure 4.1 Cost of elections per capita

Source: Ryan 2005, 9, 10, 12, 16, 19, 22, 25, 29.

logical advances in the mass media and made more exploitable by the penetration of these media among the general population. Costs have also
increased because of the use of corrupt methods that are adaptations to the
loss of programmatic appeal. Some of the more extravagant parties are
those that have largely degenerated from mass parties to electoral
machines. The goal of the party, the purpose of political participation, is to
hold power for the sake of power.[7] As put by some political leaders (young
and old), the purpose of political parties is "to win elections".[8] This is the
perspective of the professional politician who has lost any purpose that is
larger than the interests of self and party. Power is seen as an end in itself,
not a means of accomplishing a programme. Thus, the party is unapologet-
ically regarded by such members as nothing more than a self-serving interest group and a vehicle for realizing egotistic goals, such as power-holding
and converting political capital to personal wealth. Perhaps this is an
unkind formulation of the problem. However, it further explains the
decline in voluntary participation within the parties, the perceptions of

rank corruption in government and the state, and the emergence of the mentalities that motivate and tolerate this level of corruption.

Funding Elections as Opportunity-seeking Behaviour

Providing funding to the parties may be regarded as a way of accessing legal, grey and illegal opportunities. For some, funding the parties is public-spirited behaviour, but for others, it is opportunity-seeking behaviour. For some with criminally acquired wealth, it offers business opportunities and a pathway into the mainstream. Political power opens up economic opportunity and regulates access to these opportunities. State contracts may be used to create and legitimize large numbers of upwardly mobile entrepreneurs. A distinctive feature of this route is that not much starting capital (financial and human) is required; political capital is a good enough substitute for the other forms of capital. This avenue is thus also very important for those who have been excluded from the sphere of legitimate entrepreneurial activity.

This process may be elaborated as public policy that openly seeks to create opportunities for those who were previously excluded from formal business activity. It may also be signaled in public rhetoric and executed in informal, corrupt ways as political coalition building that includes organized crime. In the latter case, access is conditioned by party loyalties. Members of socially marginalized groups are able to accesses opportunities as party affiliates. Thus, a kind of "crony-capitalism" or grey opportunity structure is constructed. People access these opportunities as clients of the party officials.

Jamaican politics has long had an element of patron-client mobilization (see Stone 1980). Degeneration into machine politics has, however, emphasized it.[9] The parties thus tend to attract *active* support largely (but not solely) on the expectation of personal benefits. A national survey of the Jamaican population conducted in 1991 provided ample evidence in support of this. Party supporters were primarily interested in and actively sought a wide range of direct personal benefits from their members of parliament. It was estimated that of those seeking direct benefits, 52 per cent wanted jobs and 44 per cent wanted contracts. Others wanted credit, money, help with accessing state welfare benefits (to circumnavigate the state bureaucratic procedures) and money for funerals and emergencies such as money for prescription drugs (Stone 1991a, 10). The party supporters wanted the member of parliament to either give them access to the state benefit or to deliver the benefit personally. These are tremendous pressures.

The Stone thesis does not adequately explain the patterns of campaign funding. We have therefore incorporated it as one element in a larger framework of explanation that was elaborated in the previous chapter to explain the nexus between organized crime and political corruption.

Corrupt Use of Funds

If political loyalty is expected to be rewarded with personal benefits, the vote is seen as "tradable" and is expected to yield a more direct and immediate return. Andrew Holness, member of parliament for a Kingston constituency, reported that a survey conducted in his constituency found that 28 per cent of the voters would change their voting preference if paid to do so. Some 27 per cent said that they would change their preference if offered "a direct benefit" (Holness 2007). This is a significant minority that is willing to engage in an illegal trade in votes. In the general elections of 2007, some persons were negotiating fees for their votes even while they were in the lines at the polling stations (personal communication with one of the party candidates). The demand for bribes stimulates a supply. For example, in 2003, during the campaign for the election of the deputy leader of the JLP for Area 2, Dennis Minott, a constituency representative of the party alleged that "there was widespread bribery of JLP delegates in the Portland Eastern constituency" (Office of the Political Ombudsman 2004, 9). The supply of bribes also creates further demand – a demand for illegality that criminal networks are only too willing to supply on behalf of their political candidates.

Vote selling would seem to suggest a loss of self-efficacy, a notion that the vote has little significance after it is used and no power to change the lives of the "sellers". By this behaviour, the idea that political representatives and state actors cannot be held to account for their performance, for the allocation of state resources, and for the degree of responsiveness (or unresponsiveness) to the priorities of the population is further reinforced. The practice assumes that the politician is corrupt and self-serving and thus the voters seek to increase the cost of the office being contested, and to demand an instant return on their vote. Low self-efficacy is combined with the expectation of corruption as the outcomes of normal politics. This is the logic of the commercialization of politics.

High Cost of Elections and the Pressures for Corrupt Accumulation

Given the material demands that are placed on politicians (and the attendant high cost of electoral engagement and representation), there appears to be an increased resort to corrupt methods of funding the parties and candidates. This increased resort to corrupt funding corresponds with the rise of organized crime networks and is conditioned by a poor regulatory and enforcement framework. It is a fortuitous conjunction for organized crime. Members of the political elite and the criminal elite may become willing partners in the plunder of the state for money and power.

Poor regulation and enforcement have facilitated the corrupt accumulation and use of funds. In Jamaica, party financing and expenditure are regulated by the Representation of the Peoples Act. It makes the party candidates legally accountable, but ignores the party, gives it no standing in law, and thus no accountability to the law. Candidates are required under the law to disclose both campaign income and expenditure, and to limit their campaign expenditure to J$3 million. None of this is enforced. Jamaican politics thus operates in a very permissive environment. This has allowed the unimpeded involvement of organized crime and other types of illicit entrepreneurs and racketeers in both the accumulation and use of campaign funds.

This problem of regulatory laxity could well be illustrated by using a few cases from the Jamaican experience, but to avoid diversionary controversies, we take the case of Ernesto Samper in Colombia. In 1998, Ernesto Samper, then president of Colombia, was forced to resign four years after being elected. He was scandalized in the American and international press for allegedly taking some US$6 million dollars from the Cali drug cartel to finance his campaign. Strong pressures for his removal came from the opposition Conservative Party within Colombia and from the American government which has invested heavily in the war on drugs in Colombia. Put more generally, there were power centres within as well as external to Colombian society that opposed the practice of using drug money to fund elections, and which wished to limit the political influence of the Colombian drug cartels, or at least wished to exploit the political opportunities that the exposure of Samper presented. In the absence of these power centres, or rather of disputes with them, the problem would perhaps have gone unnoticed internationally and maybe even locally as is the case in so many other countries where similar practices have persisted.

As Maingot notes, the case against Samper was weak (Maingot 2004, 137, citing Thoumi 1995). He was charged with illicit enrichment, falsifying documents and electoral fraud.[10] Colombian laws prohibit personal enrichment from illicit money. However, Samper did not use the drug funding for his personal enrichment. It was used for electoral campaigning. As the laws did not proscribe such activity, nothing illegal was done, no laws were broken. This is the standard by which corrupt public officials expect their behaviour to be judged. Thus, the typical response of state officials to valid charges of corruption and racketeering in jurisdictions, where the regulatory framework is weak and does not criminalize such practices, is simply that no laws were broken. Moreover, as Maingot reports, the funds had been channelled to Samper via front companies of the drug cartels in a context where there was no money-laundering legislation. Again, no laws were broken.

This was a clear case of a weak and permissive system that did not seek to regulate such activity, even in the face of the serious challenges that Colombian organized crime presented for that country and of the history of its attempts to penetrate its home political system. Samper, however, paid a political price for accepting this type of funding. It pronounced the death sentence on his political career.

In Jamaica, as the regulatory framework regarding party financing remains weak and the enforcement will and capacity even weaker, issues of corruption in party financing, and even funding by drug dealers and organized crime networks, are usually treated as being a purely political issue. As politics, its impact is usually mitigated by the strong tribal loyalties to the parties. The "truth" is always a party truth, or the truth as defined by the party. This means that any effort to hold to account corrupt politicians and parties that take dirty money is immediately taken as an assault on the party by persons whose accountability-seeking behaviour is taken as sufficient to define them as being affiliated to the opposing party. The motivation is never to protect the interest of the public and country, but rather to advance the agenda of the political opposition who tend to be regarded as being equally guilty of similar practices. This preempts and silences any exposure by civil society actors who do not wish to risk being caught in this trap.

Those who persist and refuse to be silenced are easily discredited in the way described above or as agents of foreign institutions and agendas. This is easy to do if anti-corruption non-governmental organizations are weak, led by minorities, and are dependent on external financial support. Thus, despite the enduring concerns among all sections of the population with the issues of crime, corruption and the crime-politics nexus, groups that confront these issues lack broad support. Changing the attitudes to these problems, breaking the patterns of disinterestedness and social facilitation, and dislodging the protective shield of tribal loyalties are perhaps conditions for greater accountability.

Nine Theses

Having contextualized the problem and identified some of its driving forces, this section of the paper presents some of the ideas about the actual and potential co-optive impact of illegal funding on the political process. This is done in the form of nine theses. These are assertions, but underlying them are observations. These theses are treated as simply an economical way of summarizing the existing knowledge about the subject and stimulating discussion and focused research. They will have served their purpose if they help to extend the debate.

These ideas are grouped as follows: those treating with the impact of criminal funding on the outcomes of intra- and inter-party elections; those on its impact on the power balance within the parties; and, most importantly, those anticipating the effects of political debts incurred and the prospects for co-option and influence on public policy.

Thesis 1. *Criminally acquired wealth is becoming more fungible. It may now be used to purchase electoral candidacy.*

In both political parties, in both the distant past and recent time, there have been cases in which party candidacy has been purchased by persons who acquired much of their wealth from drug trafficking and who have succeeded in laundering much of it (personal correspondence with members of the leadership of both parties).

This purchase does not appear to take the form of a conscious sale of the post by the party leader or leadership. Rather, it takes the form of the prospective candidates being selected because they are able to show that they are able and willing to self-finance campaigns and not rely on central party funding. There are instances of reputed traffickers who have put themselves forward as candidates, and cases of their proxies being put forward – sometimes successfully and sometimes unsuccessfully.

Thesis 2. *The flow of criminally acquired funds into the parties and the campaigns of selected candidates suggests a new power relationship between the criminal networks and the parties or candidates. The criminal, as party-client, has become the patron of party candidates. With the emergence of organized crime, the great asymmetries of power between street criminal and politician have been diminished and a balance of power that is more favourable to the criminal networks now exists.*

The weakening of the state and the discrediting of politics on one hand, and the rise of organized crime and the strengthening of its hold on the communities of the poor on the other, have helped to alter this power balance. New reciprocities and interdependencies between organized crime and the holders of political office have emerged, reciprocities that have the effect of strengthening the influence of organized crime within the political parties and political process, and fostering greater corruption among the political and state bureaucratic elites.

Thesis 3. *While criminal funding may not have a significant impact on the outcome of national elections, it now has a decisive impact on some candidate selections and particular contests in some constituencies.*

These include garrison and non-garrison constituencies where drug trafficking is a major business and where the influence of the criminal networks is grounded in patronage, the provision of welfare services and other benefits that have already been described in chapter 1. Organized crime networks fund the local party machinery and its candidates. In return, the networks are awarded state contracts. This, in turn, further strengthens their position in the local party machinery as they are now able to award jobs to party activists, for instance on road works and other government programmes. In some constituencies, candidates on both sides are funded by drug traffickers. The upshot of this is that, in those cases, the leaders of organized crime have become the determining influence in candidate selection.

Thesis 4. *Regardless of the extent of legitimate contributions, criminal funding may have a significant impact on internal party elections and may help to shape or reshape the dominant coalitions within the parties. At minimum, it has veto power in some localities.*

This was discussed in an earlier chapter with reference to internal elections in both political parties. These included the contest for the deputy leader of the JLP and the election for the president of the PNP in 2006. The story of these and other experiences need not be repeated here.

Thesis 5. *Candidates will opt for funding that does not incur political debts. They will opt for funding arrangements that maximize their political autonomy.*

Plundering the resources of the state is the best way to ensure maximum political autonomy. This may be treated as a form of self-funding. The funds, however, cannot simply be taken from the coffers of the state. The money has to be spirited out (the word is intended to connote not just speed, but also mystery and stealth) via contracts for services, and this requires corrupt partners who are able to provide services to the state. Organized crime is a good and reliable partner in this business.

This type of "self-funding" encourages party permeation of the state, that is, the planting of party affiliated and personally loyal persons in high positions in the state bureaucracy as facilitators or potential facilitators of this activity.[11] Political administrators who benefit from these activities develop an interest in maintaining poor systems of accountability within the state.

Self-funding methods include the use of the "tied contractor". This is a symbiotic relationship between contractor and politician with the state being host to both. Here it is the candidate or politician who has the power in the relationship. It is his influence that secures the contract and the debt is incurred to him. Tied contractors do not compete for state contracts. Public tendering becomes a sham. Absence of accountability of these firms typically results in poor quality work and service delivery and affects programmes ranging from road repairs to garbage collection.

State corruption thus involves little, if any, public policy related debt. Funding from criminals that is otherwise secured, at best involves limited political debt. We must act on the assumption that criminal entrepreneurs, like legitimate entrepreneurs, will seek their larger interests as a group. If this is accepted, then we may imagine that they could, for example, lobby to scuttle efforts to make the police more effective, particularly in regard to their activities. However, to the extent that they are dependent on the state for laundering opportunities and are beneficiaries of state contracts, then their policy influence will be somewhat limited (and, of course, there are constraints on the ability of political actors to execute the wishes and demands of organized crime). Moreover, dons are substitutable or disposable, especially if they operate in territory where the people exhibit very strong party loyalties and they do not have the option of "switching the area".

Thesis 6. *Political debts to contributors are most heavily incurred if there is a dependency on legitimate funding from a few large sources. And when this funding comes from concentrated sector interests, the recipient parties are very vulnerable to public policy pressures.*

If the major contributors to each party are few, then there is greater personalization of the political debts. Personalization sets up expected reciprocities and cronyism. Broad corporate, institutional and group-representative contributions allow more open and transparent channels of influence. The parties thus play a more appropriate role of synthesizing and aggregating the various interests for a larger national developmental purpose.

Thesis 7. *Political debts are limited and the risk of co-option is low if there is a high ratio of corrupt and illegal funds to legitimate corporate and institutional or group contributions.*

This explains the limited influence of the Jamaican private sector on incumbents who have greater access to opportunities for corrupt funding than the Opposition. Incumbents have greater access to alternative funding and thus more power in their relationships with legitimate contributors.

Thesis 8. *The funding structure of ruling parties provides greater party and candidate autonomy of all social forces. Funding patterns tend to be more constraining and co-opting for opposition parties.*

Ruling parties enjoy the benefits of (corruptly extracted) state funding. The opposition parties have less control and influence over the allocation of state funds and must take greater risks in accepting criminal funds.

Thesis 9. *Criminal networks seek control over candidates by attempting to link them to webs of criminal relations, not just by funding them.*

These larger webs may present opportunities for a wide range of illicit activity. And where they involve organized crime, opportunities are presented for access to the supply of political violence and intimidation, electoral fraud, and perhaps illegal schemes for personal enrichment that further compromise the candidates and state officials.

Seven Proposals

Much of the discussion on how to better control the problems associated with party financing has centred on transparency measures. These are critical, but a more comprehensive treatment of the matter is required. A review of the entire regulatory framework and enforcement capacity ought to be undertaken with a view to filling the existing gaps in legislation and resolving the problems. Indeed, at the time of writing, the Electoral Commission was in the process of conducting this review. Some of the suggestions presented below are being considered by the Electoral Commission and are likely to be adopted as a part of the new regulatory framework for party financing. The suggestions presented below are simply an attempt to systematize the thinking on the issue and to explore aspects of possible solutions to the problem in their connectedness.

Proposals 1, 2, 4 and 6 are intended to dampen the demand for illegal funds. Proposal 1 also seeks to reduce the cost of election campaigns or, rather, limit the expenditure on campaigns. Proposals 5 and 6 are concerned with increasing transparency in both campaign income and expenditure so that the informal systems of accountability, including the mass media, may play a greater role in regulating this activity and controlling its negative consequences. Finally, proposals 2, 4 and 5 look at strengthening formal accountability. Together, they address the loopholes and weaknesses in both fund-raising and the use of funds.

1.   Put a legal limit or cap on party and candidate campaign expenditure, with this limit being subject to periodic reviews.

2.   Make the party, and not just the candidates, accountable in law. This may be approached in a manner similar to the way in which corporations, universities and other institutions are held accountable. It is not just candidates who raise and spend funds. The central party organizations spend more money than any single candidate, yet the latter is accountable and the former is not.

3.   Limit the size of contributions from a single source (individual or group) and ensure restrictions such that a single originating source does not use different routes to circumvent the spirit of this proposal. This is intended to limit the potential influence of both criminal and legitimate sources.

4.   Ensure greater transparency in income and expenditure by legally requiring the parties to submit to an audit of their accounts by a responsible agency such as the Electoral Commission. This should

include periodic forensic audits that are specifically charged with investigating the flow of dirty money into the treasuries of the parties and candidates via kickbacks from state contracts and other corrupt activity.

5.   Provide state funding for all parties that enjoy a minimum level of voter support. The minimum may be established by the Electoral Commission. This could be a fixed proportion of an established cap on campaign expenditure.

Receipt of state funding would force compliance with transparency and accountability requirements and allow the imposition of other funding restrictions such as, for example, decertifying candidates who use their influence to secure state contracts for criminals and party enforcers or who exhibit a pattern of violating the agreed code of conduct for electoral candidates.[12]

State funding may therefore provide a lever for the acceptance of the other proposals listed above that give effect to the principles of transparency and accountability. The existing corrupt practices of the parties, such as vote buying, are a major source of the reluctance by sections of the public to support the idea of state funding for the parties. In this regard, perhaps prior improvements in accountability should be a condition for state funding. The parties should be required to meet established transparency and accountability criteria and not just voter strength criteria in order to qualify to state funding.

There is considerable public support for state funding of the parties. An October 2006 Stone poll estimated that some 41 per cent of the population supports state funding for the parties while some 38 per cent opposed the idea (*Jamaica Observer*, 9 November 2006, 1). This is not yet a consensus issue. However, these results may be sensitive to changes in context. They show that the issue is an open one.

6.   State funding would require a proper legal framework and a regulatory body that ensures compliance with the new laws. The regulatory body should have a competent investigative arm that is adequately empowered in law to effectively carry out its work. It should not be dependent on the goodwill and assistance of the police force. The

Representation of the Peoples Act criminalizes vote buying, but it is rarely enforced by the police.

7. A collective effort by private sector contributors to make similar conditions of transparency and accountability a requirement for qualifying for funding would reinforce the leverage provided by state funding. Non-compliant candidates would risk disqualification for both private and public funding.

Conclusion

Party funding is not an administrative matter. It is profoundly political. Funding returns reflect the political appeal of the party and its candidates. For the population, making or withholding financial contributions to the parties is a way of actively expressing approval or disapproval of them. Difficulties in raising funds may force greater party responsiveness, and depending on the regulatory framework, it may be a responsiveness that disproportionately favours the more powerful subpopulations, or may force broad appeal. Fund raising outcomes may indicate the ability or inability of a party to build coalitions, and is usually a statement of the nature of these coalitions and the power balance within them. Our concern here has primarily been with organized crime entering these coalitions.

The point of party financing reform is, however, not just to put pressure on the nexus between crime and politics, although this has been the focus of this chapter. The above proposals by themselves may make it a bit more difficult for the symbiotic relationships between politicians and organized crime to thrive and to bilk the state of its resources. In so doing, the proposals may weaken the relationship between these two sets of actors.

Displacement effects and other unintended consequences must, however, be anticipated. For example, a possible consequence of the proposal to provide state funding for the parties (depending on the amount of such funding) is that it may increase the autonomy of the parties in relation to all social forces and further professionalize politics. This may not necessarily enhance the public good. A well considered and comprehensive package that does not permit "cherry-picking" of some proposals is perhaps a way of avoiding this type of problem.

5

In Lieu of a Conclusion
Prospects for Controlling Organized Crime

THUS FAR THE RESPONSES of the state to organized crime and violent crime in general have not been very effective. "Head-hunting" has not made much of an impression on the problem. A number of dons have been killed by the police. Some of the major leaders of organized crime and selected drug traffickers have been extradited to the United States, and a few have even been convicted. These achievements, to the extent that they have been within the law, should not be disregarded. However, despite these case-related triumphs, organized crime as a method of criminality, pattern of behaviour, set of criminally exploitable relationships and mentality has strengthened in Jamaica. The main networks have survived the removal of their leaders with their business operations, community support base, and political ties intact.

If head-hunting has had limited success, targeting the assets of the organized crime networks has been even less effective. A distinction must be made between targeting the criminally acquired assets of convicted leaders of an organized crime group and targeting the criminal firm. The assets and person of the former may be sequestered and successfully separated from the firm without doing great harm to the latter if the rackets and income streams remain active and the exploitable and protective relationships are not ruptured.

A condition for effective asset seizure is the existence of adequate legal instruments. Historically, the House of Representatives has never been reluctant to pass crime-control legislation. However, some difficulties were encountered in getting effective assets forfeiture legislation passed by the parliament. The Proceeds of Crime Act of 2007, which was described in chapter 2, may be regarded as the outcome of a long (more than fourteen years) and somewhat difficult process. Initially, the impetus to craft an act with this content was largely external. The provisions in the act did not have a politically influential domestic champion until after 2004 even though the violence and other negative consequences of the drug trade were so evident.[1] Various groups sought to amend the proposed legislation such that the control objectives might be made more effective. This was done with the best of intentions. For example, some provisions in the draft of the act in its earlier form were seen as an attack on banking privacy. Sections of the political elite and the public saw it as a tool that could be used by an abusive state against its political opponents. In general, the earlier effort floundered on the profound distrust of the state. The upshot of this process was the promulgation of the Drug Offences (Forfeiture of Proceeds) Act of 1994 which permitted assets forfeiture only on condition that the specified assets were linked to a specific crime (or crimes) for which there was a conviction. Experience of its inadequacy coupled with the more manifest threat of organized crime had the effect of reducing the resistance to the more problematic provisions of the Proceeds of Crime Act of 2007. Although it may not be officially admitted, the act of 2007 represents an attempt to correct the defects in the earlier legislation, most of which were anticipated.

And if passing control legislation has been dilatory, there has been even greater difficulty in getting law enforcement to act effectively. There have been cases when criminally acquired funds and property have been successfully seized by the Jamaican police, but these have been few.

Too great a proportion of the indictments that justify the seizures of criminal assets have been initiated by foreign law enforcement and concluded by foreign courts. There is a real danger that the reliance on foreign law enforcement, and particularly the use or overuse of extradition, may lead to a further avoidance of the need to significantly improve the functioning of the Jamaican criminal justice system. Otherwise healthy and valued partnerships with foreign law enforcement, if overrelied on, could have this unintended negative effect.

Despite the severity of the problems of homicide, extortion, arms and drug trafficking, the hold of organized crime on the communities of the urban poor and its damage to the reputation of the country, there has been a continued failure to adequately deal with the problem of organized crime. The experiences of the countries that have had major problems with organized crime, including Italy and Colombia, suggest that serious assaults on organized crime by the state tend to come only after there are attacks by organized crime groups on officials of the state. It is only when these groups are considered a political threat, when they make the state or a particular political administration seem impotent or challenge its authority, that the problem is treated seriously.

In the case of Jamaica, where policing has been historically state-protective and generally unresponsive to the security needs of the general population (who were regarded as the source of potential threats to the colonial state), this absence of a direct threat to the state *partly* explains the *generally* inadequate and ineffective response to organized crime and the pattern of the response.[2] It is the threat that is presented by particular organized crime groups that explains the pattern of responses, that is, the tendency to act in the main (but not exclusively) against those organized crime groups that most attract the attention of the press, tend to engage in violent conflicts, and whose political protection is most tenuous.[3]

Why is there this reluctance to act effectively in the absence of a threat to the state? Any chance of successfully responding to the problem must begin by asking why there has been this failure on the part of successive political administrations and the responsible state agencies to adequately respond to the challenges presented by organized crime. This concluding chapter attempts to answer this question.

The Obstacles to Effectiveness and Change

Effective control of organized crime does not rest solely on having a good strategy. The failure of crime control, thus far, has not been primarily an intellectual failure. There are many other obstacles to success. These include the official constructions of the problem, and very real material interests (that these constructions often serve). Far from revealing an intellectual failure, these constructions are evidence of an intellectual agility in service of the underperforming state bureaucracy and successive political administrations.

Official Constructions and the Deflection of Accountability

There has been a constant and largely successful effort to define the crime problem in ways that are favourable to the responsible institutional actors, that is, in ways that excuse their inaction and failure. Moreover, when it is difficult to excuse failure, efforts are made to define and finesse failure in ways that circumscribe and limit the discussion of failure such that fundamental questions about the dysfunctionality of the institutions are not asked. For example, the failure of the police to control crime is typically explained in terms of their poor working conditions, a need for more constables, more cars, more resources. These definitions therefore also serve as tools that are used for resource mobilizations. With these tools, failure provides a justification for more resources and better working conditions. These demands are then met, only to be followed by new failures and new demands for additional resources. This provides an incentive to repeat the cycle.

An examination of the official narratives about the crime problem will reveal a clear evolution of the arguments. Violent crime, especially homicidal violence, has been used to define the Jamaican crime problem. State officials are given to periodically stating that the crime rate "is declining" "with the exception of murder". As noted in chapter 1, in the early 1990s, the homicide problem was constructed as a problem of domestic and interpersonal violence. Politics, it was claimed, was no longer a motivating factor in violent crimes. Indeed, the violence attending direct electoral competition between the political parties has dramatically declined (Harriott 2003b, 93). The declining rate of overt political violence is however mistakenly taken as an indicator of a more generalized disengagement of political actors with street crimes. The level of political violence was taken as the sole measure or index of politically induced and politically involved criminality. The role of politics in ordinary crime, especially organized crime, was obscured. This line of argument persisted for some time, and indeed still persists, despite the extant scholarly analyses showing both arguments concerning the nature of the crime problem to be without evidential support. The domestic violence thesis for example, had the effect of minimizing the contribution of organized crime to the murder rate.[4] The thesis on the declining role of politics in crime made it difficult to see the role of political corruption in the rise of organized crime. These misrepresentations of the problem and deflection of the public gaze (at times inquiring, at times puzzlingly amused, and at times puzzlingly frustrated) occurred during the early stages of the development of organized crime when effective action to control it would have been less costly in lives and state resources.

This line of argument was partly due to poor information and analysis, and to advocacy for more effective action to be taken against the problem of domestic violence. The latter was supported by advocacy data and research. There was a happy convergence of interests. The domestic violence thesis was used to make the point, especially in the late 1990s, that there was little that the police could do as the homicide problem was, in the main, not preventable. The police, it was argued, could not conduct patrols inside of people's homes. This argument sat uncomfortably with the recorded data which also revealed that the proportion of murders that occurred in homes had been steadily declining (from at least since 1983) and the proportion of those occurring in the streets and other public places was increasing, and exceeded 55 per cent since 1988 and 65 per cent since 1997.[5] Further, the vast majority of homicide offenders and victims (usually approximating 90 per cent) have been male. If there was an epidemic of "domestic violence", then it had to be largely male on male. These seemingly obvious inconsistencies did not matter. They did not urge a re-examination of the system of recording and processing the data – except among some academic researchers. In 2002, the newly formed Peace Management Initiative[6] contributed to a reduction of the national homicide rate which declined by 8 per cent in that year, and a dramatic reduction of some 56 per cent in West Kingston, which was the focal point of the peace effort. The police took the credit for this decline in the homicide rate.[7]

In reality, this temporary decline in the rate was largely the outcome of efforts by the two political parties (within the framework of the Peace Management Initiative) to broker a peace agreement between the organized crime networks and gangs in that area of the city. Such an outcome revealed the powerful influence that the political parties still exerted on these groups. Again, in 2006 when there was a 20 per cent decline in the homicide rate, the police and the political administration quickly took the credit for this reduction in the rate as the outcome of their efforts. Striking a more personal note, Deputy Commissioner Mark Shields stated: "When I arrived here on March 1 last year we had a 50 per cent increase in homicides over and above the previous year [2004]. That was reduced to 12 to 13 per cent by the end of the year" ("Plan to Cut Murder in Jamaica", *Gleaner* 5 January 2006).

Later, even after the existence of the gang problem was accepted, organized crime still remained invisible and unnamed in the official public discourse about crime. The activities of transnational networks gave some credibility to the labelling of the violent activity of the more powerful gangs as a deportee problem. This meant that the problem was exacerbated by the deportation of convicted criminals back to Jamaica. The violent crime waves of the 1990s to the time of writing were largely attributed to the deportee problem that was visited on Jamaica by the deporting states.[8] The deportees presented real difficulties for Jamaica and the other receiving countries of the region. Their proper rehabilitation and reintegration into their home societies and a crime prevention programme that specifically targeted them would have been costly. The claims regarding their impact on the local crime rates were, however, overblown.[9] This line of argument, which followed a well-trodden path of externalizing critical problems (at times with some justification) has persisted despite the doubtful evidential basis for it.[10] Being a small, open and vulnerable country, the external economic and political processes do matter, but may be overemphasized to deflect responsibility from internal actors. An unintended consequence of this kind of discourse is that it lowers the sense of self-efficacy and confidence of the people in their ability to solve the problems of their society.

The gang problem is thus misrepresented as having been manufactured abroad, or at least violently animated by the influx of unwanted elements that "were socialized abroad" or who "learnt and mastered their criminal craft abroad". The problem is externalized. Externalization has many political uses. It implies minimization of the internal social roots of the problem and thus the scope of the response required and the extent to which public policy is implicated in the development of the problem. It deflects the analysis away from the ties between crime and local power structures.

Another political purpose of this discourse is getting assistance from the deporting countries for the resettlement of the deportees. This is a political objective that is quite legitimate, but which may be pursued and perhaps achieved without distorting the realities of the crime problem. In order to achieve this latter political objective, the law enforcement challenges that the deportees present are magnified. It has been argued that it is difficult for the police to control high-end crime because of the (deportee assisted) externally accumulated resources and imported weaponry that are available to the criminal networks. Police modernization should therefore be focused on giving the police the technological edge in weaponry, mobility, communications and intelligence gathering gadgetry. Further, people are intimidated or refuse to cooperate as witnesses so it is difficult or impossible to convict the more accomplished, powerful and violent criminals. This argument may be taken in either of two directions, or both. It may be taken as a justification for police vigilantism or as an excuse for poor performance.

And yet despite these difficulties, there are the oft repeated premature and exaggerated claims of success without any reference to changes in these conditions. Such claims of success are usually not based on evaluations, but rather on short-term changes in the crime data that are not carefully analysed and are usually public relations exercises. Thus when crime rates fall, this is purportedly due to police action, and when they rise, it is because other agencies have underperformed and because the resources that are available to the police are inadequate. Such is the politics of crime control.

These arguments misrepresent the problem, mask incompetence and corruption, and assist the avoidance of accountability. They rely on the construction of misleading measures of success and self-serving interpretations of changes in the accepted indicators. For example, declining homicide rates are taken as an indicator of success. And increasing homicide rates are also taken as a measure of success. In instances of the latter, the population is told that increased lethal violence is the result of the arrest of major drug dealers and the consequent fracturing of organized crime networks and gangs and competition among them. Increased violence is thus an indicator of success in controlling organized crime. There is some plausibility to these arguments. It is well known that the removal of leaders of organized crime groups may indeed precipitate increased competitive violence within and between these groups. Leadership means control over considerable resources, so despite the risks involved, there will be candidates who are willing to vie for leadership of organized crime groups. Increased violence is however less likely when the targeted networks are of the corporate type. These are not involved in predatory activity, such as extortion rackets, are not tied to territory, and are given to using the police to protect their business. This was the case with a number of those who were extradited. The misrepresentation is however not in the claim that the removal of leaders of organized crime may result in new rounds of competitive violence for succession (although this is not always the case), but rather in the promotion of the idea that this violence indicates success in neutralizing the particular firms that were targeted and in controlling organized crime as a general phenomenon. The evidence (higher homicide rates and lower homicide rates) is presented as tactics affirming. In other words, the data hardly matters; it becomes supporting evidence for success regardless of its direction.

Sources of Political Unresponsiveness

Despite improvements in recent years, the responses of the responsible state agencies (the Jamaica Constabulary Force, the Financial Investigations

Division of the Ministry of Finance, the Income Tax Department, the Contractor General's Department, the Director of Public Proscecutions, the Courts and the Department of Corrections) to organized crime have generally been inadequate. The sources of this administrative unresponsiveness are to be found not just in internal departmental weaknesses, but also in environmental factors. Most responsible, however, are the successive political administrations. Political unresponsiveness frames administrative unresponsiveness, and both have shared environmental sources. The sources of political administrative unresponsiveness include self-interest and interdependencies with organized crime, societal tolerance of corruption and enterprise crimes (weak civic and political will), fear of conflict and state incapacity. The problems of the will to act are underpinned by objective difficulties.

Interests

The unresponsiveness of recent political administrations to high-end crime is in part rooted in the interests of individual institutional actors and powerful coalitions within these administrations that secure corrupt and criminally acquired benefits for their parties. Political corruption has compromised the policy process and the administrative capacity and resilience of the state, and may indeed be transforming the very character of the state itself. It has corroded the systems of accountability within the state – even while the political administration appeared to be strengthening these systems by nominally passing laws and forming new control institutions. An example of this is the process involved in the attempts to draft the National Investigative Authority Act which has as one of its stated goals the formation of an agency that is dedicated to the investigation of corruption and organized crime. The draft of 2007, however, prohibits any investigation of contracts that are awarded by the government without the approval of cabinet. It states as follows: "The Authority may not investigate matters relating to Government contracts and supply of equipment to the Security Forces" (National Investigative Authority Act, 2007, 2).[11]

All major contracts are awarded by the cabinet of the Government of Jamaica. It therefore means that by the proposed act, the members of the

cabinet would have secured for themselves immunity from the investigation of any impropriety on their part (while acting as members of the
cabinet). This provision would also protect those core activities of organized crime that exploit its links to the state and the politically powerful.
Thus, motivated by self-protection, a corrupt leadership would be able to
divert the attention of law enforcement away from high-end crime and
institutionalized corruption and restrict its probes to those that are directed
at the criminality of individuals and groups that do not have official protection. This approach by the political administration acts as an unintended
inducement for unaffiliated crime networks to seek political affiliation and
protection. It weakens the general ability of law enforcement to effectively
respond to high-end crime.

Given the strong ties between organized crime and sections of the political elite, any administration that acts methodically with resolve to control
organized crime runs the risk of political retaliation by organized crime
groups and, perhaps, associated conflicts within the administration. The
Bulbie and Zekes cases, which were discussed in chapter 1, provide examples of the risks that are involved. Some of the most significant battles
against crime and for effective crime control therefore have to be fought
within the political parties. To borrow from the language of war, this is a
critical front in any crime-control campaign.

Political resistance and retaliation are unlikely to be limited to intra-elite
conflicts and struggles. Effective control of organized crime may have
broader political effects that are generated by its economic consequences.
The economic effect of putting the major drug-trafficking groups out of
business is unlikely to be lost on any political administration. Crime-
control efforts that are likely to have a significant immediate negative
impact (even if short term) on the economy are unlikely to be met with
enthusiasm. There are no reliable estimates of the contribution of the drug
trade to the Jamaican economy. The financial inflows from the trade are
however thought to be significant given the market value of the quantum of
drugs that are produced, exported, and trans-shipped through the country.

The extent of money laundering and its effects on the Jamaican economy are also unknown. Laundering involves not just the proceeds from the
efforts of Jamaican organized crime networks and corruptly acquired

funds, but also criminally acquired funds that may be lured from abroad. The spread of the benefits from such enterprise leads to an indifference to the sources of financing.

As discussed in chapter 1, at the local community level, there are welfare systems that are funded by the resident organized crime groups and which (when coupled with the ability to deliver violence) enable the local dons to secure and deliver the votes to the party of their choice. The political representatives are therefore very sensitive to any political fallout and instability that may result from a weakening of this system. These material interests tend to sap the will of the enmeshed political administration and that of the sections of the population that benefit from enterprise crimes, either directly or indirectly, and who are painfully aware of these benefits.

Civic Will

The relationships of interdependence between organized crime networks, on one hand, and the various combinations of businesses, communities, and the political parties, on the other hand, and reliance on organized crime as an instrument of public policy weaken both the civic and political will to control organized crime.

The criminal "economy" and the legitimate or formal economy are so interlocked that profound interdependencies between the two have developed and, as discussed in earlier chapters, have been most evident in construction and finance. These interdependencies tend to weaken the civic will and popular support for the control of entrepreneurial crimes. This reality, for example, found unexpectedly open and frank expression in the responses of spokespersons for established business firms to "Operation Kingfish", a major law enforcement drive against organized crime (and in particular, the arrest, on drug-trafficking charges, of Leebert Ramcharan, a "businessman" and "drug Kingpin" who operated his businesses in the city of Montego Bay).

In 2006, Anthony Holness, the chief executive officer of Hardware and Lumber, a reputable company that supplies materials for housing and other construction projects, reported the impact of Operation Kingfish on their accounts as follows:

The people who are involved in [drug trading] are major developers . . . They build large houses, they build shopping centres, and they do townhouse development and we benefit from that business. Unfortunately, it is the environment in which we live . . . It's just the reality.

There was a direct decline in our sales at the hardware stores in Montego Bay and [its] environs . . . There is no question that it is significant, but I won't attempt to quantify. I am not sure that is something we want to disclose.[12] ("King Fish Success – and a Business Dilemma", *Gleaner*, 14 June 2006)

This was clearly a lament. It was not just the hardware businesses which felt that they were beneficiaries of the drug trade; others also benefited from it. Ramcharan was a major supplier of foreign currency to the local business community (personal correspondence with a former foreign currency trader). His visible and hidden firms were very much part of the normal business landscape of the city.

Where there is a high degree of tolerance of corruption and crime, the grey activities of organized crime are more easily defined as *normal business*. Construction racketeering, for example, is seen by many who work in that sector as normal. Its methods have spread from criminal firms to legitimate ones, especially to those firms that are politically connected. Invoice padding and false billing are regarded as normal business practices especially when used to defraud the state.

So, too, are corrupt procurement practices and the associated acceptance of kickbacks seen as *normal politics*. The defence of the Trafigura affair was an attempt to redefine corruption as normal politics. The argument was that ruling parties have tended to take contributions from companies that conduct business with the government. As the practice was customary, it therefore ought to be considered as acceptable. Strong party loyalties are harnessed in defence of these practices, which in turn reinforces both the practices and loyalties. To the extent that the defence of corrupt practices is politically successful, its practitioners are assured that the loyalty of the party supporters can be relied on in future cases. When confronted with evidence of its misdeeds, the parties become communities of belief whereby truth becomes the party's truth. Any true accusations of corruption and collusion with criminal networks are dismissed as political manoeuvres on the part of the party's opponents and "enemies".

Consequently, the corrupt practices of the party and individual party members are shielded and accountability subverted. Defence of the party against true charges of corruption by its members are then advertised as proof of their unshakable loyalty, and therefore an entitlement to new (corrupt) rewards.[13] Given the strong party loyalties and the degree of interdependence among the underground, the interrelatedness of the informal and formal economies, and the dependence of some of the urban communities on organized crime networks, political and social facilitation of entrepreneurial criminality may therefore be expected to remain very problematic. Thus, if political transformation is one front in any crime-control campaign, building civic support for such a campaign is another.

Despite the normalization of entrepreneurial crimes, where and whenever there are civil society pressures, these are easily neutralized by fierce party loyalties which, as described above, act as a protective device. In its most extreme form, this loyalty must be personalized. Loyalty to the party as an institution and fidelity to its principles are not enough as it need not be conflated with loyalty to individual leaders and permits the excoriation of individuals who violate those principles and who may bring the institution into disrepute. The notions of loyalty that are more compatible with corruption take it to mean uncritical public support. Thus any criticism of the activity of the government or Opposition is interpreted as being motivated by narrow party political hostility to them. Consequently, the rational deliberative space is dissolved, or at least considerably shrunk. Independent voices are thereby silenced, not because they lack the courage to challenge the criminality of the powerful, but because they fear being labelled as partisans. This is a kind of tribal handcuff that restrains and silences.[14] Perhaps the biggest obstacle to the control of organized crime is the tolerance of it or, worse, its social and political facilitation.

Political Will

The political administration is responsible for public safety. In order to fulfil this responsibility, it must ensure that the state has the capacity and the moral authority to enforce the laws and in so doing protect the citizenry. This is a core function of the state. Any state, or more narrowly, any political administration that is unable and/or unwilling to provide adequate protection for its citizens from predatory criminality and to ensure public order is a failing state or at least a failing political administration.[15] Political administrations are responsible because they influence the outcomes via public policy and other political choices – including the choice not to act. For example, they may choose to neglect social crime prevention programmes as this may mean reallocating resources at a political cost that they are unwilling to bear. They may choose not to collaborate with other political parties and influential civil society actors, thereby foregoing national unity, with the consequence that crime-control policy remains ineffective.

In a context where critical institutional actors have developed an interest in sustaining high-end criminality and where tackling criminality means making some trade-offs and risking dislocation, political leadership that has the strength of character to take difficult decisions is required. Among the political elite there is a fear of conflict and of the political (and economic) fall out from the effective control of high-end crime. Given past experiences, political resistance from the more dependent urban communities may be anticipated. Such developments could possibly weaken the level of political support for the political administration in the communities of the urban poor. The violent demonstrations in support of leaders of organized crime such as Donald Phipps and Donovan Bennett, and the extended armed clashes between the state security forces and gunmen in the urban communities presents images of instability. And these developments occur in a context where these communities are typically politically homogenous and strongly affiliated to the political parties. It follows that if there is a loosening of the political influence of the parties in these areas (and a loosening of their ties to these criminal groups), then even greater instability should be expected. The suppression and control of territorially based organized crime involves political risks.

The above examples are very public and open confrontations, but there are also other less dramatic potential negative consequences of controlling organized crime. For example, as was discussed in chapter 2, breaking up the organized crime networks means terminating the welfare and other services that they provide to their communities. This would also have other consequences such as increased robberies and other predatory crimes (these provide replacement income for dependent young males and gang members). Such consequences would put pressure on state officials to replace the lost welfare support. Failure to respond positively to these pressures could precipitate anti-government activism. These are potential consequences that may sap the political will to act.

There are also potential conflicts between the state agencies and the political administration. The latter are perhaps most averse to these types of conflicts, especially conflicts with the police force. As organized crime systematically uses corruption to influence the behaviour of law enforcement officers, any effort to seriously respond to organized crime will collide with corruption within the ranks of the police force (and other state agencies). If there is a systematic attempt to reduce the level of corruption within the police force and state bureaucracy, then political resistance by the beneficiaries of corruption may be anticipated. Such measures typically precipitate conflict, and in the absence of a two-party consensus, these conflicts are easily politicized.

There is considerable experience of police-government conflicts. These conflicts have involved ideological, policy, administrative as well as trade union matters. From the viewpoint of any political administration, there is the constant threat of the police becoming oppositionist. With regard to the problem of corruption, if it acts, the government may be portrayed as compromising the security of the country by engaging in a witch hunt within the police force and victimizing the members of the security forces. Anti-corruption measures are easily presented as their opposite, that is, as efforts that weaken the ability of the police to control crime. These ideas resonate with sections of the public that are not always well informed on these matters. It is therefore not surprising that after some twelve years of police reform and modernization, the Jamaica Constabulary Force is no more effective in controlling crime than it was at the beginning of the process. Again, reluctance on the part of the political administration to act is informed by the fear of conflict with a powerful group that could exact a costly political price for efforts to do what is necessary to improve the law enforcement capability of the state.[16]

Underlying the fear of conflict is the facility with which constructive projects may founder against the deep political and social divisions in the society, the low level of trust and confidence in the institutions, and a politics that puts party interests first. Conflicts are thus easily generated and politically exploited.

Incapacity of the State

Even when there is the political will to act against organized crime, there still remains the real problem of the incapacity of the state to implement policy. Being a developing country, there are resource constraints and consequently the underfunding of crime-control programmes and the criminal justice system. There are also issues of technical and managerial competences, antiquated systems and inefficient and ineffective methods of work. The culture of the state bureaucracy is not performance and results oriented. Coupled with incapacity is unresponsiveness to the public. Unresponsiveness is not just a matter of a poor work ethic and poor work attitudes; it is also an adjustment to incapacity.

Performance of the state is related to the social and political context. If the people are alienated from the institutions of the state, if service to the public is not valued, and if accountability is not treated seriously, then it will be difficult to get the police and other state agencies to work effectively and to achieve their goals.

There are many competing demands on the state, yet limited resources. Thus while crime control may be a major concern, there is usually no corresponding shift in resource allocations including human resource allocations. There are always crises that have to be responded to, many immediate needs that require urgent attention, and corresponding constituencies to be satisfied. This is a formula for ineffectiveness.

The Jamaican criminal justice system is therefore unable to achieve the stated objectives that justify its existence (the prevention and control of crime).[17] Given its poor record of controlling violent crime, it is understandable that the population is not sanguine on matters of crime control. A survey that was conducted in 2006 indicated that only 12.6 per cent of a representative sample of the population felt that "the war against crime is being won". Some 85.4 per cent disagreed with this claim. This was in the context of a 20 per cent decline in the homicide rate in 2006, and claims by the government and the police force that crime was "under control". The incapacity of the state is understood by the population. Some 62 per cent felt that "the state is unable to enforce the laws", and only 7 to 8 per cent have "a lot of confidence in the police" (Powell 2007, 55).

Despite the low level of public confidence, there is no sustained pressure on the political administration to have the problems fixed. This is because the public is unable to imagine better state administered alternatives, and have available to them non-state disciplinary alternatives such as the jungle courts of the dons (as described in chapter 1) and self-help justice. The development of a stronger, that is, more effective and just state system that is able to protect the people and to police with their consent remains a strategic developmental challenge.

Conclusion

Social and political facilitation insulates and reinforces organized crime. It is an expression of a weak state system and troubled social system. If the foundational institutions of the state, polity and society such as the police force, the political parties, and indeed norms of everyday social behaviour, have become sites of accommodation with and struggle against enterprise criminality, then this reflects the extensiveness and enormity of the challenge with which the society is confronted. This challenge has become not just a matter of crime control, but of a regeneration of the society and its critical institutions.

Organized crime has developed in Jamaica in response to the demand for illegal services. It has, however, reinforced itself by efficiently meeting some of the more basic legitimate demands and needs of the marginalized sections of the society. In order to weaken organized crime and make it more vulnerable to police action, the state must fulfil its basic functions and better deliver these services. It must provide better police service and protection for the people who need it most. It must make the justice system more accessible to the marginalized urban poor so that they need not go to the local don for justice. It must undertake programmes that aim to better integrate the communities of the urban poor and which will give the state a valued institutional presence in the communities, and indeed help the people to transform these communities. In order to achieve this, new opportunities will have to be created by and for the people. These are not easy to accomplish, but the possibilities must first be seen before they can be grasped. In these chapters, we have tried to strengthen the possibilities by sketching them.

Notes

Introduction

1. This was computed from estimates of the level of criminal victimization of the Jamaican population that were derived from a survey by the author that was conducted in 2000 and reported on in Harriott 2003a. Subsequent estimates by the Centre for Leadership and Governance at the University of the West Indies for 2006 have confirmed this estimate.
2. See the National Squatter Survey Jamaica, Final Report (2004).
3. In popular discussions, the relationship of poverty to crime is a most controversial one. For an empirical treatment of the matter, readers may see Ellis (1992).
4. It is, of course, quite difficult to get to the apex of anything – if the rewards are high. Researchers have shown that for most street level drug-dealers the realities are quite harsh.
5. This includes the efforts of the National Committee on Crime and Violence (2002).

Chapter 1

1. Cuba has a different political tradition from the Commonwealth Caribbean. Its encounters with authoritarian politics allows the maximum leader to protect (or crush) organized crime groups more effectively than in a democratic polity where the police and courts are independent. The latter is not always truly the case in democracies where the independence and competence of law enforcement may be compromised by the political administration.

2. Organized crime groups vary in their internal structural arrangements and levels of discipline. Within Jamaica, the most durable groups tend to be highly organized, but outside of Jamaica, some of them may operate more loosely as networks.

3. A large informal sector and endemic corruption blurs the boundaries between the "upper world" and the "underworld" but the distinction is nevertheless real and useful.

4. The concept of the garrison is elaborated on later in the text.

5. See the *Jamaica Observer*, 14 July 2004, 1 and 3, for a report on the disorder and violent responses to Smith's death.

6. Donald Phipps was convicted for murder in April 2006.

7. This translates roughly as "This is our thing". The description is striking not just because of how it represents the relationship between the community and organized crime, but also because of the choice of words. Translated into Italian it reads *cosa nostra*. These observations are taken from the author's field notebook for a larger research project on homicides in Jamaica.

8. The point is elaborated on in a study of homicide which will be completed shortly.

9. See Ministry of National Security (2007, 5–16).

10. It has been argued that organized crime may assist the activity of international terrorist groups – if the price is right. The logic of this reasoning is, however, not very cogent. Any such alliance would do irreparable damage to organized crime, its political links, its reputation in the international markets as anti-American and would precipitate more robust international law enforcement cooperation against it. See Bagley (2004) for a discussion of this issue.

11. I refer to the movie *The Harder They Come* written by Perry Henzell and Trevor Rhone.

12. See *Gleaner*, 2 May 1978, 1.

13. "Social banditry" is quite distinct from organized crime, but Blok (1974, 99–102) describes the pathways of "upward mobility" in nineteenth-century southern Italy by which elements of the former may have evolved into the latter. Even if a direct line of continuity cannot be established, it may reasonably be argued that despite the significant differences between these two phenomena, social banditry was a precursor to organized crime.

14. Figueroa (1994) has already alerted us to this prospect. His conclusions are based on his analysis of the patterns of garrison voting.

15. If computations are made using Figueroa's operational definition which takes a pattern of homogenous voting as the definiens, then the percentages are likely to be lower. This definition is however open to the contention that a pattern of homogenous voting may be produced in different ways. A conceptual definition

that considers the garrison a mode of political administration in which criminal networks, usually organized crime, form a part of the dominant coalition and are fully integrated into the party structures, is applied, then the figures are as reported in the text. This concept of the garrison is elaborated on later in this chapter.

16. This has already occurred in the case of the Opposition protests against the proposed gas price increases which were held in 1999.

17. There have been at least two such cases in recent times (personal communication with the author).

18. See *Gleaner*, 19 July 1992, 15A. In the world of organized crime "disrespectful" behaviour warrants a violent response. And as democracy is not a value, a democratic challenge may be considered simply a challenge to the established leader and thus disrespectful.

19. As will be discussed later, Seaga claimed that "dirty money" was used in the campaign to remove his allies from leadership positions. There were also allegations that intimidation and violence were used.

20. Criminalized is put in quotation marks because this is not typically how the word is used. The common usage is that the behaviour is legally proscribed. Here it is not meant that politics is legally proscribed but, as indicated above, that criminal methods are adopted in politics. It may be better to invent a new word for this second meaning but until then we may accept the two ways in which the word is used.

21. The ascriptive statuses are excluded.

22. For a discussion of the extent of corruption in the police force, see the speech by the commissioner of police at the annual meeting of the Police Federation in 2005 (*Gleaner*, 6 June 2005).

23. Communication by a very senior member of the Jamaica Constabulary Force whose unit has special responsibility for investigating organized crime. This offer should not be taken literally. It was perhaps simply a way of opening up a discussion on alternate solutions to his dilemma. The statement may be translated as follows: "I am willing to pay very handsomely if you are willing to help me avoid extradition."

24. For a rather generous review of the performance of the Peace Management Initiative, see *The Peace Management Initiative Jamaica* in South-South Regional Cooperation for Determining Best Practices for Crime Prevention in the Developing World, 2006, 108–27.

25. This is, for example, the first essay on the activities of Jamaican organized crime within Jamaica.

26. See Tyrone Reid, " 'I Want Proof'– Haye-Webster denies Association with 'Bulbie' ", *Gleaner*, 2 November 2005.

27. See, for example, "The Yardies: England's Emerging Crime Problem", Roy Ramm, detective chief superintendent, International and Organized Crime Branch, Scotland Yard, http://www.textfiles.com/law/yardies.text.
28. On the face of it, this term could also be read as an attempt to grapple with the complexities of the Jamaican networks but there is not much in the written record to support this idea. It was not a debate about its flexibility, adaptability and complexity of its relationships but rather of its relative lack of sophistication (when, for example, compared with American organized crime). In other words, it reflects a kind of structural formalism and the confusion that follows from it.
29. "Inner city" may be regarded as a term borrowed from social ecology. It is used here simply to avoid using the word ghetto which is usually taken as a stigmatizing epithet.
30. Tales of their "good works" and the celerity and efficiency of their policing methods are periodically reported on national radio via the talk show programmes.
31. For a discussion of "corner crews" in Jamaica, see Levy (2005).
32. Extensive treatment of this issue is beyond the scope of this work.
33. Stone used these words to describe the mobilizational methodology of the political parties, not organized crime.
34. The groupings that became organized crime networks were not even involved in the local retail trade in ganja (marijuana). This was left to individual "hustlers".
35. This assumption is rather dubious, but the data gives some indication of production levels.
36. This is possibly an overestimate, but even if it is a gross overestimate, it suggests that the reality is truly problematic. These data were reported by the minister of national security, Dr Peter Phillips, in a speech at the University of the West Indies, Mona, and which was subsequently published in *Jamaica: The Way Forward – Presentations at the Political Leadership Forum 2005* (Kingston: Sir Arthur Lewis Institute of Social and Economic Studies, 2006).
37. For a discussion of the violence of these networks in the United States, see Headley 1997.
38. The term "mafia", as used here, does not refer to the culturally specific form of organized crime that is native to Sicily, but rather a generic type that may be found in a variety of settings as a kind of violent entrepreneur or supplier of violent services that further distinguishes itself from ordinary predatory criminal networks by its relationship to mainstream state and political actors.
39. There are some significant exceptions. The point is elaborated on in a larger work that is currently in progress.
40. See the Survey of Living Conditions (Government of Jamaica) for the period.
41. A number of surveys of the living conditions and unemployment rate in some of

these communities were conducted by the Kingston Restoration Company. Some were done by students but they provide useful data on these communities.

42. Computed from data on reported homicides that were provided by the Jamaica Constabulary Force and population estimated based on data that was provided by the Planning Institute of Jamaica. This is an estimate, as the reported homicides represent approximately 5 per cent less than the true number of homicides and the estimate of the population for the Kingston Metropolitan Area was 593,448.

43. In the early twentieth century, the western sections of Kingston were already stigmatized as criminal haunts. See Moore and Johnson (2000).

44. See Stone (1985) for a discussion of the garrison phenomenon.

45. This point is elaborated on in a larger work by the author on Jamaica's homicide problem.

46. In the context of patrimonial relations or a grounding of the don's authority in highly personalized familial type relations, both designations may be equated. Prime Minister is a father or mother figure. The Caribbean has had this tradition in its politics. "Papa Doc" François Duvalier of Haiti and "Uncle" Eric Gairy of Grenada were two of the most notorious cases.

47. This case was reconstructed from personal correspondence with the owner-manager of the firm.

48. The conduct described in this case is illustrative not inferential. More work on this issue is required to discern and confirm that the subtleties that generate authority are clear patterns.

49. For a discussion of the impact of these variables on violent crimes see Francis et al. (2004), and Frost and Bennett (1998). Readers should note that while, for example, there has been some reduction in the level of inequality, official measures of unemployment are notorious for underestimating and masking this phenomenon.

50. Later researchers who wish to explore these relationships will have the benefit of access to official documentation by using the Freedom of Information Act.

51. See the Erwin Angus report on the operations of the National Housing Development Corporation Limited and Operation Pride (2002) for a description of the types and scale of these kinds of fraud.

52. The bulldozing of Back-o-Wall, which is the area on which Tivoli Gardens was built, is documented in the pages of the *Gleaner*. The similar clearance of sections of Trench Town was done in the early 1970s and this too is documented in the *Gleaner*.

53. There is not much hard evidence of this. However, the author has witnessed a contribution from a known don that occurred openly at a party conference. Personal correspondence with members of the Jamaican intelligence services and the political elite also suggests that this is truly a significant problem.

54. See "Zekes' Family Under the Microscope", *Gleaner*, 31 May 2005.

55. For a critical commentary on this development see Dawn Rich, "He that Hath Ears better Hear", *Gleaner*, 9 May 1999, 9A.

56. Computed from data provided by the *Economic and Social Survey of Jamaica* for the respective years. Suicides are excluded.

57. This type of specialization is more evident in Colombia where guerrilla and paramilitary forces are able to extort the drug-producing and trafficking networks.

58. This paper represents a limited exploration of this process. It pulls from a larger work that is being undertaken by the author.

59. This was the first election that was based on universal adult suffrage.

60. See Lacy (1977) for a discussion of political violence during this period.

61. A similar situation has now developed in Venezuela.

62. This was a way of meeting some of the demands for foreign exchange, stabilizing the exchange rate and ending the black market trade in dollars.

63. A similar comment was made by Edward Seaga to foreign reporters about Lester Coke, a former leader of the Shower posse. Seaga was then the leader of the Opposition (the JLP) and the comment was made at Brown's funeral and is reported in the film *The Yardies*. I thank my colleague Professor Bernard Headley for bringing this to my attention.

64. A recording of this interview exists and I have viewed it more than once but I hope that readers will kindly pardon me for not citing it here.

65. This is being developed in a manuscript that is still in progress.

66. In the case of the National Housing Development Cooperation, for example, Danhai Williams was charged with defrauding the agency of $450 million (*Gleaner* 15 December 2005, 1); see also "Solid Waste Scandal: $2 Billion Breach at National Solid Waste Authority", *Gleaner*, 28 July 2005.

67. Some ways of doing this are discussed in chapter 2 with reference to the experiences of other countries.

68. Estimate computed by the author for a study that is in progress.

69. These data were prepared in tabular form with the names of the individuals given. This table is, however, not presented here because listing the names of those that have never been convicted of a crime may present legal difficulties.

70. Such a prospect would raise a number of moral issues that are related to dons being permitted to materially benefit from their crimes, and the likely impact of such a policy on the moral authority of law enforcement. These issues, however, need not be discussed here.

71. I thank my colleague Professor Barry Chevannes for insisting that I find a legally acceptable device for operationalizing my proposal that organized crime networks be denied access to state contracts, and Professor Alfred Francis for bringing this device to my attention.

72. The popular journalistic writings tend to highlight "zero tolerance" public order policies and COMSTAT as the reasons for the decline in the crime rate in New York City. For a discussion of these two aspects in the academic literature see Kelling and Coles (1996) and Silverman (1999) respectively.

73. Investing billions of dollars in inner-city transformation before breaking the hold of organized crime on these networks, only transfers a significant proportion of these funds to them. For example, workers on housing projects may be required to pay over a percentage of their salaries to these networks.

74. See the report of the National Committee on Political Tribalism, 1997.

Chapter 2

1. Strategy is about ends-means relationships and the processes by which the latter are moved to achieve the former. A developed strategy sets out clear goals, the programmatic activity required to achieve those goals, and the critical institutional actors and how their activity would be orchestrated, as well as the resource requirements and how these would be mobilized.

2. This is one of the reasons why the police tend to make so many premature claims of success.

3. Computed from data presented in the *Economic and Social Survey of Jamaica* for the years 1994 to 2006.

4. See, for example, the *Economic and Social Survey of Jamaica*.

5. See the *Economic and Social Survey of Jamaica* for the years 1996 to 2006. During this period, the number of incidents of reported crimes declined from 52,771 to 31,306 or rates of 2097.8 to 1173.7 incidents per 100,000 citizens.

6. Bennett was introduced in chapter 1 and "Pang" was a leader of a group in the Grant's Pen area of the city of Kingston.

7. Lower-level operatives from different networks who have worked as drug dealers in the United States were interviewed. They said that they were able to corrupt and form enduring working relationships with street police in cities along both the West and East coasts of that country.

8. One expression of party tribalism in Jamaica is that large enough numbers of the members of the parties treat it as a community of beliefs. They are therefore not predisposed to accept negative facts about their parties and its members. For example, truthful claims that their party gives organized crime firms contracts may therefore be disbelieved even in the face of overwhelming evidence in support of this claim. To accept this truth claim is to run the risk of having doubt cast on one's loyalty to the party. And if the party leader claims that garrisons do not exist, then to use the word similarly signals that one does not truly belong to

the "tribe". Exposure of the party-organized crime nexus, like the exposure of corruption, may therefore be blunted by tribal loyalties.

9. There were acts of solidarity that took the form of armed attacks on members of the security forces. See the reports in the *Gleaner*, 24 and 25 September 1998, 1.

10. That he was terminally ill should not be taken as a truth claim, but rather as a belief that was used to explain his behaviour and to encourage an assault on his leadership.

11. There is no known evidential support that directly links the attack on the car in which the parliamentarian was travelling and the death of Bennett. My point is simply that it represented a code violation that one could reasonably expect to have consequences.

12. See the Report of the Independent Commission Against Corruption (Hong Kong).

13. This may not be a widely held view but it is an often repeated apology for particular pro-government organized crime groups.

14. In an attempt to alleviate this problem, a special rape unit was set up in the police force. This unit is more supportive and appears to have generated greater confidence among rape victims.

15. This pressure to simply help, and to help in personalized ways, constitutes a pressure "from below" on agents of the state to subvert the rules and to act corruptly.

16. From personal notes that were taken on a visit to Haiti in July 2007. The word "gang" is placed in quotation marks because many regard their violence against the United Nations Peacekeeping force and the Haitian police as just resistance to the overthrow of their government and because they are not involved in ordinary criminal activity. The estimate of seven hundred was done in July 2007. By then the situation was considered by UN and Haitian state officials to be stable.

17. Stille (1995) provides a discussion of the issues related to the maxi-trials.

18. For a discussion of the effects of youth unemployment on violent crime in Jamaica and the Caribbean, see Francis et al. 2004.

19. These agencies and institutions include the Small Business Loan Board, Jamaica National Investment Programme, the Jamaica Development Bank, and the National Commercial Bank (when it was state controlled).

20. This may be found in Italian law.

21. Japanese law provides for this (see Hill 2003).

22. Operation Kingfish investigators come to mind. Operation Kingfish is a special police operation aimed at Jamaican organized crime networks. The police officers and investigators who are assigned to this operation are specially selected.

23. It may be argued that the types of rackets associated with organized crime were being run by American-born robber barons prior to this, or that the robber baron was at least the native fore-runner of American organized crime. The war

profiteer Cornelius Vanderbilt (1794–1877) and cotton smuggler James Fisk (1834–1872) are often cited as examples of this.

24. Chu (2000) claims that, prior to this, its antecedents were evident in the Fujian province of China.

25. In some states there have been efforts to reduce partisan political influences on the judicial appointments. There has, for example, been considerable public debate about how to ensure this in the state of New York.

26. The period of prohibition began in January 1920 when the United States Congress passed the National Prohibition Act and ended in 1933 when the Act was repealed.

27. Decriminalization should not be regarded as a panacea for all of the problems of criminal violence and organized crime, but simply as one element in a larger strategy of control.

28. Problem solving is practised fairly widely in the United States, United Kingdom and elsewhere, but I am not aware of it being applied to the prevention of organized crime in these jurisdictions.

Chapter 3

1. Other studies done by various bodies had also identified a link between corruption and development. These include the World Bank, the International Chamber of Commerce, the International Federation of Accounts, the International Monetary Fund, the Organization for Economic Cooperation and Development and Transparency International regarding the possibilities of corruption.

2. Although we are using this conceptualization of corruption, which represents the dominant discourse on corruption, we are aware of its limitations as outlined by Warren (2004).

3. The Centre for Leadership and Governance is an institution in the Department of Government at the University of the West Indies (Mona). Its mandate is to contribute to the strategic transformation of the University of the West Indies by strengthening the Mona campus's responsiveness to national needs, broadening graduate student training in policy-relevant research, enriching instructional material for Faculty of Social Sciences courses, and enhancing the university's interaction with the society on leadership and governance issues.

4. This should not be taken to mean that we are suggesting that cost over-runs are never honest claims.

Chapter 4

1. Organized crime is present in both of these latter groups but these groups include other types of actors. Many favoured contractors who systematically engage in corrupt practices are not criminals in the social or legal definitions of the word. They are clearly distinguishable from organized crime in their accumulative activities although their corrupting effects partially overlap.
2. Their histories are long relative to those of other parties in the developing world, many of which emerged during the final stage of the anti-colonial struggle. It is also long relative to the age of the country as an independent nation.
3. For evidential support of these claims see Powell (2007).
4. The ruling PNP was exposed as having received a gift of some J$30 million (just under US$500,000) from Trafigura Beeher, a transnational company based in Holland that does business with the Jamaican government.
5. For purposes of this computation, the campaign is taken as the twenty-one-day period ending on election day. In reality, intense political campaigning can last up to six months. The above is therefore an underestimate of the true cost. The estimate also excludes contributions in kind and the use of state resources by the ruling party.
6. It is not clear how comparable these data are. Ryan does not define what is meant by the campaign period, neither does he state how the figures are computed. My calculations, which were intended to update the data, may therefore represent a somewhat different reality from the data presented by Ryan in 2005.
7. This does not preclude an appreciation of the instrumental value of power by the members of the party for the members of the party.
8. This quote is taken from a public statement by a leader of the Peoples National Party Youth Organisation (PNPYO). A similar attitude may be found among political activists in several countries of the Caribbean.
9. The parties have also at times employed class and race mobilization, as well as appeals to nationalism, socialism and anti-communism.
10. These are the types of charges that Jamaican law allow. They are quite unlike, for example, the provisions in Italy which permit more serious organized crime related charges.
11. I include "potential facilitators" because I am aware of cases that have "gone bad" for corrupt political administrators who misjudge the character of their appointees.
12. See the *Agreement and Declaration on Political Conduct*, and the *Code of Political Conduct*.

Chapter 5

1. In 2004, Peter Phillips became the minister of national security. He was then a very influential figure in the government.
2. The word "generally" is emphasized as in specific cases the response has been adequate enough to secure convictions or extradition.
3. The pattern of party bias in policing has been considerably eroded, but has not yet been broken. This should not be taken to mean that there have not been periods of relatively unbiased policing when support for the governing party was not as powerful a protective factor for party affiliated high-end criminals.
4. In the case of the domestic violence thesis, evidence in support of it was provided by the police force, but these data were poorly coded and lacked validity.
5. This was computed from a data set that was created by the author from information recorded by the police for another research project on homicides.
6. The Peace Management Initiative was formed in January 2001 and enjoyed the active support of the two major political parties and was funded by the state.
7. See "Forbes Upbeat about Crime", *Gleaner* 19 January 1999. The data on changes in the homicide rate are taken from the "Jamaica Constabulary Force Crime Statistics Year End 2002 vs. 2001" which was provided by the Statistics Unit of the Jamaica Constabulary Force.
8. This became a Caribbean issue as officials in other territories made similar claims. At the time I was a member of the Caribbean Task Force on Crime and these concerns were forcefully brought to our attention.
9. Here I am echoing the views expressed in the report of the Caribbean Task Force on Crime. This report was submitted to the heads of government of the region. Consistent with the principle of disclosure, readers should be aware that this author was involved in drafting the report of the task force.
10. See, for example, the debates on the sources of the economic crises of the 1970s which may be found in the parliamentary debates that are documented in the Jamaica *Hansard*. For a more developed articulation of the issue see also Manley (1982).
11. At the time of writing, the draft act was under review by a new political administration and it has been proposed that the investigative authority be permitted greater independence and freedom to act.
12. The company later apologized for the statement.
13. This perverse "logic" may not be very clear to readers who are not familiar with the dark side of Jamaican politics. Corrupt politicians tend to emphasize loyalty to them and the party as a primary value. Good party members are therefore, most of all, loyal party members. And good party members anticipate rewards for approved conduct. This is similar to the values that connect the leaders of organ-

ized crime with their support base. Citizens who are loyal to them and shield them from the police expect to be rewarded. The disloyal who become police informants expect to be punished.

14.   This idea should be easily understood by Jamaican readers. "Tribal" roughly refers to the strong party loyalties and social ties, such that party interests trump all other interests.

15.   "Failing" must be distinguished from "failed". The idea expressed here is not original; it is a fairly common idea.

16.   The Jamaica Constabulary Force does not resist efforts to improve its "crime-fighting" capabilities by providing it with more and better equipment. I however do not equate law enforcement with crime-fighting.

17.   It may be argued that the system has more profound control "functions" and that these objectives simply form a legitimating discourse.

References

Abadinsky, H. 1990. *Organized Crime*. Chicago: Nelson-Hall.

Albanese, J. 2004. North American Organized Crime. *Global Crime* 6, no. 1.

Albanese, J., and D. Das. 2003. A Framework for Understanding. In *Organized Crime: World Perspectives*, ed. J. Albanese, D. Das and A. Verma. Upper Saddle River, NJ: Prentice Hall, 2003.

Alleyne, D., and I. Boxill. 2003. The Impact of Crime on Tourist Arrivals in Jamaica: A Transfer Function Analysis. In *Understanding Crime in Jamaica*, ed. A. Harriott, 133–56. Kingston: University of the West Indies Press, 2003.

Anderson, E. 1990. *Code of the Street: Decency, Violence, and the Moral Life of the Inner-city*. New York: W.W. Norton.

Anderson, P. et al. 2004. Report on the 2003 Housing Census of Denham Town and Midtown. Mimeo. Department of Sociology, Psychology and Social Work, University of the West Indies, Mona.

Bagley, B. 2004. Latin American and Caribbean Organized Crime. *Global Crime* 6, no. 1: 32–53.

Bayley, D.H. 1966. The Effects of Corruption in a Developing Nation. *The Western Political Science Quarterly* 19, no. 4: 719–32.

Beare, M.E. 1997. Corruption and Organized Crime: Lessons from History. *Law and Social Change* 28, no. 2: 155–72.

Blake, D. 2002. *Shower Posse: The Notorious Jamaican Criminal Organization*. New York: Diamond.

Blok, A. 1974. *The Mafia of a Sicilian Village, 1860–1960: A Study of Violent Entrepreneurs*. Prospect Heights, IL: Waveland Press.

Blom, T. 2001. The Netherlands: Criminalization Plus Expediency, and the Special Case of Cannabis. In *European Drug Laws: the Room for Manoeuvre*, ed. N. Dorn and A. Jamieson. London: Drugscope.

Bogues, A. 2002. Nationalism and Jamaican Political Thought. In *Jamaica in Slavery and Freedom: History, Heritage and Culture*, ed. Kathleen Monteith and Glen Richards, 363–87. Kingston: University of the West Indies Press.

Bowling, B., and C. Phillips. 2006. Young Black People in the Criminal Justice System. Submission to the House of Commons Home Affairs Committee. Mimeo.

Buscaglia, E., and J. van Dijk. 2003. Controlling Organized Crime in the Public Sector. *Forum on Crime and Society* 3, nos. 1 and 2: 3–34.

Caribbean Group for Cooperation in Economic Development (CGCED). 2000. Challenges of Capacity Development: Towards Sustainable Reforms of Caribbean Justice Sector. Vol. 2. Report prepared under the auspices of the Caribbean Group for Cooperation in Economic Development (CGCED).

Carter Center. 1999. *Combating Corruption in Jamaica: A Citizen's Guide*. Atlanta: The Carter Center.

Charap, J., and C. Harm. 1999. Institutionalised Corruption and the Kleptocratic State. Working paper. International Monetary Fund, Washington.

Charles, C. 2003. Business Ethics in Jamaica and the Problem of Extortion by Counter-societies. Typescript. City University of New York.

Chu, Y. 2000. *The Triads as Business*. London: Routledge.

Collier, M.W. 2000. Explaining Political Corruption: The Case of Jamaica. Typescript. Florida International University.

Crenshaw, M. 2001. The Causes of Terrorism. In *Violence: A Reader*, ed. Catherine Besteman. New York: New York University Press.

Cressey, D. 1969. *Theft of the Nation*. New York: Harper and Row.

Davidson, J. 1997. *Gangsta: The Sinister Spread of Yardie Gun Culture*. London: Vision Paperbacks.

Donais, T. 2003. The Political Economy of Stalemate: Organised Crime, Corruption and Economic Deformation in Post-Dayton Bosnia. *Conflict, Security and Development* 3, no. 2: 359–82.

Dowdney, L. 2003. *Children of the Drug Trade: A Case Study of Children in Organised Armed Violence in Rio de Janiero*. Rio de Janeiro: 7 Letras.

Ellis, H. 1992. *Identifying Crime Correlates in a Developing Society: A Study of Socio-economic and Socio-demographic Contributions to Crime in Jamaica, 1950–1984*. New York: Peter Lang.

Figueroa, M. 1994. Garrison Communities in Jamaica 1962–1993: Their Growth and Impact on Political Culture. Paper presented at symposium Democracy and Democratization in Jamaica: Fifty Years of Adult Suffrage. Faculty of Social Sciences, University of the West Indies. 6–7 December.

Findlay, M. 1999. *The Globalization of Crime*. Cambridge: Cambridge University Press.

Francis, A., G. Gibbison, A. Harriott and C. Kirton. 2004. *Crime and Development in Jamaica*. Report for the World Bank.

Frost, B., and R. Bennett. 1998. Unemployment and Crime: Implications for the Caribbean. *Caribbean Journal of Criminology and Social Psychology* 3, nos. 1–2: 1–29.

Gambetta, D. 1993. *The Sicilian Mafia: The Business of Private Protection*. Cambridge: Harvard University Press.

Gordon, D. 1987. *Class, Status and Social Mobility in Jamaica*. Kingston: Institute of Social and Economic Research, University of the West Indies.

Griffith, I. 1997. *Drugs and Security in the Caribbean: Sovereignty Under Siege*. University Park: Pennsylvania University Press.

Harriott, A. 1998. Public Opinion and the Jamaica Constabulary Force. Unpublished report presented to the Ministry of National Security and Justice.

———. 2000. *Police and Crime Control in Jamaica: Problems of Reforming Ex-colonial Constabularies*. Kingston: The University of the West Indies Press.

———. 2003a. Fear of Criminal Victimization in a Reputedly Violent Environment. *Social and Economic Studies* 52, no. 1: 35–72.

———. 2003b. Social Identities and the Escalation of Homicidal Violence in Jamaica. In *Understanding Crime in Jamaica: New Challenges for Public Policy*, ed. A. Harriott, 89–112. University of the West Indies Press.

———. 2005. The Jamaican Crime Problem: Taking a New Turn and Presenting New Challenges. *Ideaz* 1, no. 2: 44–52.

———. 2006. Globalization and Crime: The Jamaican Experience. In *Jamaica Human Development Report*, ed. S. Vasciannie. Kingston: Planning Institute of Jamaica.

———. 2007a. Dis a fi wi Ting: The Rise of Organised Crime in Jamaica. Paper presented at the annual meeting of the Academy of Criminal Justice Sciences, Seattle.

———. 2007b. Risk Perceptions and Fear of Criminal Victimization among Visitors to Jamaica: Bringing Perceptions in Line with Reality. *Journal of Ethnicity and Crime* 5, nos. 2–3: 93–108.

Harrison, L.E., and S.P. Huntington. 2000. *Culture Matters: How Values Shape Human Progress*. New York: Basic Books.

Headley, B. 1994. *The Jamaican Crime Scene: A Perspective*. Mandeville: Eureka Press.

———. 1997. The Jamaican Posses in America: An Emergent Force in US Organised Crime. Paper presented at the annual meeting of the Law and Society Association, May, St Louis, Missouri.

———. 2002. *A Spade Is Still a Spade: Essays on Crime and the Politics of Jamaica*. Kingston: LMH Publishing.

Hill, P. 2003. *The Japanese Mafia: Yakuza, Law and the State*. Oxford: Oxford University Press.

———. 2004. The Changing Face of the Yakuza. *Global Crime* 6, no. 1: 97–116.

Holness, Andrew. 2007. Strengthening Social Capital. Presentation to the Social Policy Forum, King's House, Jamaica. 13–14 April.

Huntington, S.P. 1968. *Political Order in Changing Societies*. New Haven: Yale University Press.

Jacobs, J. 1999. *Gotham Unbound: How New York City Was Liberated from the Grip of Organized Crime*. New York: New York University Press.

Jamaican Economy since Independence Project (JEP). 2006. The Jamaican Economy since Independence: A Working Paper. Typescript.

Jessop, R. 2000. The Crisis of the National Spatio-temporal Fix and the Ecological Dominance of Globalizing Capitalism. *International Journal of Urban and Regional Studies* 24, no. 2: 323–60.

Johnson, H., and J. Soeters. 2008. Jamaican Dons, Italian Godfathers and the Chances of a "Reversible Destiny". *Political Studies* 56: 166–91.

Johnston, M. 1982. *Political Corruption and Public Policy in America*. Monterey: Cole.

———. 2005. *Syndromes of Corruption: Wealth, Power, and Democracy*. Cambridge: Cambridge University Press.

Josephs, J. 1999. Jamaican Posse and Transnational Crimes. *Journal of Gang Research* 6, no. 4: 41–47.

Kelling, G., and C. Coles. 1996. *Fixing Broken Windows: Restoring Order and Reducing Crime in Our Communities*. New York: The Free Press.

Kelly, R.J., ed. 1986. *Organized Crime: A Global Perspective*. New Jersey: Rowman and Littlefield.

Kenney, D., and J. Finckenauer. 1995. *Organized Crime in America*. Belmont, CA: Wadsworth.

Khan-Melnyk, A. 1994. Politics and US-Jamaican Drug Trade in the 1980s. In *Drug Trafficking in the Americas*, ed. B. Bagley and W. Walker III. New Brunswick, NJ: Transaction Publishers.

Kleinknecht, W. 1996. *The New Ethnic Mobs*. New York: Free Press.

Lacy, T. 1977. *Violence and Politics in Jamaica 1960–1970*. Manchester: Manchester University Press.

Leff, N.H. 1964. Economic Development through Bureaucratic Corruption. *American Behavioral Scientist* 8, no. 3: 8–14.

Levy, H. 2005. Peacemaking on the Front Line. *Caribbean Journal of Social Work* 4 (August): 14–27.

Leys, C. 1965. What Is the Problem About Corruption. *Journal of Modern African Studies* 3, no. 2: 215–24.

Lipset, S.M., and G.S. Lenz. 2000. Corruption, Culture, and Markets. In *Culture Matters: How Values Shape Human Progress*, ed. L.E. Harrison, and S.P. Huntington. New York: Basic Books.

Liu, B. 2001. *The Hong Kong Triad Societies Before and After the 1997 Change-over*. Hong Kong: Net e-Publishing Ltd.

Liverpool, F. 2007. Paper presented at regional seminar sponsored by the Organization of American States. Montego Bay, Jamaica. 20–21 March.

Lotspeich, R. 2002. Crime and Corruption in Transitional Economies: Lessons for Cuba. *Journal of Policy Reform* 6, no. 2: 71–87.

Lupsha, P. 1988. Rational Choice: Not Ethnic Group Behaviour: A Macro Perspective. *Law Enforcement Intelligence Analysis Digest* (Winter): 1–8.

Maingot, A. 1994. The Drug Trade in the Caribbean: Policy Options. In *Drug Trafficking in the Americas*, ed. B. Bagley and W. Walker III. New Brunswick, NJ: Transaction Publishers.

————. 1999. The Decentralization Imperative and Caribbean Criminal Enterprises. In *Transnational Crime in the Americas*, ed. Tom Farer. New York: Routledge.

————. 2004. *The Challenge of the Corruption-Violence Connection*. In *Caribbean Security in the Age of Terror*, ed. I. Griffith. Kingston: Ian Randle.

Manley, M. 1982. *Jamaica: Struggle in the Periphery*. London: Third World Media.

Mason, E.S. 1978. *Corruption and Development*. Development Discussion Paper No. 50. Cambridge: Harvard Institute of International Development.

McFarlane, J. 1998. Transnational Crime, Corruption, and Crony Capitalism in the Twenty-first Century: An Asia-Pacific Perspective. *Transnational Organized Crime* 4, no. 2: 1–30.

McWalters, I. 1999. The Link Between Organized Crime and Corruption: A Hong Kong Perspective. Paper presented at the ninth International Anti-corruption Conference, Global Integrity: 2000 and Beyond. Durban. 10–15 October.

Merton, R. 1967. *On Theoretical Sociology*. New York: Free Press.

Minnaar, A. 1999. A Symbiotic Relationship? Organised Crime and Corruption in South Africa. Paper presented at the ninth International Anti-corruption Conference, Global Integrity: 2000 and Beyond. Durban. 10–15 October.

Ministry of National Security. 2007. *National Security Strategy*. Kingston: Ministry of National Security.

Moore, B., and M. Johnson. 2000. *"Squalid Kingston" 1890–1920: How the Poor Lived, Moved and Had Their Being*. Kingston: Social History Project, University of the West Indies, Mona.

Munroe, T. 1999. *Renewing Democracy into the Millennium*. Kingston: The University of the West Indies Press.

National Advisory Committee on Crime and Violence (NACCV). 1984. *Report of the National Advisory Committee on Crime and Violence*.

————. 1990. *Report of the National Advisory Committee on Crime and Violence*.

————. 2002. *Report of the National Advisory Committee on Crime and Violence*.

National Institute of Justice (NIJ). 2007. *Asian Transnational Organised Crime and its Impact on the United States*. Special Report. US Department of Justice.

Naylor, R. 2003. Follow the Money: Methods in Crime Control Policy. In *Critical*

Reflections on Transnational Organized Crime, Money Laundering, and Corruption, ed. M. Beare. Toronto: University of Toronto Press.

Nettleford, R. 1989. *Jamaica in Independence: Essays on the Early Years*. Kingston: Heinemann Caribbean.

———. 1971. *Manley and the New Jamaica: Selected Speeches and Writings, 1938–1968*. London: Longman.

Nice, D.C. 1986. The Policy Consequences of Political Corruption. *Political Behavior* 8, no. 3: 287–95.

Nye, J.S. 1967. Corruption and Political Development: A Cost-Benefit Analysis. *American Political Science Review* 61, no. 2: 417–27.

Office of the Political Ombudsman. Report of the Office of the Political Ombudsman 2003–4.

Onuf, N. 2001. Speaking of Policy. In *Foreign Policy in a Constructed World*, ed. V. Kubalkova. London: M.E. Sharpe.

Planning Institute of Jamaica (PIOJ). 2005. *Economic and Social Survey of Jamaica, 2004*. Kingston: PIOJ.

Police Executive Research Forum (PERF). 2001. Violent Crime and Murder Reduction in Kingston. Report for the American Chamber of Commerce–Jamaica, Washington DC.

Powell, L. 2007. *Probing Jamaica's Political Culture*. Vol. 1. Kingston: Centre for Leadership and Governance, University of the West Indies, Mona.

Radzinowicz, L. 1979. *The Growth of Crime: The International Experience*. London: Penguin Books.

Reppetto, T. 2004. *American Mafia: A History of its Rise to Power*. New York: Henry Holt.

Robotham, D. 1998. Vision and Volunteerism: Reviving Volunteerism in Jamaica. Grace, Kennedy Foundation Lecture. Kingston: The Grace, Kennedy Foundation.

———. 2000. Blackening the Jamaican Nation: The Travails of a Black Bourgeoisie in a Globalized World. *Identities: Global Studies of Culture and Politics* 7, no. 1: 1–37.

Rose-Ackerman, S. 1999. *Corruption and Government: Causes, Consequences and Reform*. Cambridge: Cambridge University Press.

Ryan, S. 2005. Disclosure and Enforcement of Political Party and Campaign Financing in the CARICOM States. In *From Grassroots to the Airwaves: Paying for Political Parties and Campaigns in the Caribbean*, ed. S. Griner and D. Zovatto. Washington: Organization of American States.

Santino, U. 2003. Mafia and Mafia-type Organizations in Italy. In *Organized Crime: World Perspectives*, ed. J. Albanese, D. Das and A. Verma. Upper Saddle River, NJ: Prentice Hall.

Schulte-Bockholt, A. 2006. *The Politics of Organized Crime and the Organized Crime of Politics: A Study of Criminal Power*. New York: Lexington Books.

Shelley, L. 1998. Organized Crime and Corruption in Ukraine: Impediments to the Development of a Free Market Economy. *Demokratizatsiya* 6, no. 4: 648–63.

———. 2000. Is the Russian State Coping with Organized Crime and Corruption? In *Building the Russian State: Institutional Crisis and the Quest for Democratic Governance*, ed. V. Sperling. Colorado: Westview Press.

———. 2001. Crime and Corruption. In *Development in Russian Politics*, ed. Z.G. Stephen White and Richard Sakwa. Houndsmills: Palgrave.

———. 2003. Russia's Policy Challenges: Security, Stability, and Development. In *The Challenge of Crime and Corruption*, ed. S.K. Wegren. New York: M.E. Sharpe.

———. 2005. The Government Bureaucracy, Corruption and Organized Crime: Impact on the Business Community? http://www.reec.uiuc.edu.

———. 2006. Money Laundering, Organized Crime and Corruption. http://www.respondanet.com/english/anti_corruption/publications/documents/dellasoppa.01.doc.

Shigui, Q. 1992. Group and Joint Crime Distinctions in Law and Practice. In *Enterprise Crime: Asian and Global Perspectives*, ed. A. Lodl and Z. Longguan. Chicago: Office of International Criminal Justice, University of Illinois.

Silverman, E. 1999. *NYPD Battles Crime: Innovative Strategies in Policing*. Boston: Northeastern University Press.

Sives, A. 2003. The Historical Roots of Violence in Jamaica: The Hearne Report 1949. In *Understanding Crime in Jamaica: New Challenges for Public Policy*, ed. A. Harriott, 49–62. Kingston: University of the West Indies Press.

Small, G. 1995. *Ruthless: The Global Rise of the Yardies*. London: Warner Books.

Smith D. 1978. Organized Crime and Entrepreneurship International. *Journal of Criminology and Penology* 6, no. 2: 161–77.

Steligson, M.A. 2006. The Measurement and Impact of Corruption Victimization: Survey Evidence from Latin America. *World Development* 34, no. 2: 381–404.

Stille, A. 1995. *Excellent Cadavers: The Mafia and the Death of the First Italian Republic*. London: Vintage.

Stinchcombe, A. 1968. *Constructing Social Theories*. New York: Harcourt, Brace and World.

Stone, C. 1980. *Democracy and Clientelism in Jamaica*. New Brunswick, NJ: Transaction Books.

———. 1985. *Class, State and Democracy in Jamaica*. Kingston: Blackett Publishers.

———. 1988. Race and Economic Power in Jamaica. In *Garvey: His Work and Impact*, ed. R. Lewis and P. Bryan. Kingston: Institute of Social and Economic Research, University of the West Indies.

———. 1989. Power, Policy and Politics in Independent Jamaica. In *Jamaica in Independence: Essays on the Early Years*, ed. Rex Nettleford. Kingston: Heinemann Caribbean.

———. 1991a. Report of the Stone Committee Appointed to Advise the Jamaican Government on the Performance, Accountability and Responsibility of the Elected Parliamentarians. Kingston: Bustamante Institute of Public and International Affairs.

———. 1991b. Survey of Public Opinion on the Jamaican Justice System. Unpublished report to the US Agency for International Development. Kingston, Jamaica.

Theobald, R. 1990. *Corruption, Development and Underdevelopment*. Basingstoke: Macmillan.

Thrasher, F. 1994. What Is a Gang? In *Classics of Criminology*, ed. J. Jacoby. 2nd ed. Prospect Heights, IL: Waveland Press.

Tilly, C. 2002. War Making and State Making as Organized Crime. In *Violence: A Reader*, ed. Catherine Besteman, 35–60. New York: New York University Press.

Transparency International. 1999–2007. *Transparency International Annual Report*. Berlin: Transparency International.

Uchiyama, A. 2003. Organized Crime: A Perspective from Japan. In *Organized Crime: World Perspectives*, ed. J. Albanese, D. Das, and A. Verma. Upper Saddle River, NJ: Prentice Hall.

United Nations Development Programme (UNDP). 2002. *Human Development Report 2002: Deepening Democracy in a Fragmented World*. New York: UNDP.

United Nations Office of Drugs and Crime (UNODC). 2002. Results of a Pilot Survey of Forty Selected Organized Crime Groups in Sixteen Countries. Mimeograph.

van der Heijden, O. 2003. Organized Crime: A Perspective from the Netherlands. In *Organized Crime: World Perspectives*, ed. J. Albanese, D. Das, and A. Verma. Upper Saddle River, NJ: Prentice Hall.

Van Dijk, J. 2006. Organized Crime and Collective Victimization. Paper for International Conference on Corruption and Organized Crime: Bridging Criminal and Economic Policies, Center for Democracy. Sofia, Bulgaria. 23–24 June.

Volkov, V. 2002. *Violent Entrepreneurs: The Use of Force in the Making of Russian Capitalism*. Ithaca: Cornell University Press.

von Lampe, K. 2003. Criminally Exploitable Ties: A Network Approach to Organized Crime. In *Transnational Organized Crime: Myth, Power and Profit*, ed. E. Viano, J. Magallenes, and L. Bridel. Durham, NC: Carolina Academic Press.

Waller, L., P. Bourne, I. Minto and J. Rapley. 2007. *A Landscape Assessment of Political Corruption in Jamaica*. Kingston: Caribbean Policy Research Unit.

Warren, M. 2004. What Does Corruption Mean in a Democracy? *American Journal of Political Science* 48, no. 2: 328–43.

Wei, S.J. 2000. How Taxing Is Corruption on International Investors? *The Review of Economics and Statistics* 82, no. 1: 1–11.

Wilson, J. 1989. Corruption: The Shame of the States. In *Political Corruption: A Handbook*, ed. A.J. Heidenheimer, M. Johnston and V.T. Le Vine. New Brunswick, NJ: Transaction.

Wilson, W. 1996. *When Work Disappears: The World of the New Urban Poor.* New York: Vintage.

West Kingston Commission (WKC). 2002. Report of the Commission of Inquiry into the Upsurge of Violence Since May 2001 in the Kingston Metropolitan Area.

Wolfe, L., et al. 1993. Report of the National Task Force on Crime. Kingston. Government of Jamaica.

Woodiwiss, M. 2003. Transnational Organized Crime: The Strange Career of An American Concept. In *Critical Reflections on Transnational Organized Crime, Money Laundering, and Corruption*, ed. M. Beare. Toronto: University of Toronto Press.

World Bank. 1997. *World Development Report.* New York: Oxford University Press.

Zhang, X. 1992. Enterprise Crime and Public Order. In *Enterprise Crime: Asian and Global Perspectives*, ed. A. Lodl and Z. Longguan. Chicago: Office of International Criminal Justice, University of Illinois.

Index

accountability
in abuses of power, 95
avoidance of, 167
in campaign income and expenditure,
157, 159
as condition for state funding of political parties, 158–59
in construction sector contractual
system, 88, 134–35, 158
in co-option strategies, 72
deflection of responsibility, 163–67
and institutional corruption, 24, 25,
125, 128–29
in political funding, 73–74
subversion of, 68
in trusteeships, 74, 184n72
Adair, Derrick (Shabba), 18
Allen, Janice, 55
Andem, Joel, 71
Andreotti, Giulio, 51, 110
anti-corruption programmes, 87, 88–90,
90–92
arrogance, qualities of, 77–78

Barth, Dennis (Copper), 18
Bennett, Donovan (Bulbie), 15–16, 83,
169, 173
black market foreign exchange, 66,
183n62

Brazil, Comando Vermelho, 18
business, formal
"Black Bourgeoisie" project, 98
disruption of relationships as crime
control strategy, 85–87
extortion of, 40–41
facilitation of, 98, 185n19
and legal activities of organized crime,
35–36
linkage to enterprise crime, 33–35
as money-laundering facility, 36,
39–40, 133
relationship to organized crime, 80,
100–101
trusteeships, in systems of accountability, 74
business victimization survey, 40

CAPRI (Caribbean Policy Research
Institute)
public sector agencies, perceived
corruption in, 123–25
"Taking Responsibility Survey", 121,
122–29
Centre for Leadership and Governance
trust, crime and criminality survey,
121, 122–29
Charles, Pearnel, 20
China, 18, 66

citizens' rights, 96
civic activism, 1, 10–11
coalitions, control of political process,
  20–22
code of silence, 8, 95
Coke, Lester, 183n63
Colombia, 183n57
  exit routes as crime control strategy,
    86
  foreign exchange controls, 66
  law enforcement efforts, 162
  regulatory framework of election
    funding, 150–51
  relationships of political parties to
    organized crime, 51, 143
community governance
  and clientelistic model of enterprise
    crime, 32–33
  co-policing of garrison communities,
    87
  co-rulership as crime control strategy,
    84
  dons as community gatekeepers, 46–49
  functional displacement of community
    support, 93–97
  in garrison communities, 2, 15–16,
    18–19, 28
  jungle courts, 30, 34, 44–45, 53, 93,
    176
  political administration of garrisons,
    33–34, 51–52
  and pro-social activities of organized
    crime, 18–19, 34
  quasi-governmental aspects of crime
    networks, 41, 43–44, 45, 56, 59, 89,
    101, 170
  self-policing of garrison communities,
    43, 45–46, 53–55, 181n30
  social hierarchy, 12–14
  state provision of services, 92–97

street protests, 20. *See also* garrison
  communities
construction sector
  corruption in, 129–35
  "Corruption in Construction and
    Post-conflict Reconstruction"
    report, 131–33
  cronyism, direct contracting and,
    135–37
  extortion of, 40–41
  front firms, 35–36, 134, 170–71
  gross domestic product, contribution
    to, 131
  money laundering in, 133
  procurement criteria, leaking of, 135,
    137–38
  racketeering in, 133–34, 171
  structure of, 132
  transparency in contractual system, 88,
    134–35, 158
contracts
  awarding of, 21–22, 68, 98, 100–101,
    129–31, 154, 183n66
  benefits to ruling party, 156
  and construction sector corruption,
    129–35
  contractual system, accountability in,
    88, 134–35, 158
  direct contracting, 135–37
  "fit and proper" standard, 73
  National Contracts Commission,
    135
  perceived corruption in awarding,
    126–27
  procurement criteria, leaking of, 135,
    137–38
  procurement practices, corruption in,
    171
  procurement process, improvement to,
    140–41

state accountability as crime control strategy, 88

"tied contractor", as self-funding method, 155

trusteeships, in systems of accountability, 74, 184n72

convictions

immunity from, 6, 68–71

as means of achieving crime control, 80–81

co-option strategies, in crime control, 71, 72

corruption, 5, 182n53

acadamic discourse of, 115–16

academic research on, 116–20

anti-corruption programmes, 87, 88–90, 90–92

apologetics as reinforcement of, 91–92

Corruption Perceptions Index, 67, 128

Corruption Prevention Act, 69

corrupt political authority, view of by crime networks, 118–19

criminalization of politics, 20–22, 100, 180n20

defined, 116

disruption of relationships as crime control strategy, 85–87

expectation of as outcome of politics, 150

factors in prevalence of, 138–40

global GDP and, 117

grey activities, naturalization of, 100, 171

institutional corruption. *See* institutional corruption

of law enforcement, 9, 184n7

perceived causes of, 125–26

perceived corruption in state bureaucracy, 123–25

political funding as opportunity-seeking behaviour, 148–49

political patronage, 128

in popular culture, representation of, 128

relationship of political parties to organized crime, 49–56, 67–68

relationship of power motive to, 29–30

reporting rates, 7

and Westminster parliamentary system, 128

World Values Survey, 139–40

corruption, Jamaican perceptions of, 115–41, 186n1

corruption defined, 122–23

Corruption Perceptions Index, 67, 128

perceived causes of, 125–26

politicians, perceived involvement of in crime, 127–28

public sector agencies, perceived corruption in, 123–25

research design, 120–21

Corruption Perceptions Index, 67, 128

crime and criminality

academic studies on post-independence political violence, 2–3

apologetics for, 67

controlling, reports on, 3–4

high crime vs. low crime, 1–2

ideological perspective of, 4–5

legitimization of through corruption, 119

peace-making strategies, 25–26, 71–72

perceived corruption in contract procurement, 126–27

as political protective strategy, 22

role of politics in, 2–3, 9

social restraints, erosion of, 23

street violence, 4

crime and criminality (*continued*)
  transformation of in Jamaica, 14,
    16–17
crime control legislation, 104–6
  conspiracy laws, 74, 105–6
  Corruption Prevention Act, 69, 105
  Drug Offences (Forfeiture of
    Proceeds) Act, 161
  forfeiture of assets, 73, 160–61
  Freedom of Information Act, 182n50
  Interception of Communication Act,
    105
  Larceny Act, 68–69
  Maritime Drug Trafficking Suppres-
    sion Act, 105
  modernization of, 73–74
  Money Laundering Act, 69, 105
  National Investigative Authority Act,
    168–69, 188n11
  Operation Kingfish, 170–71, 185n22,
    188n12
  Proceeds of Crime Act, 69, 105, 161
  proposed areas of attention, 106
  RICO laws, 74, 110
  Terrorism Prevention Act, 105
crime control policies
  approaches to, 71–75
  deterrence theory, 109
  human rights violations, 114
  implementation of, 175–76
  law enforcement, effective strategies
    for, 72–73
  moralistic approach to, 109
  national consensus on, 10–11
  negative consequences of, 169–70,
    173–74
  opportunity theory, 109
  overview, 113–14
  as phenomenon research, 111, 186n28
  political unresponsiveness to, 167–68

  political will, role of in effective
    administration, 172–75
  potential conflicts as result of, 174–75
  public confidence in, 176
  success of, exaggerated, 166–67
crime control strategies, 84–107
  anti-corruption programmes, 87,
    88–90, 90–92
  community governance, state provi-
    sion of, 92–97
  co-policing of garrison communities,
    87
  crime commissions, creation of, 112
  disruption of criminal influences,
    98–104
  features of organized crime, relevance
    of, 79–80
  functional displacement of community
    support, 93–97
  law enforcement instruments, 104–7
  measures of success in, 80–83, 160–62
  obstacles to, 163–76
  political facilitation, disruption of, 85–87
  political protection of crime networks,
    disrupting, 88–90
  political transformation, need for, 172
  public education, 92
  tax violations, prosecution for, 82
crime-fighting, unconventional, 71
crime networks
  activities of, 35–41
  and business of violence, 23–24
  Clansman, 15, 25, 50
  community support of, 8, 15–16, 41,
    80, 93–97
  corrupt political authority, view of,
    118–19
  criminal as party-client, 153
  criminal conglomerates as full service
    providers, 36–37

criminalization of politics, 20–22, 100
deportees as cause of, 165–66
diversification of funding streams, 99
dons as criminal entrepeneurs, 15–16
effect of transnationalization on,
  38–39
evolution of in national contexts,
  17–18
as extra governmental tools, 118
Gideon Warriors, 71
governance of garrison communities,
  15–16, 18–19
Group 69, 61–62
immunity from law enforcement,
  68–71, 113
integration into formal economic
  system, 15–16, 99–100, 170–72
managed violence, 15–16, 17
new capitalism of, 119–20
One Order, 15, 25
opportunity structure of, 43–44, 59
organizational features of, 26–28,
  179n2
organizational models of, 32–35, 41
party elections, impact of criminal
  funding on, 154, 156
patrimonial relationship of authority,
  45–46, 182n46
peace-making strategies, 25–26, 71–72
penetration of local economy, 15–16
performative violence, 58
political protection of, 88–90, 170,
  188n3
political retaliation by, 169
pro-social activities of, 18–19, 34, 41,
  59, 89
quasi-governmental aspects of, 41,
  43–44, 45, 56, 101, 170
relationship to political parties, 49–56,
  67–68, 152–56, 165–66, 169

relationship to urban poor, 42–43,
  179n7
as security threat, 5, 24–25
Shower Posse, 62, 89, 183n63
socio-structural roots of, 60–63
Spanglers, 52, 61–63, 70, 90, 169
specialization of, 101
Super Dons, 22–23
targeting-up strategies, 82–83
violence, logic of, 56–58
violence-related services to political
  parties, 31–32, 57, 76, 180n19. *See
  also* organized crime
crime rates
reduction in as measure of success,
  81
reporting rates, 7, 81, 93, 178n1,
  185n14
and socio-economic conditions, 7–9
substitution and displacement effect,
  81
criminal enterprises, drug-related
as organized-disorganized crime, 27,
  82, 181n28
criminal entrepeneurs
differentiation between violent
  specialists, 80
dons as, 15–16
facilitation of, 170–72
rural-based, 64–65
criminal justice system
clearance rates as indicator of immunity, 69
deal brokering, 55
modernization of, 8, 73–74
political interference with, 87
public confidence in, 6–7
weakness of, 5–7, 68–71
criminal victimization, reporting rates,
  7, 81, 93, 178n1, 185n14

criminology
  academic interpretations, 77
  authenticity discourse against, 4–5
  on drug trafficking, 13
  organized crime definitions, 28–31
cronyism
  crony capitalism, 148–49
  and direct contracting, 135–37
  and institutional corruption, 125, 126
  and political debts, 155–56
Cuba, 13, 178n1 [ch. 1]
customs department, perceived corrup-
    tion in, 123–25

decriminalization, 186n27
  of drugs, 91, 109
  peacemaking as discourse of, 71–72
deterrence theory of crime control, 109
dissent, silencing of, 20–21, 180n18
dons
  as actors on the national stage, 53
  behaviour patterns, 89
  as community gatekeepers, 41, 46–49,
    100, 101
  as criminal entrepeneurs, 15–16
  criminal records of, 6, 70–71, 179n6,
    183n69
  front firms of, 134, 170–71
  front of, 35–36
  as heroic figures, 18, 83
  jungle courts, 30, 34, 44–45, 53, 93,
    176
  patrimonial relationship of authority,
    45–46, 93, 181n30, 182n46
  political administration of garrisons,
    33–34, 51–52
  political protection of, 88–90, 170,
    185n11
  protection offered by, 34
  rankin as predecessor, 49

role of in co-option strategies, 72
  Super Dons, 22–23
drug trafficking
  anti-corruption programmes, 91
  cannabis, 14, 37–38, 63
  cocaine, 37–38, 63
  criminal relationships with, 33
  criminology research, 13
  drug seizures, 37–38
  effect on mainstream economy, 8–9,
    12, 66
  as enterprise crime, 100
  international drug markets, 5, 16,
    37–38, 39, 58–60, 63–66
  market orientation of organized
    crime, 28–29
  as organized-disorganized crime, 27,
    82, 181n28
  recreational drugs, 35
  subcultural tolerance of, 14
  in United States, 109
  and youth unemployment, 8–9,
    178n3, 178n4

economic system
  corruption, consequences of, 117
  integration of organized crime into,
    12, 15–16, 99–100, 170–72
  trusteeships, in systems of accountabil-
    ity, 74
elections and electoral process
  candidate selection, impact of criminal
    funding on, 154
  cost of per capita, Caribbean, 146–47
  criminalization of politics, 20–22, 100,
    180n20
  electoral fraud, 187n10
  Jamaican history of, 143
  party financing reform proposals,
    156–59

political competitiveness, in evolution of gangs, 61–63
political influence of crime networks, 12–13, 16, 142–44
Representation of the People's Act, 106
vote buying, 22, 145, 158
voter intimidation, 22, 31–32, 35, 106, 143
voter mobilization, 88
vote selling, 149–50
empowerment process, disruption of, 84
enterprise crime, 3
activities of, 35–41
corporate model, 32, 41, 167
economic dependencies of, 86
in growth phase of maturation, 100–101
linkage to formal business, 33–35
market orientation of organized crime, 28–29
organizational models of, 32–35
patron-client model, 32–33, 41
protection rackets, 40–41
typology of, 31–35
enterprise theory, 63
Escobar, Pablo, 51
exit routes, 86
extortion, 28
and business of violence, 23, 56
business victimization survey, 40
Larceny Act, 68–69
predatory criminality of, 35, 36, 37, 40–41, 183n57
statistical invisibility in reporting, 7, 69, 81

financial system
and black market foreign exchange, 66
and legal activities of organized crime, 36
penetration of by organized crime, 14
penetration of local economy by crime networks, 15–16
firearms markets, 28, 39, 80
forfeiture of assets, 80, 105, 110, 112

gang violence
and Peace Management Initiative, 25, 165, 188n6
political competitiveness, in evolution of gangs, 61–63
in politicization of criminality, 22
youth gangs, 26, 27, 31
ganja trafficking. See drug trafficking, cannabis
garrison communities, 14
Arnett Gardens, 51
candidate selection, impact of criminal funding on, 154
community support of crime networks, 15–16, 41, 56–57, 80, 93–97
co-policing of, 87
co-rulership as crime control strategy, 84
dismantling, 75, 80
dons as community gatekeepers, 41, 46–49, 100, 101
governance of, 15–16, 18–19, 28, 41, 43
homicide rates, 45
jungle courts, 30, 34, 44–45, 53, 93, 176
as mafia republics, 43–46
Matthew's Lane, 70, 90
patron-client relationship model, 100
political administration of, 33–34
political influence of crime networks, 142–44

garrison communities (*continued*)
  political resistance to crime control
    policies, 173–74
  and pro-social activities of organized
    crime, 18–19, 34, 41, 59, 89
  role of local influence on political
    process, 20–22, 179n14, 179n15
  self-policing of, 53–55, 181n30
  and social banditry, 18–19, 70, 179n13
  as social housing, 51–52
  socio-economic conditions of, 5–7,
    14, 42–43, 75–76
  targeting-up strategies, 82–83
  Tivoli Gardens, 51, 62, 182n52
  violence as defence of, 26
  violence within, 43, 44–45
globalization, effect on transnationalization of crime, 38–39, 59–60, 63, 66
good governance, implications of corruption on, 13, 24, 117, 118–20, 129
Grange, Olivia, 25–26
Guyana, 53

Haiti, 95–96, 185n16
Haye-Webster, Sharon, 25–26
head-hunting, 82, 160
high politics, 1
Holness, Andrew, 149
  on Operation Kingfish, 170–71
homicide rates, 9, 69
  crime control policies, success of, 167,
    188n7
  deflection of responsibility, 163–65
  Jamaican compared to Caribbean and
    Latin America, 56
  in Kingston, 43, 45–46, 182n42
  Peace Management Initiative, 25, 165,
    188n6
  substitution and displacement effect
    on, 81–82

Hong Kong
  anti-corruption strategy, 91
  cigarette smuggling by triads, 66
  law enforcement efforts, 83, 107–8,
    112
  triads, origins in territorial isolation,
    59
human rights violations, 114

illegal opportunities
  anti-corruption programmes, 90–92
  diversification of funding streams by
    crime networks, 99
  expansion of, 65–66
illicit goods and services, demand for,
  32, 35–41, 79
immunity, from convictions, 6, 68–71,
  113
India, 51, 111–12
institutional corruption, 179n3
  and criminally acquired wealth,
    24–25
  and cronyism, 125, 126
  relationship of power motive to, 29–30
  and rural-based criminal entrepeneurs,
    64
  trusteeships, in systems of accountabil-
    ity, 74, 184n72
international law enforcement
  conventions and agreements, 104–5
intimidation tactics
  criticism as cause of, 20–21, 180n18
  on party leaders, 20
  voter intimidation, 22, 31–32, 35, 106,
    143
  wire-tapping, police use of, 106
Italy, 18, 179n13
  anti-Mafia legislation, 110
  anti-mafia prosecutions, 83, 96
  exit routes, 86

law enforcement efforts, 107–8, 112, 162

relationship of political parties to organized crime, 51, 110

Jamaica Constabulary Force
Organized Crime Unit, formation of, 26

Jamaican diaspora, permeation of criminal partnerships in, 39

Jamaicans for Justice, 55

Japan, 51, 53, 110–11

jungle courts, 30, 34, 44–45, 53, 176

justice system. *See* criminal justice system

Khan, Shaheed, 53

Knight, K.D., 24

law enforcement
approaches to crime control, 71
cash-defined crime, 106
corruption of, 9, 112, 174–75, 184n7
of crime control legislation, 106–7
crime control strategies, 82–83
deal brokering, 55
deflection of responsibility, 163–67
effective strategies for crime control, 72–73, 85–87, 161–62
head-hunting, 82, 160
human cost of effective enforcement, 57–58
immunity from, 6, 68–71, 113
in inner city, 43
and institutional corruption, 24
insulation from political influences, 87
international conventions and agreements, 104–5
international cooperation, weakening of, 63

international experiences in, 83, 107–13, 162

Larceny Act, 68–69

Operation Kingfish, 170–71, 185n22, 188n12

on Operation Kingfish, 188n12

Organized Crime Unit, formation of, 26

and organized-disorganized crime, 27–28

organizing principles of case-solving, 84–85

party bias in, 188n3

peace-making strategies, 25–26, 71–72

peace-making strategies, involvement in, 22

plea-bargaining, 82

politicization of criminality, as protective strategy, 22

reform, 8

response overreach, 113

targeting-up strategies, 82–83, 110

weakness of, 14, 76

legal authority, tradition of subverting, 16

legitimacy, soft definition of, 53–54

low politics, 1

mafia, 5, 13, 59, 83, 96, 181n38

Martin, Ivanhoe (Rhygin), 18

mediation services, of dons, 46–49

Ministry of National Security and Justice, crime networks as security threat, 5, 24–25

Minott, Dennis, 149

Mitchell, Carl (Byah), 89

money laundering
black market foreign exchange, 66, 183n62
in construction sector, 133
economic consequences of, 169–70

money laundering (*continued*)
  in legal activities of organized crime,
    36, 39–40
  Money Laundering Act, 69, 105
  in party financing, 151, 155

narco-terrorism, 13
national security, crime as threat to, 5,
  24–25
National Security Strategy, and international terrorism, 17
Netherlands, 111, 186n28
Nigeria, 51

opportunity theory of crime control,
  109
organized crime
  activities of, 35–41
  aspects of, 17
  controlling, approaches to, 71–75
  and corporate sector, 4
  defined, 26–31
  enforcement function of, 52–53
  as enterprise crime, 3, 28–29
  evolution of, 17–18, 99–104
  factors in development of, 58–60
  foundational relationships of, 41
  as high crime of criminal elite, 1–2
  immunity from law enforcement, 6,
    68–71, 113
  integration in formal economy, 15–16,
    99–100, 170–72
  international drug markets, 5, 16,
    37–38, 39, 58–60, 63–66
  maturation of, 99–100, 102t–3t
  as motor of violent crimes, 22–26
  organizational features of, 26–28,
    179n2
  organizational models of, 32–35, 41
  penetration of Jamaican politics by,
    12–14

performative violence, 58
policing methods of, 30
political influence of, 16, 49–56,
  67–68, 152–56, 165–66, 169
socio-structural roots of, 60–63
territoriality of in political activities,
  20–22, 29–30
transnationalization of, 3, 38–39
typology of, 31–35. *See also* crime
  networks
organized-disorganized crime, 27, 82,
  181n28
originating conditions, comparison to
  sustaining conditions, 59–60

parish councils, perceived corruption in,
  123–25
party financing, 65, 73–74, 180n19,
  182n53
  autonomy as form of self-funding,
    154–55
  campaign funding, 88
  candidate control through criminal
    funding, 156
  candidate selection, and criminal
    funding, 154
  clean money vs. tainted money vs.
    dirty money, 143, 180n19,
    187n4
  contribution limits, 157
  election campaign spending per
    capita, Caribbean, 146–47
  feedback effect of corrupt funding,
    21–22
  funding as opportunity-seeking
    behaviour, 148–49
  illegal funding, theses on, 152–56
  illegal funding sources, political
    influence of, 142–44
  indifference to sources of, 170

internal party elections, impact of
criminal funding on, 154
money laundering, 151
as party capture by special interests,
145–46
political debts, 142, 153, 154, 155–56,
156
reform proposals, 156–59
regulatory framework of funding,
150–52, 157
Trafigura affair, 146, 171, 187n4
transactional nature of party-citizen
encounters, 145–46
voter support, and state funding,
158–59
party politics, 180n19
anti-corruption programmes, 88–90
criminal partnerships in, 2, 9, 12–14,
140–41
crony capitalism, 148–49
intimidation of party leaders, 20
Jamaican multi-party system, back-
ground of, 144
linkage to violent entrepeneurs,
31–32, 35
local influence on political process,
20–22, 179n14
patron-client relationship model, 41,
100
peace-making strategies, involvement
in, 25–26, 71–72
political affiliations in development of
organized crime, 61–63
political debts, 142, 153, 154, 155–56
political patronage, 128
political tribalism, 88, 152, 171–72,
184n8, 188nn13–14
relationship to organized crime,
49–56, 67–68, 73–74, 80, 165–66,
169, 182n53

uncivil politics, 13
and violence-related services, 31–32,
57, 76, 180n19
voter support, and state funding,
158–59
Patterson, P.J., 52
peace-making strategies, 22, 25–26,
71–72
pacification, as peace-building, 94–95,
185n16
Peace Management Initiative, 25, 165,
188n6
Phillips, Peter, 16, 188n1
Phipps, Donald, 16, 67, 70, 88–90, 173,
179n6
plea-bargaining, 82
police and policing
abuses of power, 95, 107, 113–14
anti-corruption programmes, 87
citizen involvement in, 94–96
co-policing of garrison communities,
87
corrupt relationships with, 174–75,
184n7
crime control strategies, 82–83,
162
deflection of responsibility, 163–67
drug seizures, 37–38
enforcement of crime control legislation, 106–7
hierarchy of organized crime, in
developing policing strategies, 27–28
immunity from, 68–71, 101
and institutional corruption, 24
inter-personal violence as domestic
violence, 25
law enforcement reform, 8
modernization of, 73–74, 165, 189n16
Operation Kingfish, 170–71, 185n22,
188n12

police and policing (*continued*)
  Organized Crime Unit, formation of, 26
  party bias in, 188n3
  peace-making strategies, involvement in, 22, 25–26, 71–72
  perceived corruption in, 123–25
  politicization of criminality, as protective strategy, 22
  public confidence in, 6–7
  in reduction of protection rackets, 80
  self-policing of garrison communities, 43, 45–46, 53–55
  wire-tapping, 106
political activism, 61–63, 64–65
political change, and commoditization of violence, 32
political facilitation
  benign view of crime, 67–68
  of crime networks, 176–77
  as crime of conspiracy, 88
  disruption of as crime control strategy, 85–87
  of entrepeneurial criminality, 170–72
political influence, consolidation of in Jamaica, 65
political mobilization
  corruption and, 128
  in crime control strategies, 111, 113
  evolution of crime networks in national contexts, 17–18
  as protective strategy, 22
  of urban poor in garrison communities, 14
political patronage, 16–17, 128
political system
  degeneration of, 20–22, 179n14, 179n15
  influence of organized crime on, 99–100

  internal influence on, 17–18
politics, 179n13
  academic studies on post-independence political violence, 2–3
  and black market foreign exchange, 66
  class-colour-gender divide in, 5–6
  and clientelistic model of enterprise crime, 32–33
  colonial legacy in post-independence, 60–61
  commercialization of, 150
  conspiracy laws, 74
  corruption as normal, 171
  drug trafficking as international relations issue, 13
  high vs. low politics, 1, 13
  import restrictions, 66
  Ministry of National Security and Justice, 24–25
  patron-client mobilization in, 148–49
  peace-making strategies, involvement in, 25–26
  Peace Management Initiative, 25, 165, 188n6
  penetration of by organized crime, 9, 12–14
  perceived corruption in state bureaucracy, 123–25
  post-colonial restructuring of opportunity, 129
  professionalization of, 145
  relationship of social conditions to organized crime, 61–63
  relationships of political parties to organized crime, 49–50, 52–56
  voluntarism, decline of, 145, 147–48
  vulnerabilities of to organized crime, 5–10
pornography, 35
posses, 13

power
  in corruption of political participa-
    tion, 147–48
  and political corruption, 29–30
  relationship to authority, 48–49, 53–54
  violence as projection of, 56
predatory criminality, 28–29, 35, 174,
  183n57
private sector corruption, 5
prostitution, 35, 99
protection rackets
  business victimization survey, 40
  in elections and electoral process, 61–63
  pacification, as systematic peace-build-
    ing, 94–96
  provided by organized crime, 28–29,
    34, 35, 79, 99
  reduction of through policing, 80
  statistical invisibility in reporting, 81
  threat of violence, 40–41
public opinion, in crime control policies, 10–11, 112
public policies
  disruption of criminal influences as
    crime control strategy, 98–104
  effect of education on social mobility,
    98
  effect on socio-economic conditions,
    49–50
public sector, 5
  perceived corruption in, 123–25

racketeering, 3
  in construction sector, 133–34
  reporting rates, 7
  role of in corrupt funding, 22
Radzinowicz, Leon, 5
Ramcharan, Leebert, 170–71
rankin, as predecessor to don, 49
real estate rackets, 37

RICO laws, 74, 110
rural-based criminal entrepeneurs,
  64–65
Russia, 119. *See also* USSR
Ryan, Selwyn, 143–44

Samper, Ernesto, 143, 150–51
Seaga, Edward, 20, 180n19, 183n63
security services
  provided by organized crime, 28–29,
    44–45
Shields, Mark, 165
Smith, Oliver (Bubba), 15
social banditry, 18–19, 70, 89, 179n13
social change, and commoditization of
  violence, 32
social exclusion
  and social change, integration of,
    92–97
  and street crime, 7
  of urban poor in garrison communi-
    ties, 43–46
social facilitation
  benign view of crime, 67–68
  of crime networks, 59, 66, 80, 176–77
  disruption of empowerment process as
    crime control strategy, 84
  disruption of relationships as crime
    control strategy, 85–87
  of entrepeneurial criminality, 170–72
social hierarchy, penetration of organized crime in, 12–14
social integration, as means of disrupting
  crime influences, 98–104
social support
  of crime networks, 14, 15–16, 17,
    33–34, 76, 80, 179n7
  dismantling, 75, 80, 92–97
  political influence of garrison com-
    munities, 20–22

social support (*continued*)
  political resistance to crime control
    policies, 173–74
  as source of immunity, 70
socio-economic conditions
  disruption of criminal influences as
    crime control strategy, 98–104
  effect of public policies on, 49–50
  and formation of youth gangs, 26, 27,
    31
  poverty, 7, 42–43, 178n3
  relationship to organized crime, 5–7,
    14, 42–43, 75–76
  role of in sustaining street crime,
    7–9
  and rural-based criminal entrepeneurs,
    64
  transformation of, 75
squatter settlements, 7
state agencies
  legitimacy discourse against, 4–5
  responsiveness of, 7–9
state corruption, 14
  National Housing Development
    Cooperation, 68, 183n66
  National Solid Waste Management
    Authority, 68, 183n66
  relationship of political parties to
    organized crime, 67–68
Stevens, Andrew (Andrew Pang), 83
street crime, 2, 7–9
street violence, 4

Taiwan, 51
targeting-up strategies, 82–83, 110
tax violations, prosecution for, 82
territoriality
  community gatekeepers, 41
  dynamics of, 12, 34–35, 80
  of enterprise crime, 33–34

of organized crime in political activi-
    ties, 20–22, 29–30
  in phases of organized crime, 100–103
  of rural-based criminal entrepeneurs,
    64–65
  and violence, 56–57
terrorism, 13, 17, 179n10
Thailand, 51
tourism
  dependence of economy on, 5
  effects of crime on, 8, 99
  hotel construction, 131
  and legal activities of organized crime,
    35–36
transparency
  campaign accounts audit, 157–58, 159
  in campaign income and expenditure,
    157
  in construction sector contractual
    system, 134–35
  and institutional corruption, 24, 25,
    125
trusteeships, in systems of accountability,
    74, 80, 184n72

underemployment, 5, 7, 49–50
unemployment
  in crime control policies, 75
  employability, levels of, 7
  post-independence urban migration,
    60–61
  relationship to organized crime, 5–7,
    14, 42–43
  and youth gangs, 31
United Kingdom
  crime networks in, 13
  Jamaican organized crime in, 12
  law enforcement efforts, 40, 83
  RICO laws, use of in crime control,
    74

stereotyping of immigrant communities, 39
United States
alcohol prohibition policy, 66, 109
crime networks in, 13, 29
illicit drug market in, 63
Jamaican organized crime in, 12, 37, 39
law enforcement efforts, 40, 83, 107, 108–10, 112
legal activities of organized crime, 36
political parties and organized crime, 50–51
RICO laws, use of in crime control, 74, 110
robber barons, 185–86n23
stereotyping of immigrant communities, 39
urban poor
co-rulership of, 9
demographic characteristics of, 42–43
effect of criminally acquired wealth on, 12
impact of drug trafficking on, 9
improvements to built environment of, 97
integration of in political system, 19
integration of into main stream society, 75
marginalization of, 14
patron-client relationship model, 41, 100
and pro-social activities of organized crime, 59, 89
role of social disadvantage in development of organized crime, 60–61
and social banditry, 18–19, 70, 179n13
social integration of, 92–97
USSR, Thieves World, 17. *See also* Russia

violence
business of, 23–24, 31–32, 80
commoditization of, 32
in communities of urban poor, 42–43
in growth phase of maturation, 101
inter-personal violence as domestic violence, 25
logic of, 56–58
managed violence, 15–16, 17
of narco-terrorism, 13
outsourcing of, 64–65
performative violence, 58
for political purposes, 9, 180n19
roots of, 56–57
specialization in, 57, 80, 183n57
use of in garrison communities, 19, 20
violent criminality
effect of public policies on, 49–50
externalization of, 165–66
post-independence conditions conducive to, 60–61, 75–76
rate of, 14, 22–26
typology of violent entrepeneurs, 31–35
violent entrepeneurs
deportees and, 165–66
differentiation between criminal entrepeneurs, 80
tensions with drug-enterprise criminals, 64–65, 183n57
typology of, 31–35
Vollmer, August, 109
voter intimidation, 22, 31–32, 35, 106, 143
votes, illegal trade in, 22, 145, 149–50, 158

wealth, criminally acquired
in formal economy, 12
as illegal funding source, 143–44

wealth (*continued*)
   and institutional corruption, 24, 52
   laundering of. *See* money laundering
   in purchase of electoral candidacy,
      153
   and status acquisition, 22–23
welfare projects, 19, 34, 170
   state provision of, 92, 173–74
white-collar crime, 4
women, in underground economy, 19

yardies, 13
youth (male)
   opportunity structure of organized
      crime, 43–44, 59

referent power of organized crime on,
   13
replacement income of through
   crime, 174
youth gangs, 26, 27, 31
youth unemployment
   in crime control strategies, 97
   effect of public policies on, 49–50, 75
   employability, levels of, 7
   lure of drug trafficking, 8, 178n3,
      178n4
   post-independence urban migration,
      60–61
   relationship to organized crime, 5–7,
      14, 42–43

www.ingramcontent.com/pod-product-compliance
Lightning Source LLC
Chambersburg PA
CBHW020703270326
41928CB00005B/239